MW00592321

New Zealand Literature to 1977

AMERICAN LITERATURE, ENGLISH LITERATURE, AND WORLD LITERATURES IN ENGLISH: AN INFORMATION GUIDE SERIES

Series Editor: Theodore Grieder, Curator, Division of Special Collections, Fales Library, New York University

Associate Editor: Duane DeVries, Associate Professor, Polytechnic Institute of New York, Brooklyn

Other books on world literatures in this series:

BLACK AFRICAN LITERATURE IN ENGLISH—*Edited by Bernth Lindfors*

ASIAN LITERATURE IN ENGLISH—*Edited by George Anderson**

AUSTRALIAN LITERATURE TO 1900—*Edited by Barry G. Andrews and William H. Wilde*

MODERN AUSTRALIAN POETRY, 1920-1970—*Edited by Herbert C. Jaffa*

MODERN AUSTRALIAN PROSE, 1901-1975—*Edited by A. Grove Day*

ENGLISH-CANADIAN LITERATURE TO 1900—*Edited by R.G. Moyles*

MODERN ENGLISH-CANADIAN POETRY—*Edited by Peter Stevens*

MODERN ENGLISH-CANADIAN PROSE—*Edited by Helen Hoy**

INDIAN LITERATURE IN ENGLISH, 1827-1979—*Edited by Amritjit Singh, Rajiva Verma, and Irene Joshi**

IRISH LITERATURE, 1800-1875—*Edited by Brian McKenna*

IRISH LITERATURE, 1876-1950—*Edited by Brian McKenna**

SCOTTISH LITERATURE IN ENGLISH—*Edited by William Aitken**

WEST INDIAN LITERATURE IN ENGLISH—*Edited by Priscilla Tyler**

AUTHOR NEWSLETTERS AND JOURNALS—*Edited by Margaret Patterson*

*in preparation

The above series is part of the

GALE INFORMATION GUIDE LIBRARY

The Library consists of a number of separate series of guides covering major areas in the social sciences, humanities, and current affairs.

General Editor: Paul Wasserman, Professor and former Dean, School of Library and Information Services, University of Maryland

Managing Editor: Denise Allard Adzigian, Gale Research Company

New Zealand Literature to 1977

A GUIDE TO INFORMATION SOURCES

Volume 30 in the American Literature, English Literature, and World Literatures in English Information Guide Series

John Thomson

Senior Lecturer in English
Victoria University
Wellington, New Zealand

Gale Research Company
Book Tower, Detroit, Michigan 48226

Library of Congress Cataloging in Publication Data

Thomson, John E.
New Zealand Literature to 1977.

(American literature, English literature, and world literatures in English ; v. 30) (Gale information guide library)
Includes indexes.
1. New Zealand literature—Bibliography. I. Title.
Z4111.T45 [PR9624.3] 016.82 74-11537
ISBN 0-8103-1246-8

VITA

John Thomson is a senior lecturer in English at Victoria University of Wellington, New Zealand. He took honours degrees at that university and at the University of Oxford, and a Ph.D. at the University of Otago, New Zealand. Late-eighteenth-century English fiction and New Zealand literature have been his areas of special study. He is general editor of the New Zealand Playscripts series, and recently published a biographical and literary study of the poet Denis Glover (DENIS GLOVER. Wellington: Oxford University Press, 1977).

CONTENTS

Contents

INTRODUCTION

"The literature relating to New Zealand," wrote T.M. Hocken, introducing his BIBLIOGRAPHY of 1909, "is not only unusually interesting but is unusually extensive." As Hocken well realized, however, this "literature" included very little imaginative writing in verse and even less in prose. "The birth of the poet," he said, "is still awaited. Perhaps his advent is not far distant, and may, indeed, be heralded by that yearly increasing burden of song, which here and there is lightened by undoubted talent, rhythm, and beauty." The not entirely undistinguished literary activity which accompanied the economic depression of the 1890s proved, alas, to be no dawn chorus, and it was not until the greater depression of the early 1930s that imaginative literature (although the image of feathered songsters was now totally inappropriate to this new, socially radical group of writers) was truly born, and lived and flourished.

Hocken, with the great English Victorian novelists in mind by way of comparison, had found nothing at all to say for the country's prose fiction. But as he wrote, New Zealand's most notable author was offering some of her earliest short stories for publication. That was in another country, though, and Katherine Mansfield, for all that she much later was to influence many New Zealand short-story writers, was not at the time a part of the country's literary culture.

So a bibliography of New Zealand's imaginative literature is very largely a record of what has been published in the last fifty years, and the present work, while not ignoring the writing of the first hundred years of settlement, reflects that emphasis. Critical discussion was still slower to develop, very little being worthy of attention before the founding of the periodical LANDFALL (see p. 218) in 1947. Only in the last decade has a significant number of critical monographs and collections of essays been published. It has therefore been possible in this bibliography, while covering material published up to the end of 1977, to be more inclusive than might be expected, and, in the absence of a developed body of critical writing, to list articles and biographical notes of at times more journalistic than scholarly quality and, as well, to list unpublished masters and doctoral theses. This inclusiveness seemed all the more desirable given the lack of any other bibliography devoted to New Zealand literature. A corollary has been the inclusion of both primary and secondary material without regard to its availability. A few (though fortunately only a few) of the items listed in this book are rare even in New Zealand libraries.

This bibliography could not possibly have been prepared, however, within the space of two years without the invaluable assistance of many of the general and specialized bibliographical tools listed in chapter 1. I am also indebted to friends who drew obscure items to my attention, and particularly to those who suggested, for inclusion in the section on nonfiction, books which I might otherwise have overlooked altogether. And although, despite this assistance, the preparation of this bibliography may have encountered some of the vicissitudes of the pioneering farmer, it is hoped that the finished book will prove as wholesome as the farmer's produce.

Chapter 1

BIBLIOGRAPHIES AND OTHER WORKS OF REFERENCE

Entries in this chapter are arranged alphabetically under subject headings.

A. BIBLIOGRAPHIES

The essential bibliography for the study of New Zealand literature will be A.G. Bagnall's NEW ZEALAND NATIONAL BIBLIOGRAPHY TO THE YEAR 1960 (see p. 2.) Of the five projected volumes, only three have yet appeared. Volume 1, covering the years before 1890, is not expected to be available before the early nineteen-eighties, and in its absence the more important of the rather dated existing bibliographies for that period have been listed in detail.

The bibliographical exercises carried out by students at the Library School of the National Library of New Zealand form a variable but often very useful source of specialized, usually annotated, information. These short bibliographies are generally not published but can be borrowed within New Zealand from the National Library through the interloan service. Copies of the originals are sometimes held by other libraries.

Maori literature, and Maori culture generally, increasingly influence New Zealand writing in English. Although writing in Maori and translations from Maori (apart from a few exceptions in chapter 7) will not be listed in this book, bibliographies relating to Maori writing, including myths and legends, have been included in this section as an initial guide to further study.

1. General

Bagnall, A.G. A REFERENCE LIST OF BOOKS AND OTHER PUBLICATIONS ASSOCIATED WITH THE NEW ZEALAND CENTENNIAL 1840-1940. Wellington: Dept. of Internal Affairs, 1942.

> The books listed are mostly of a historical kind, but also included are the few relevant items of literary interest.

_____, ed. NEW ZEALAND NATIONAL BIBLIOGRAPHY TO THE YEAR 1960. Vol. 2: 1890-1960, A-H. Vol. 3: 1890-1960, I-O. Vol. 4: 1890-1960, P-Z. Wellington: Government Printer, 1969-75.

This indispensable compilation is "primarily a catalogue of printed books and pamphlets; periodicals and annual reports are omitted." Volume 1 will cover the period to 1889 and include a selection of periodical articles; volume 5, the index volume, will also include a supplement with additions and corrections.

"Bibliographical Work in Progress." NEW ZEALAND LIBRARIES. Vol. 25, 1962-- . Annual.

This series of bibliographical articles records work published as well as work in progress.

CURRENT NATIONAL BIBLIOGRAPHY OF NEW ZEALAND BOOKS AND PAMPHLETS PUBLISHED IN 1950-65. Wellington: National Library of New Zealand, 1951-66. Annual.

This was published with the INDEX TO NEW ZEALAND PERIODICALS (see p. 11. It included subject references. After 1966, it was issued separately under the title NEW ZEALAND NATIONAL BIBLIOGRAPHY (see p. 3).

Harris, John. GUIDE TO NEW ZEALAND REFERENCE MATERIAL AND OTHER SOURCES OF INFORMATION. 2nd ed. [Wellington]: New Zealand Library Association, 1950.

Two supplements were compiled by A.G. Bagnall and published in 1951 and 1957. These as well as the original work are now dated.

Hocken, T.M. A BIBLIOGRAPHY OF THE LITERATURE RELATING TO NEW ZEALAND. Wellington: Government Printer, 1909; rpt. Wellington: Newrick Associates, 1973.

This bibliography of books on all subjects relating to New Zealand is arranged chronologically and has a rather unsatisfactory subject index. The brief annotations show Hocken to have been unimpressed by his country's imaginative literature in its early days. Various attempts were later made to fill the gaps in Hocken. A.H. Johnstone compiled a supplement (Auckland: Whitcombe & Tombs, 1927; rpt. Wellington: Newrick Associates, 1975) which added to Hocken's book and included a very selective list of works published between 1909 and 1926. L.J.B. Chapple's A BIBLIOGRAPHICAL BROCHURE CONTAINING ADDENDA AND CORRIGENDA TO EXTANT BIBLIOGRAPHIES OF NEW ZEALAND LITERATURE (Dunedin: Reed, 1938) was also chiefly concerned with supplementing the nineteenth-century items in Hocken's bibliography. "Titles Not in Hocken's Bibliography" by Shafto (pseud.), HISTORY AND BIBLIOGRAPHY, 1 (December 1948), 229-33, adds a few new items.

Volume 1 of the NEW ZEALAND NATIONAL BIBLIOGRAPHY TO THE YEAR 1960, covering the period to 1889, will supersede Hocken and his followers.

Johnstone, A.H. CANTERBURY BOOKS 1847-1955: A BIBLIOGRAPHY. Christchurch: Whitcombe & Tombs, 1956.

Although this chronological list includes literary works, whether by Canterbury authors or about Canterbury, its usefulness to the student of literature is diminished by the absence of a subject index.

NEW ZEALAND BOOKS IN PRINT. Wellington: New Zealand Book Publishers Association, 1957-- . Triennially.

[New Zealand Broadcasting Corporation.] ARCHIVES SECTION GENERAL CATALOGUE NO. 1. Timaru: 1967.

This catalogue, prepared for use within the Broadcasting Corporation, includes under authors' names details of the not very numerous readings by and about writers held in the archives section. It has not been updated.

New Zealand Library Association. A BIBLIOGRAPHY OF NEW ZEALAND BIBLIOGRAPHIES. Preliminary ed. Wellington: 1967.

This bibliography is based on a bibliographical exercise carried out by S.J. Cauchi at Library School. It is valuable to the student of literature for its coverage of general bibliographies, manuscripts, newspapers, theses, libraries, Maori literature, theatre, and biography, as well as of imaginative literature.

_____. UNION LIST OF THESES OF THE UNIVERSITY OF NEW ZEALAND 1910-1954. Comp. D.L. Jenkins. Wellington: 1956.

Supplements by different compilers and under slightly differing titles were issued in 1963, 1969, and 1972.

NEW ZEALAND NATIONAL BIBLIOGRAPHY. Wellington: National Library, 1968-- . Monthly, with annual cumulations.

A comprehensive list of all books and pamphlets published in New Zealand as well as books published overseas either relating to New Zealand or by New Zealand authors. The yearly volumes include annual publications and a subject index, and give details both of new serials and of those which have ceased publication. Also listed in recent issues are art prints and sound recordings and the addresses of New Zealand publishers. The first volume, published in 1968, covered the year 1966.

Rimmer, Anne H., and William A. Siddells. "A Bibliography of New Zealand Library School Bibliographies, 1946-1972." Bibliographical exercise, Library School, Wellington, 1972.

This valuable compilation gives both descriptive and evaluative annotations.

Turnbull, M.M. A BIBLIOGRAPHY OF LIFE ON THE GOLD FIELDS OF THE SOUTH ISLAND OF NEW ZEALAND AS DESCRIBED IN BOOKS, PAMPHLETS AND OFFICIAL PAPERS. Wellington: National Library Service, 1961.

The material is arranged by provinces, and includes sections listing fiction based on personal observation.

Wood, G.A. A GUIDE FOR STUDENTS OF NEW ZEALAND HISTORY. Dunedin: University of Otago Press, 1973.

Although this guide does not attempt to serve all his needs, it is still of very real use to the research student in the field of imaginative literature.

2. Literature—General

Andersen, J.C. ANNALS OF NEW ZEALAND LITERATURE; BEING A PRELIMINARY LIST OF NEW ZEALAND AUTHORS AND THEIR WORKS. Wellington: New Zealand Authors' Week Committee, 1936.

This was the first bibliography to be devoted to imaginative literature, but it is not a very useful compilation.

"Annual Bibliography of Commonwealth Literature 1964--: New Zealand." JOURNAL OF COMMONWEALTH LITERATURE. London: Oxford University Press, 1965-- .

This journal has from its inception included an annual bibliography of New Zealand literature prefaced by a descriptive essay on the year's publications. It is the fullest and best of the annual bibliographies.

ANNUAL BIBLIOGRAPHY OF ENGLISH LANGUAGE AND LITERATURE. [London]: Modern Humanities Research Association, vol. 43, 1970-- .

There was no New Zealand contribution until 1968. Works on individual authors are listed under the author's name, but general studies of New Zealand literature are not easily found within the large section on twentieth-century English literature. Volume 43, published in 1970, covered the year 1968.

Clarkson, Susann. "A Bibliography of Writings Relating to the New Zealand Novel and Poetry." Bibliographical exercise, Library School, Wellington, 1967.

Useful mainly for its listing of periodical articles and its brief descriptive comments.

Jones, Joseph J., and R.T. Robertson. "Resources for the Study of Commonwealth Literature in English." Trial version for private circulation. Austin: University of Texas, 1959.

There is a very selective, unannotated list for New Zealand literature on pages 163-84. The book was not published other than in this cyclostyled form.

Lewin, P. Evans, comp. SUBJECT CATALOGUE OF THE LIBRARY OF THE ROYAL EMPIRE SOCIETY. Vol. 2. London: Royal Empire Society, 1931; rpt. London: Royal Commonwealth Society, 1967.

The second volume of this catalogue contains a short section on New Zealand literature. Volume 6 of a supplement to the catalogue (Boston: G.K. Hall, 1971) adds to the New Zealand section.

MLA INTERNATIONAL BIBLIOGRAPHY OF BOOKS AND ARTICLES ON THE MODERN LANGUAGES AND LITERATURES. New York: Modern Language Association of America, 1959-- .

A very selective New Zealand section first appeared in 1959 under "English Language and Literature," subsection "Australia, Canada."

New, William H. CRITICAL WRITINGS ON COMMONWEALTH LITERATURES: A SELECTIVE BIBLIOGRAPHY TO 1970, WITH A LIST OF THESES AND DISSERTATIONS. University Park: Pennsylvania State University Press, [1975].

The New Zealand section offers an unpredictably selective listing of material under the headings of "Research Aids," "General," and "Individual Authors."

Pearson, W.H. "Bibliography: The Maori and Literature." In THE MAORI PEOPLE IN THE NINETEEN-SIXTIES. Ed. Eric Schwimmer. Auckland: Blackwood & Janet Paul, 1968, pp. 373-84.

This bibliography, which covers the years 1938-65, is an updating and expansion of Pearson's earlier list published in JOURNAL OF THE POLYNESIAN SOCIETY, 67 (September 1958), 235-38, where a selective listing of pre-1938 material was also included. Ruth Ensor's bibliography (see p. 7) is much fuller for the earlier period, and includes descriptive annotations. Pearson's bibliography, on the other hand, includes verse and drama, uncollected short stories, and lighter fiction excluded by Ruth Ensor. It is divided into "Writing by Pakeha [i.e. European New Zealanders]," "Writing [in English] by Maori," and "Other References," which includes critical material.

3. Poetry

Alcock, Peter. "A Select Bibliography of New Zealand Verse and Some Related Writing, 1920-1952." Bibliographical exercise, Library School, Wellington, 1952.

Arranged chronologically within the section "General Verse," and by author in the sections "Drama in Verse," and "Anthologies." Though deliberately selective, nothing of importance is omitted.

Cuthbert, E.I. INDEX OF AUSTRALIAN AND NEW ZEALAND POETRY. New York: Scarecrow Press, 1963.

Includes only the poems in the few important anthologies of New Zealand verse, listing them by author, title, and first line.

Serle, P. A BIBLIOGRAPHY OF AUSTRALASIAN POETRY AND VERSE. Melbourne: Melbourne University Press, 1925.

No distinction is made between Australian and New Zealand writers, although title and place of publication are sometimes a guide.

Vinson, James, ed. CONTEMPORARY POETS. 2nd ed. London: St James Press; New York: St. Martin's Press, 1975.

First published under the title CONTEMPORARY POETS OF THE ENGLISH LANGUAGE, ed. Rosalie Murphy (Chicago and London: St James Press, 1970).

Walton, Margery. "A Bibliography of Poetry Published and Printed at The Caxton Club Press and The Caxton Press, Christchurch, 1934-63." Bibliographical exercise, Library School, Wellington, 1963.

Provides occasional details of edition size and type face used.

Weir, J.E. "Five New Zealand Poets: A Bibliographical and Critical Account of Manuscript Material." Thesis, University of Canterbury, 1974.

The five poets are R.A.K. Mason, D'Arcy Cresswell, Eileen Duggan, James K. Baxter, and Alistair Campbell.

Winter, J.R. "New Zealand Women Poets: Works Published Since 1970: An Annotated Bibliography." Bibliographical exercise, Library School, Wellington, 1977.

4. Fiction

Burns, James A.S. A CENTURY OF NEW ZEALAND NOVELS. Auckland: Whitcombe & Tombs, 1961.

This selective list of fiction arranged chronologically from 1861 to 1960 is useful as a quick guide, especially to the earlier period. There is no index.

Ensor, Ruth. "The Treatment of the Maori in Fiction: A Bibliography of Novels and Collected Short Stories, 1861-1967, Annotated and Arranged in Chronological Order." Bibliographical exercise, Library School, Wellington, 1968.

Excludes myths and legends, fiction written by Maori authors, and lighter fiction. The annotations, although at times little more than simple descriptions of the stories, do attempt to indicate the way the authors treat the Maori characters.

Gries, Joan C. "A Bibliography of New Zealand Prose Fiction, 1778-1948." In "An Outline of Prose Fiction in New Zealand." Thesis, Auckland University College, 1951, pp. 203-385.

A full bibliography with brief descriptive annotations added to those of the more important items which are not discussed in the thesis. The titles of the individual short stories published in collected volume form are given. The bibliography indicates the major libraries which hold a copy of each work listed and includes a "Selected Bibliography of Juvenile Fiction," a list of anthologies, and an index of authors and titles.

Horncy, Janet, and Catherine Hutchinson. "New Zealand Fiction, October 1957-1968: An Annotated List of Novels and Collected Short Stories." Bibliographical exercise, Library School, Wellington, 1968.

A continuation of Elizabeth M.M. Millen's work (see below), aiming to cover all prose fiction of the chosen period. The annotations provide an indication of the literary worth. Anthologies are included.

McKenzie, R.M. "The Short Story and New Zealand Society: A Bibliography." Bibliographical exercise, [Library School, Wellington, 1967].

A select, well-annotated list of material published between 1934 and 1967 which offers comment on "the New Zealand milieu and its influence on the form, content and style of the short story."

Millen, Elizabeth M.M. "New Zealand Fiction 1947-1957: An Annotated List of Novels and Collected Short Stories." Bibliographical exercise, Library School, Wellington, 1957.

Vinson, James, ed. CONTEMPORARY NOVELISTS. 2nd ed. London: St James Press; New York: St. Martin's Press, 1976.

5. Drama

Edridge, Sally. "Bibliography of New Zealand Drama, 1953-1963." Bibliographical exercise, Library School, Wellington, 1964.

Though superseded by McNaughton's bibliography (see below), this is still useful for its brief descriptions of the plays listed, and for its short section on "Play Production."

Hitchings, Michael. "Plays by New Zealanders." In PROMPT BOOK: A NEW ZEALAND THEATRE GUIDE. Comps. Joan Reid and Russell Reid. 2nd ed. Wellington: Joan and Russell Reid Ltd., 1959, pp. 17-23.

Hitchings lists only published plays, but he gives fuller information about the type of play and the setting than McNaughton (see below), whose bibliography otherwise supersedes this.

Hopkins, Gwen. "A Chronological Survey of Professional Theatre in New Zealand: A Select Bibliography." Bibliographical exercise, Library School, Wellington, 1968.

A useful list of books and articles on the history of professional theatre since the 1840s.

McNaughton, Howard. NEW ZEALAND DRAMA: A BIBLIOGRAPHICAL GUIDE. Interim ed. Christchurch: University of Canterbury, 1974.

A comprehensive list, by playwright's name, of plays for stage, radio, and television, the majority of them unpublished. McNaughton provides very brief details of first performances, and in most cases the number of sets and actors required.

Mathias, Rosemary. "New Zealand Amateur Theatre: A Select Bibliography." Bibliographical exercise, Library School, Wellington, 1963.

An annotated bibliography of the history of amateur theatre in New Zealand. Criticism and reviews of individual plays are excluded, as (for the most part) are items about particular theatrical groups. The list does include handbooks on play production written by New Zealanders, and items on theatre buildings and drama in schools.

Vinson, James, ed. CONTEMPORARY DRAMATISTS. 2nd ed. London: St James Press; New York: St. Martin's Press, 1977.

6. Maori Writing

Hirst, Linda. "A Select, Annotated Bibliography of Publications on the Myths, Legends and Folk Tales of the Maori." Bibliographical exercise, Library School, Wellington, 1973.

The compiler lists books and articles which recount myths, legends, and folk tales but does not include purely anthropological or critical material. Periodical articles are drawn from the JOURNAL OF THE POLYNESIAN SOCIETY (Wellington: Polynesian Society, 1892--) and TE AO HOU (see p. 219) only.

Siddle, Graeme L. "Aspects of Maoritanga: A Select Bibliography for Public Libraries." Bibliographical exercise, Library School, Wellington, 1975.

This includes sections on the Maori language and on poetry, action songs, and proverbs, and provides extensive descriptive annotations.

Taylor, C.R.H. A BIBLIOGRAPHY OF PUBLICATIONS ON THE NEW ZEALAND MAORI. Oxford: Clarendon Press, 1972.

This admirable and comprehensive bibliography includes sections on language, folklore, traditional history, and music, songs, chants, games, and recreations.

Williams, H.W. A BIBLIOGRAPHY OF PRINTED MAORI TO 1900. Wellington: Government Printer, 1924.

A supplement compiled by A.D. Somerville (Wellington: Government Printer, 1928) has been superseded by her own unpublished "A Supplement to the Williams Bibliography of Printed Maori" (Bibliographical exercise, Library School, Wellington, 1947), which attempts a complete coverage of material published between 1900 and 1947, as well as adding many items to the pre-1900 list.

7. Related Subjects

Coleridge, Kathleen A. "A Bibliography of New Zealand English." Bibliographical exercise, Library School, Wellington, 1966.

An annotated list of items on the English language as spoken in New Zealand by New Zealanders. While full comprehensiveness is not claimed, an attempt is made to draw on letters and articles in newspapers as well as in periodicals. Arrangement is under subject headings.

Foot, Sadie M. "New Zealand Libraries: A Bibliography." Bibliographical exercise, [Library School, Wellington], 1948.

Of use for the history of New Zealand libraries.

Griffith, Penelope. "Printing and Publishing in New Zealand: A Preliminary Bibliography." Bibliographical exercise, Library School, Wellington, 1974.

Although this work covers the history of printing from the earliest missionary presses and newspaper offices, only items published between 1890 and 1960 are listed. It nevertheless offers a very useful coverage of the subject, dealing with newspapers, printing history, style manuals and type specimens, and publishers and their catalogues. There are full annotations and a subject index.

Pitcher, Hazel D. "Bibliography of New Zealand Children's Books 1920-1960." Bibliographical exercise, Library School, Wellington, 1960.

This includes nonfiction as well as fiction, but excludes school texts, school readers, and school bulletins. There are brief descriptive and critical annotations.

Rennie, Kathryn. "New Zealand Journalism: A Selective Bibliography." Bibliographical exercise, Library School, Wellington, 1968.

An annotated bibliography, arranged chronologically under a variety of subject headings.

Ringer, J.B. "A Bibliography of New Zealand Juvenile Fiction 1833-1919, with Annotations and Introductory Essays." Bibliographical exercise, Library School, Wellington, 1977.

B. BIOGRAPHICAL DICTIONARIES

For basic biographical information about living writers, the reader should also consult CONTEMPORARY POETS, COMTEMPORARY NOVELISTS, and CONTEMPORARY DRAMATISTS, all edited by James Vinson, where many New Zealand authors are listed. See under "Bibliographies" (p. 1) for details of these works.

CONTEMPORARY AUTHORS: A BIO-BIBLIOGRAPHICAL GUIDE TO CURRENT AUTHORS AND THEIR WORKS. Detroit: Gale Research Co., 1962-- . Annual.

"Each year's [four] volumes are cumulated and revised about five years later." The cumulative index, which is updated every second year, directs the reader to information on those New Zealand writers who have been recently published in the United States.

McLintock, A.H., ed. AN ENCYCLOPAEDIA OF NEW ZEALAND. 3 vols. Wellington: Government Printer, 1966.

Brief biographies of a few of the major writers are included.

Scholefield, G.H., ed. A DICTIONARY OF NEW ZEALAND BIOGRAPHY. 2 vols. Wellington: [New Zealand] Dept. of Internal Affairs, 1940.

As there were few authors of importance in the earlier years of the country's history, this dictionary, which excluded living people, is of little use to the student of literature except in the case of writers more renowned in some other field--for example, politics.

WHO'S WHO IN NEW ZEALAND. 10th ed. Wellington: Reed, 1971.

Published irregularly since 1908. The various editions have drawn the usual basic information from some of the writers who were alive at the time of compilation.

C. INDEXES TO SERIAL PUBLICATIONS

Details about indexes to individual periodicals are given, under the name of the periodical, in chapter 6 (see p. 213).

General Assembly Library. A UNION CATALOGUE OF NEW ZEALAND NEWSPAPERS PRESERVED IN PUBLIC LIBRARIES, NEWSPAPER OFFICES, AND LOCAL AUTHORITY OFFICES. 2nd ed. Wellington: 1961.

INDEX TO NEW ZEALAND PERIODICALS. Wellington: National Library of New Zealand, 1948-- .

The index for the years 1941-46 was published in one volume in 1949. Articles are listed under author and subject. The earlier volumes are less comprehensive than those of recent years. Recent volumes also include material of New Zealand interest published in overseas periodicals. Publication began with the first volume covering the year 1947.

National Library of New Zealand. UNION LIST OF SERIALS IN NEW ZEALAND LIBRARIES. 3rd ed. 6 vols. Wellington: 1969-70.

This includes periodicals in all languages from all parts of the world which are held in New Zealand libraries. Although not a bibliography, and far from up-to-date on library holdings, the UNION LIST is still indispensable as a guide to New Zealand periodicals. A supplement for the period 1970-75 was published in 1976.

Park, Iris M. NEW ZEALAND PERIODICALS OF LITERARY INTEREST. Wellington: National Library Service, 1962.

A fully annotated list of periodicals, including many of only marginal literary interest, which began publication between 1850 and 1961, providing a general description of their nature, and the names of editors and important contributors.

D. GUIDES TO SPECIAL COLLECTIONS

Printed information about special collections and research material of interest to the student of New Zealand literature is both meagre and out of date. No library catalogue has been printed since those of the General Assembly Library (1897) and the Hocken Library (1912), nor are there any lists of a local literary nature. The following items are included as the most helpful guides available.

Alexander Turnbull Library. UNION CATALOGUE OF NEW ZEALAND AND PACIFIC MANUSCRIPTS IN NEW ZEALAND LIBRARIES. Interim ed. 2 parts. Wellington: 1968-69.

> Part 1 lists notifications from other libraries; part 2 lists manuscripts held by the Alexander Turnbull Library. The catalogue as a whole is already very out of date. The Turnbull Library's manuscript holdings, for example, have trebled in the last decade. To make good this major weakness in the country's reference tools, the Alexander Turnbull Library and National Archives are preparing a "National Register of Archives and Manuscripts in New Zealand," and it is hoped that this will be available in 1979. Meanwhile, the reader can at least consult the regular descriptive lists of manuscript material acquired by the Turnbull Library which have been published in the TURNBULL LIBRARY RECORD since 1967. See also the following item.

ARCHIFACTS. Nos. 1-9 (April 1974-October 1976); N.S. No. 1- (February 1977-). [Wellington]: Archives and Records Association of New Zealand, 1974-- .

> ARCHIFACTS carries a record of important accessions to, and articles on, special collections of archives in New Zealand libraries; these accessions occasionally include items of literary interest.

Coleman, Michael D., and Rosemary Chapman. MANUSCRIPTS AND ARCHIVES IN AUCKLAND UNIVERSITY LIBRARY: A BIBLIOGRAPHY. Auckland: Auckland University Library, 1971.

> Among the library's literary papers are collections of A.R.D. Fairburn and Robin Hyde material.

New Zealand Library Association. Special Libraries Section. DIRECTORY OF SPECIAL LIBRARIES IN NEW ZEALAND. 3rd ed. Wellington: New Zealand Library Association, 1974.

> This is more a guide to practical matters like library hours than to the contents of the special collections of the libraries.

Osborn, Andrew D. NEW ZEALAND LIBRARY RESOURCES. Wellington: New Zealand Library Association, 1960.

> This general guide includes an account of library weaknesses (especially in university libraries) which is, fortunately, at least partly out of date.

E. NEW ZEALAND ENGLISH

Baker, S.J. NEW ZEALAND SLANG: A DICTIONARY OF COLLOQUIALISMS. Christchurch: Whitcombe & Tombs, [1941].

Bennett, Jack. "English As It Is Spoken in New Zealand." AMERICAN SPEECH, 18 (April 1943), 81-95; rpt. in ENGLISH TRANSPORTED: ESSAYS ON AUSTRALASIAN ENGLISH. Ed. W.S. Ramson. Canberra: Australian National University Press, 1970, pp. 69-83.

Deals with pronunciation and vocabulary.

Burchfield, R.W., ed. "A Supplement of Australian and New Zealand Words." In THE POCKET OXFORD DICTIONARY. Comp. F.G. and H.W. Fowler. 5th ed. Oxford: Clarendon Press, 1969, pp. 1017-48.

The most readily accessible short list of specifically New Zealand words.

_____. A SUPPLEMENT TO THE OXFORD ENGLISH DICTIONARY. Vol. 1: A-G; vol. 2: H-N. Oxford: Clarendon Press, 1972-76.

This supplement, to be completed in two further volumes, is rich in illustrative examples of the history of words and usages peculiar to New Zealand.

Morris, E.E. AUSTRAL-ENGLISH: A DICTIONARY OF AUSTRALASIAN WORDS, PHRASES AND USAGES. London: Macmillan, 1898.

The earliest scholarly list.

Orsman, H.W. "New Zealand English." In BRITISH AND AMERICAN ENGLISH SINCE 1900. By Eric Partridge and John W. Clark. London: Andrew Dakers, 1951, pp. 93-95.

Turner, George W. THE ENGLISH LANGUAGE IN AUSTRALIA AND NEW ZEALAND. London: Longmans, 1966.

Turner gives most space to Australian English and concentrates on vocabulary.

_____. "New Zealand English Today." In ENGLISH TRANSPORTED: ESSAYS ON AUSTRALASIAN ENGLISH. Ed. W.S. Ramson. Canberra: Australian National University Press, 1970, pp. 84-101.

Wall, Arnold. NEW ZEALAND ENGLISH: A GUIDE TO THE CORRECT PRONUNCIATION OF ENGLISH, WITH SPECIAL REFERENCE TO NEW ZEALAND CONDITIONS AND PROBLEMS. 4th ed. Christchurch: Whitcombe & Tombs, 1961.

______. "New Zealand Speech." In AN ENCYCLOPAEDIA OF NEW ZEALAND. Vol. 2. Ed. A.H. McLintock. Wellington: Government Printer, 1966, pp. 677-81.

Williams, H.W. A DICTIONARY OF THE MAORI LANGUAGE. 7th rev. ed. Wellington: Government Printer, 1971.

> The standard Maori dictionary, first compiled by W. Williams and published in 1844.

F. MISCELLANEOUS REFERENCE WORKS

The following works are useful sources of factual information about New Zealand.

McLintock, A.H., ed. AN ENCYCLOPAEDIA OF NEW ZEALAND. 3 vols. Wellington: Government Printer, 1966.

New Zealand Department of Lands and Survey. GAZETTEER OF NEW ZEALAND PLACE NAMES. Wellington: 1968.

> A very extensive gazetteer, providing grid references to Lands and Survey Department maps.

NEW ZEALAND OFFICIAL YEARBOOK. Wellington: Dept. of Statistics, 1893-- . Annual.

> First published as OFFICIAL HANDBOOK OF NEW ZEALAND in 1875, it became the NEW ZEALAND OFFICIAL YEARBOOK in 1893. It includes a vast range of statistical information. A select bibliography of both old and new books on all subjects, as well as a selection of titles of imaginative literature, has appeared each year since 1964.

Reed, A.W. PLACE NAMES OF NEW ZEALAND. Wellington: Reed, 1975.

> Describes the origins and meanings of place names.

Wards, Ian, ed. NEW ZEALAND ATLAS. Wellington: Government Printer, 1976.

> This contains a wide variety of descriptive essays and photographs as well as maps.

Chapter 2

LITERARY HISTORY AND CRITICISM

Since there is only a handful of full-length studies of any aspect of New Zealand literature, a generous selection of critical articles is included in this chapter, as well as all relevant theses.

Note, however, the exclusion of the following kinds of material: surveys or reviews of "the year's work" in poetry and fiction, except where wider literary considerations are introduced; introductions to anthologies (the most important of these are mentioned in chapter 3); articles on the theatre (as distinct from drama); articles about individual periodicals (these will be found in chapter 6); material on publishers and publishing, except where it reflects influences at work on creative writing; and essays or books on culture and society.

The material is arranged alphabetically by author under the headings of poetry, fiction, and drama, with an introductory general section. Annotation is provided for the more important items, and also for entries where the title is not self-explanatory.

A. GENERAL STUDIES

Alcock, Peter. "Eros Marooned: Ambivalence in Eden." In MARRIAGE AND THE FAMILY IN NEW ZEALAND. Ed. Stewart Houston. Wellington: Hicks Smith & Sons, 1970, pp. 242-75.

> Describes the family in New Zealand literature.

______. "Informing the Void: Initial Cultural Displacement in New Zealand Writing." JOURNAL OF COMMONWEALTH LITERATURE, 6 (June 1971), 84-102.

> Alcock attempts to trace the roots of the new literary growth of the thirties in the work of the Victorian and Edwardian eras.

"All Our Own Works." NEW ZEALAND LISTENER, 23 September 1960, p. 8.

Notes on the publishing success of various books, past and present (mostly nonfiction).

Arvidson, K.O. "The Emergence of a Polynesian Literature." WORLD LITERATURE WRITTEN IN ENGLISH, 14 (April 1975), 91-115; rpt. MANA REVIEW, 1 (January 1976), 28-48.

Arvidson concentrates on the work of the Maori writers Hone Tuwhare and Witi Ihimaera, and the Samoan Albert Wendt.

Bagnall, A.G. "Newspaper Anticipations." EX LIBRIS (Wellington), no. 2 (December 1960), 8-11.

Notes on the variations in the texts of some books which first appeared in newspapers.

Baxter, James K. "Conversation about Writing." NEW ZEALAND MONTHLY REVIEW, 6 (September 1965), 28.

______. "Why Writers Stop Writing." HILLTOP, no. 2 (June 1949), 26-27.

Bennett, Jack. "Landfall in Unknown Seas." LISTENER (London), 21 January 1960, pp. 123-25.

On "certain aspects" of New Zealand literature, especially the immigrant writer's response to a new and empty land.

Bertram, James. TOWARDS A NEW ZEALAND LITERATURE. Dunedin: Hocken Library, University of Otago, 1971.

On the attitudes of New Zealanders, from Dr. T.M. Hocken on, towards the notion of a national literature.

______. "Violence in New Zealand Literature." In VIOLENCE. Ed. J.M. Barrington. Wellington: Dept. of Justice for The Royal Society of New Zealand, 1971.

An abridged version of this lecture appeared as "The Violent Pen" in the NEW ZEALAND LISTENER, 15 January 1973, pp. 8-9.

Bland, Peter. "The Poets Come to Town; Or, The Katipo in the Carpet Slippers." NEW ZEALAND LISTENER, 7 June 1963, p. 4.

Describes recent work by city-dwelling poets.

Bradbrook, M.C. "Distance Looks Our Way: Rhymes and Stories of New Zealand." In her LITERATURE IN ACTION: STUDIES IN CONTINENTAL AND COMMONWEALTH SOCIETY. London: Chatto & Windus, 1972, pp. 83-115. Rpt. as "Distance Looks Our Way." In READINGS IN COMMONWEALTH LITERATURE. Ed. William Walsh. Oxford: Clarendon Press, 1973, pp. 114-23.

Burton, Ormond. SPRING FIRES: A STUDY IN NEW ZEALAND WRITING. Auckland: Book Centre, 1956.

> Burton outlines the historical and social pressures he believes have inhibited good writing in the past, and argues that "passionate enthusiasm" of a quasi-religious nature is required.

Cameron, W.J. "The National Character." In his NEW ZEALAND. Englewood Cliffs, N.J.: Prentice-Hall, [1965], pp. 38-57.

> Cameron uses fiction as well as nonfiction "as an approach to national character."

Canby, H.S. "Literature in a New Land." NEW ZEALAND LISTENER, 17 August 1945, p. 10.

Chaffey, E.V. "Publishing in New Zealand." NEW ZEALAND LIBRARIES, 8 (April 1945), 36-42.

> An informative essay based on the experience of the publishers Whitcombe and Tombs.

______. "Whitcombe and Tombs Ltd." NEW ZEALAND LIBRARIES ASSOCIATION. PROCEEDINGS, 1945, pp. 49-50.

Copland, R.A. "New Zealand: The Contemporary Scene." ENGLISH (London), 15 (Autumn 1965), 225-28.

Curnow, Allen. "New Zealand Literature: The Case for a Working Definition." In THE FUTURE OF NEW ZEALAND. Ed. M.F. Lloyd Prichard. Christchurch: Whitcombe & Tombs for the University of Auckland, 1964, pp. 84-107. Rpt. in ESSAYS ON NEW ZEALAND LITERATURE. Ed. Wystan Curnow. Auckland: Heinemann Educational Books, 1973, pp. 139-54.

> A lecture in which Curnow discusses what is meaningful in the phrase "New Zealand literature."

Curnow, Wystan. "High Culture in a Small Province." In ESSAYS ON NEW ZEALAND LITERATURE. Ed. Wystan Curnow. Auckland: Heinemann Educational Books, 1973, pp. 155-71.

> An essay on "the [unhappy] fate of intellectual and imaginative excellence in a welfare state."

______, ed. ESSAYS ON NEW ZEALAND LITERATURE. Auckland: Heinemann Educational Books, 1973.

> Nine essays, all separately listed in this guide under the appropriate heading, and all previously published except the editor's own.

Davin, Dan. "New Zealand Literature." BOOKS (London), no. 367 (September-October 1966), 161-63.

Edmond, Lauris. "A Plain Teacher's Guide to New Zealand Literature." ENGLISH IN NEW ZEALAND, (July 1976), 16-20.

"Even Writers Must Eat." NEW ZEALAND LISTENER, 4 March 1966, p. 4.

An article on the New Zealand writer's monetary rewards.

Fairburn, A.R.D. "Should Writers Be Encouraged?" NEW ZEALAND LISTENER, 10 December 1943, pp. 8-9.

An essay on book reviewing in New Zealand.

______. "Some Aspects of N.Z. Art and Letters." ART IN NEW ZEALAND, 6 (June 1934), 213-18.

An historically important essay which accurately forecasts the value of American literature as a source of models for New Zealand writers.

______. THE WOMAN PROBLEM AND OTHER PROSE. Auckland: Blackwood & Janet Paul, 1967.

Essays on society and culture, including literary matters.

Fry, Alexander. "It's a Small World." NEW ZEALAND LISTENER, 26 September 1958, pp. 4-5.

A survey of the "little" literary magazines of the previous twenty-five years.

Gabites, G.L. "Centennial Survey: A Note on Canterbury Writing." NEW ZEALAND LISTENER, 8 December 1950, pp. 10-11.

Gillespie, Oliver N. "New Zealand Authors." TOMORROW, 30 October 1935, p. 20.

A note decrying New Zealanders' sense of inferiority towards their literature.

Gillespie-Needham, Dulcie N. "The Colonial and His Books: A Study of Reading in Nineteenth Century New Zealand." Thesis, Victoria University of Wellington, 1971.

Glover, Denis. "Pointers to Parnassus: A Consideration of the Morepork and the Muse." TOMORROW, 30 October 1935, pp. 16-18.

An essay on the need for New Zealand writers to tell the truth for their own country rather than pretty romances for overseas readers.

Gonley, W.K.J. "New Zealand Life in Contemporary Literature." Thesis, University of New Zealand, 1932.

Gordon, Ian. "A Chair of New Zealand Literature." NEW ZEALAND LISTENER, 8 March 1963, p. 4.

"I do not think the time is ripe for the establishment of a Chair in New Zealand literature," Gordon asserts.

_____. "Has New Zealand Any Literature?" NEW ZEALAND LISTENER, 8 October 1943, p. 6.

_____. "Hunting New Zealandisms." NEW ZEALAND LISTENER, 22 November 1957, p. 4.

Notes on specifically New Zealand words and usages to mark the beginning of work on the new supplement to the OXFORD ENGLISH DICTIONARY (see p. 13).

_____. "Writer's Dilemma in New Zealand." JOHN O' LONDON'S WEEKLY, 7 May 1954, pp. 453-54.

An article on the question, "Whom am I writing for?"

Hall, D.O.W. "Writers of Otago." HOME AND BUILDING, 22 (March 1960), 21-25, 107.

_____, et al. "Literature." In AN ENCYCLOPAEDIA OF NEW ZEALAND. Ed. A.H. McLintock. Vol. 2. Wellington: Government Printer, 1966, pp. 320-43.

The other authors of this essay are W.J. Gardner, Nola Millar, W.H. Oliver, and Joan Stevens.

Hanlon, P.J. "The Development of Literature in New Zealand: A Study of Cultural Conditions in New Settlements." Thesis, University of Edinburgh, 1955.

Harris, John. "Book Publishing in New Zealand." NEW ZEALAND LIBRARIES, 6 (October 1942), 41-44.

A very brief essay with some statistical sampling.

Hingley, Bert, Dennis McEldowney, and Bill Manhire. "Critical Look at N.Z. Literary Criticism." NEW ZEALAND BOOK WORLD, no. 4 (September 1973), 5-8.

Holcroft, M.H. CREATIVE PROBLEMS IN NEW ZEALAND. Christchurch: Caxton, 1948.

Holcroft's thesis: "There will be no novels of real importance until writers begin to share a vision of the land which places the people against true landscapes of the mind."

______. DISCOVERED ISLES. Christchurch: Caxton, 1950.

This trilogy comprises THE DEEPENING STREAM: CULTURAL INFLUENCES IN NEW ZEALAND (Christchurch: Caxton, 1940), THE WAITING HILLS (Wellington: Progressive Publishing Society, 1943), and ENCIRCLING SEAS (Christchurch: Caxton, 1946). Holcroft's essays range well beyond purely literary matters, but at the heart of his argument is his vision of the geographical and cultural isolation of the artist and his inescapable if not always conscious awareness of the immigrant's sea voyage to New Zealand and of the emptiness of the hills and mountains the immigrant found here. Although highly individual, these books were widely admired by writers of the forties, and almost equally widely criticized by writers of the fifties. Holcroft's metaphysics were unfavorably scrutinized by D.M. Anderson in "Mr. Holcroft's Islands," LANDFALL, 6 (March 1952), 5-20. Taken as a whole, the trilogy is the most considerable work of literary and cultural criticism written about New Zealand.

______. ISLANDS OF INNOCENCE: THE CHILDHOOD THEME IN NEW ZEALAND FICTION. Wellington: Reed, 1964.

Hyde, Robin. "The Singers of Loneliness." T'IEN HSIA MONTHLY, 7 (August 1938), 9-23.

Interestingly, Robin Hyde gives more space to nineteenth- than to twentieth-century writing.

Johnson, Louis. "Poetry Yearbook and the New Zealand Literary Fund." COMMENT, 5 (January 1964), 30-33.

This is chiefly about censorship and the literary fund; but, written by the editor of the YEARBOOK, the article also provides sidelights on poetry and publishing in the early sixties.

Jones, Joseph J. "Frontier to Metropolis." NEW ZEALAND LISTENER, 19 March 1954, pp. 18-19.

An American's view of what he sees as a "frontier" literature.

Jones, Lawrence. "Some Second Thoughts on New Zealand and American Literature." REVIEW (Dunedin), 1966, pp. 39-51.

Comparisons of some American and New Zealand fiction and poetry.

Keane, Hilda. "Possibilities of New Zealand Literature." NEW ZEALAND ILLUSTRATED MAGAZINE, 1 (February 1900), 391-94.

A rhetorical, defensive paper in which the author pointed to the literary possibilities latent in New Zealand scenery and in Maori romance: an unhappily accurate forecast of what was to come during the next three or more decades.

Lawlor, Pat. BOOKS AND BOOKMEN: NEW ZEALAND AND OVERSEAS. Wellington: Whitcombe & Tombs, 1954.

Lawlor includes a variety of essays on books, printers, and writers in New Zealand, chiefly from the point of view of a book collector.

Long, D.S. "Literary Notes." ARTS AND COMMUNITY, 8, no. 5 (1972), 22-23.

On New Zealand literary periodicals.

______. "The New Zealand Literary Magazines." WORLD LITERATURE WRITTEN IN ENGLISH, 14 (April 1975), 168-74.

______. "The New Zealand Little Magazines." SECOND COMING, 3, no. 1-2 (1974), 22-33.

______. "The Publication of Contemporary New Zealand Literature." NEW ZEALAND LIBRARIES, 37 (December 1974), 290-97.

A descriptive listing of the small presses in New Zealand and overseas which publish works by New Zealand authors.

______. "The Publication of Contemporary New Zealand Literature." NEW ZEALAND LIBRARIES, 39 (February 1976), 18-22.

Of interest for its list of overseas magazines which publish the work of New Zealand writers.

McCormick, E.H. LETTERS AND ART IN NEW ZEALAND. Wellington: Dept. of Internal Affairs, 1940.

______. "Literature in New Zealand." Thesis, University of New Zealand, 1929.

______. "New Zealand: A Colony of the Mind." SATURDAY REVIEW OF LITERATURE (New York), 28 (December 1945), 28-30.

______. NEW ZEALAND LITERATURE: A SURVEY. London: Oxford University Press, 1959.

In this succinct and appreciative survey, McCormick may appear to undervalue the work written after 1930, to which he gives only a third of his space; but he properly makes room in the earlier periods for books of history, travel, and anthropology. This work remains the only full-length account of New Zealand literature.

______. "The State As a Publisher of Books and Periodicals." NEW ZEALAND LIBRARIES, 9 (March 1946), 25-32.

A critical examination of the proposal for a state literary fund put forward by M.H. Holcroft in THE WAITING HILLS (see p. 20).

______. "The Voice of a Silent Land: New Zealand Writing." BOOKS ABROAD (Oklahoma), 29 (Summer 1955), 285-88.

A compact survey of the work of the previous twenty-five years.

McEldowney, Dennis. "Scholarly Publishing in New Zealand." SCHOLARLY PUBLISHING (Toronto), 1 (October 1969), 107-11.

______. "Ultima Thule to Little Bethel: Notes on Religion in New Zealand Writing." LANDFALL, 20 (March 1966), 50-59.

McEldowney covers the period from settlement on, but is especially perceptive about the most recent decades.

Mackay, Jessie. "Concerning New Zealand Letters." ART IN NEW ZEALAND, 1 (March 1929), 161-65.

A defensive and puzzled essay on the incontrovertible poverty of New Zealand writing in its first ninety or so years.

Mander, Jane. "Creative Writing in Australia and New Zealand." LITERARY DIGEST INTERNATIONAL BOOK REVIEW, 1 (May 1923), 32, 63-64.

Marris, C.A. "Our Younger Generation of Writers." In ANNALS OF NEW ZEALAND LITERATURE. Ed. J.C. Andersen. [Wellington]: New Zealand Authors' Week Committee, 1936, pp. 18-19.

Mulgan, Alan. GREAT DAYS IN NEW ZEALAND WRITING. Wellington: Reed, 1962.

A collection of thirteen essays on a variety of New Zealand books and literary topics.

______. LITERATURE AND AUTHORSHIP IN NEW ZEALAND. London: Allen & Unwin, 1943.

A short history of New Zealand literature, with two brief chapters on the effects of publishers and audience-response on authors.

______. "Literature and Landscape in New Zealand." NEW ZEALAND GEOGRAPHER, 2 (April 1946), 189-206.

A rather superficial treatment, but the examples are interestingly various.

Murray-Smith, Stephen. "An Australian Look at the New Zealand Book." AUSTRALIAN BOOK REVIEW, 4 (February 1965), 53-54.

A publisher's view of the nonfiction as well as the imaginative literature of New Zealand to be found in Australia. In the April issue, John Hooker showed how few books in fact reached Australian shops.

Nesbitt, Bruce. "Literary Nationalism in Australia and New Zealand 1880-1900." Thesis, Australian National University, 1968.

New, William H. "New Zealand: Escape into Distance." In his AMONG WORLDS: AN INTRODUCTION TO MODERN COMMONWEALTH AND SOUTH AFRICAN FICTION. Erin, Ont.: Press Porcepic, 1975, pp. 133-56.

An essay which contrasts two reciprocal elements in New Zealand literature: an optimistic fantasy of an ideal new land, and a painful reality of an uncultured conventional society.

"New Zealand Books Today." NEW ZEALAND LISTENER, 16 September 1955, pp. 6-7.

Remarks on the growing interest in New Zealand literature with contributions from Ian Gordon, A.G. Bagnall, and K.J. Sheen.

"New Zealand in the New World." TIMES LITERARY SUPPLEMENT, 16 August 1957, pp. xxxviii-xxxix.

A general review of contemporary literature and culture, with stress on the importance of the periodical LANDFALL (see p. 218).

Palmer, Nettie. "New Zealand and Australia." MEANJIN PAPERS, 3 (Summer 1944), 165-68.

A short essay on the resurgence of New Zealand literature and on the lack of literary relations between the two countries.

Pearson, W.H. FRETFUL SLEEPERS AND OTHER ESSAYS. Auckland: Heinemann Educational Books, 1974.

This is mainly a collection of book reviews, but it contains several important essays, including "Fretful Sleepers: A Sketch of New Zealand Behaviour and Its Implications for the Artist," first published in LANDFALL, 6 (September 1952) and reprinted in LANDFALL COUNTRY, ed. Charles Brasch (Christchurch: Caxton, 1960).

______. "The Maori and Literature 1938-65." In THE MAORI PEOPLE IN THE NINETEEN-SIXTIES. Ed. Eric Schwimmer. Auckland: Longman Paul, 1968, pp. 217-56; rpt. in ESSAYS ON NEW ZEALAND LITERATURE. Ed. Wystan Curnow. Auckland: Heinemann Educational Books, 1973, pp. 99-138.

This valuable article is as much a history of racial attitudes as of the literature in which the Maori appears. Pearson also deals with writing in English by Maori authors. The extensive bibliography which accompanied the article on its first appearance is not reprinted by Curnow.

______. "The Recognition of Reality." In COMMONWEALTH LITERATURE: UNITY AND DIVERSITY IN A COMMON CULTURE. Ed. John Press. London: Heinemann Educational Books, 1965, pp. 32-47; rpt. in his FRETFUL SLEEPERS AND OTHER ESSAYS. Auckland: Heinemann Educational Books, 1974, pp. 137-50.

Phillips, Enid B.V. "New Zealand's Rich Store of Children's Books." NEW ZEALAND JOURNAL OF AGRICULTURE, 77 (December 1948), 629-33.

Plomer, William. "Some Books from New Zealand." In FOLIOS OF NEW WRITING, no. 4 (Autumn 1941), 55-61; rpt. in PENGUIN NEW WRITING, no. 17 (April-June 1943), 149-54.

An English reader's response to a variety of books by New Zealand writers, in particular Frank Sargeson.

"Printer to the Arts." NEW ZEALAND LISTENER, 4 November 1966, pp. 10-11.

An article on the printer and publisher Harry H. Tombs.

Ramson, W.S. "Australian and New Zealand English: The Present State of Studies." KIVUNG, 2 (April 1969), 42-56.

Already so out-dated as to be of primarily historical interest.

Reed, A.H. & A.W., Ltd. THE HOUSE OF REED: FIFTY YEARS OF NEW ZEALAND PUBLISHING. Wellington: 1957.

______. THE HOUSE OF REED 1957-1967. Wellington: 1968.

Reeves, Trevor. "New Zealand Small Magazines and Presses." COMMONWEALTH NEWSLETTER (Aarhus), no. 6 (June 1974), 9-12.

______. "A Survey of Recent New Zealand Writing." ARIEL, 5 (July 1974), 16-37.

Reid, Ian. "Depression Literature." In NEW ZEALAND'S HERITAGE. Ed. Ray Knox. Wellington: Paul Hamlyn, [1971-73], pp. 2276-80.

Reid, John C. CREATIVE WRITING IN NEW ZEALAND: A BRIEF CRITICAL HISTORY. [Auckland]: 1946.

______. "A False Literary Dawn." In NEW ZEALAND'S HERITAGE. Ed. Ray Knox. Wellington: Paul Hamlyn, [1971-73], pp. 1593-96.

Describes the literature of the 1890s.

______. "Letters in Otago." In A CENTURY OF ART IN OTAGO. Ed. Harry H. Tombs. Wellington: Harry H. Tombs, [1948], pp. 92-101.

______. "Literature." In THE PATTERN OF NEW ZEALAND CULTURE. Ed. A.L. McLeod. Ithaca, N.Y.: Cornell University Press, 1968, pp. 17-48.

______. "The Literature of New Zealand." In THE COMMONWEALTH PEN: AN INTRODUCTION TO THE LITERATURE OF THE BRITISH COMMONWEALTH. Ed. A.L. McLeod. Ithaca, N.Y.: Cornell University Press, 1961, pp. 63-77.

______. "New Zealand Literature." In AUSTRALIA AND NEW ZEALAND. G.A. Wilkes and John C. Reid. University Park: Pennsylvania State University Press, [1970?], pp. 155-233.

A survey by genres.

______. "New Zealand Literature." ASIAN PACIFIC QUARTERLY, 4 (Summer 1972), 31-41.

______. NEW ZEALAND NON-FICTION: A SURVEY WITH NOTES FOR DISCUSSION. Wellington: Price Milburn, 1968.

Written for school use. Reid discusses and prints extracts from books of travel, history, literary criticism, and other genres.

______. "New Zealand Writing Today." BOOKS (London), no. 12 (December 1953), 145-50.

______. "Vom Werden eigenen Schrifttums" [The evolution of an indigenous literature]. INSTITUT FUER AUSLANDSBEZIEHUNGEN, STUTTGART. MITTEILUNGEN, 6 (January-February 1956), 22-26.

"Report from New Zealand." TIMES LITERARY SUPPLEMENT, CHILDREN'S BOOKS SECTION, 1 July 1955, p. xviii.

A historical survey of the publication of New Zealand children's books.

Rhodes, H. Winston. "Australian and New Zealand Literature." MEANJIN QUARTERLY, 27 (June 1968), 184-93.

A comparative study of the historical, social, and geographical influences at work on the literature of the two countries.

______. "Author's Week." TOMORROW, 13 May 1936, pp. 20-22.

Reflections on New Zealand literature. O.N. Gillespie took issue with a number of points in TOMORROW, 27 May 1936, pp. 21-22.

______. "New Zealand Literary Criticism." NEW ZEALAND LIBRARIES, 10 (July 1947), 123-28.

A call for the avoidance of generalisation and abstraction, and for "the joys of discovery and the pleasures of interpretation" instead.

______. "On Swearing." TOMORROW, 1 August 1934, pp. 12-13.

A plea for less dove-like prattle in literature, less pussy-footing in criticism.

______. "Race Relations and Literature." MEANJIN QUARTERLY, 32 (September 1973), 260-67.

Rhodes distinguishes between the meaning of "the search for identity" for Maori and European writers in New Zealand, and discusses the special importance of Maori tradition in literature written by Maori writers.

______. "These Two Islands." TOMORROW, 19 July 1939, pp. 600-602.

Rhodes misses in New Zealand writers signs of a "fierce love of one's own native land."

Richards, Ray. "The New Zealand Publisher: His Opportunities and Limitations." BOOKSELLER (London), 24 August 1974, pp. 1530-34.

This discussion takes in all books, not just imaginative literature.

Robertson, R.T. "Early America-Early New Zealand: Some Comparisons of Early American Literature with the State of Writing in New Zealand." HILLTOP, no. 1 (April 1949), 20-22.

Ronai, Paulo. "Literary Life in Erewhon." NEW ZEALAND LISTENER, 18 February 1949, pp. 15-16.

A translation of a general article on New Zealand literature which first appeared in LETRAS E ARTES (Rio de Janiero).

Rutherford, Anna. "Recent Writing in Australia and New Zealand." BOOKS, n.s. no. 5 (Autumn 1971), 10-16.

S., E.G. "Note on the Literature of the Modern Maori." MATE, no. 4 (February 1960), 22-23.

Selles, Colette. "L'intégration des Maoris en Nouvelle-Zélande: réalité et littérature." Thesis, University of Toulouse (Le Mirail), 1973.

Seymour, R. "A Present Tendency in New Zealand Literature." NEW ZEALAND NEW WRITING, no. 4 (March 1945), 31-34.

An essay which points to a gap between the conception of the island-dweller held by Holcroft, Curnow, and McCormick and the true "normal, uninteresting but well-adjusted New Zealander."

Shadbolt, Maurice. "The Other Side." OVERLAND, no. 58 (Winter 1974), 44-49.

On recent New Zealand writing--"from an address to the Adelaide Festival."

Simpson, E.C. A SURVEY OF THE ARTS IN NEW ZEALAND. [Wellington]: Wellington Chamber Music Society, 1961.

Part 4--"Literature"--comments briefly on P.E.N., the New Zealand Literature Fund, scholarships, and the outlets provided by periodicals and the broadcasting service.

Sinclair, Keith. "The Intelligent Reader's Guide to New Zealand Criticism." HERE AND NOW, 3 (September 1953), 26.

Smithies, R.J. "New Zealand Literature: A Brief Survey." In NEW ZEALAND OFFICIAL YEARBOOK, 1964, pp. 1152-57.

Stead, C.K. "The Hulk of the World's Between." In DISTANCE LOOKS OUR WAY: THE EFFECTS OF REMOTENESS ON NEW ZEALAND. Ed. Keith Sinclair. [Auckland]: Paul's Book Arcade for the University of Auckland, 1961, pp. 79-96.

An excellent essay. O.E. Middleton wrote an extensive critical note, "Writing and Belonging," in REVIEW (Dunedin), 1971, pp. 45-51.

______. "A Poet's View." ISLANDS, 3 (Spring 1974), 314-25.

A personal and discursive essay on the author's discovery of New Zealand writing in the 1950s, and on his own experience as a poet.

Vennell, Owen St. John. PATRONAGE AND NEW ZEALAND LITERATURE: AN INVESTIGATION OF THE NEW ZEALAND LITERARY FUND. [Wellington: Dept of Internal Affairs, 1977.]

Vogt, Anton. "The Distant View." NEW ZEALAND LISTENER, 8 June 1962, p. 37.

Volkerling, Michael. "Images of Society in New Zealand Writing: An Examination of the Social Concerns of New Zealand Writers, 1960-1970." Thesis, University of Auckland, 1975.

Walsh, William. "New Zealand." In his COMMONWEALTH LITERATURE. London: Oxford University Press, 1973, pp. 93-109.

Wattie, Nelson. "The Effect of Isolation on New Zealand's Cultural Traditions." COMMONWEALTH NEWSLETTER, no. 10 (September 1976), 21-26.

The article does not have the scope which its title implies.

Wild, J.M. "The Literary Periodical in New Zealand." Thesis, University of New Zealand, 1951.

Wilson, Phillip. "A New Literature of the South Pacific." AMERICAN QUARTERLY (Philadelphia), 6 (Spring 1954), 66-71.

An essay on the local historical and social influences on New Zealand literature.

B. POETRY

Ashworth, Arthur. "Contemporary New Zealand Poetry." SOUTHERLY, 10 (1949), 2-16.

Barnhill, Helen M. "The Pakeha Harp: Maori Mythology in the Works of Four Early New Zealand Poets." Thesis, University of Otago, 1972.

The four poets discussed are Alfred Domett, Arthur Adams, Jessie Mackay, and Blanche Baughan.

Baxter, James K. ASPECTS OF POETRY IN NEW ZEALAND. Christchurch: Caxton, 1967.

In this fine lecture, Baxter identified distinguishing traits in what he called the transitional poets (those of the thirties) and the post-transitional poets (those of the forties and fifties).

______. THE FIRE AND THE ANVIL: NOTES ON MODERN POETRY. Wellington: New Zealand University Press, 1955.

Three lectures on problems of criticism, inspiration, and symbolism: the first two are in part and the third entirely about New Zealand poetry.

______. "Notes Made in Winter." NEW ZEALAND POETRY YEARBOOK, 10 (1961-62), 13-15.

An attack on the "disease of formalism" Baxter found in New Zealand poetry.

______. "Poetry in New Zealand." YEAR BOOK OF THE ARTS, 2 (1946), 111-14.

An essay on the New Zealand poet's sense of insecurity.

______. RECENT TRENDS IN NEW ZEALAND POETRY. Christchurch: Caxton, 1951.

A talk given at a New Zealand writers' conference.

Bertram, James. "New Zealand Landfall." NEW STATESMAN, 10 September 1960, pp. 352-53.

On the excellence of and the popular support given to New Zealand poetry.

______. "Poetry Comes of Age." In NEW ZEALAND'S HERITAGE. Ed. Ray Knox. Wellington: Paul Hamlyn, [1971-73], pp. 2399-403.

An illustrated survey spanning the years 1920 to 1945.

Broughton, W.S. "Problems and Responses of Three New Zealand Poets in the 1920s." In PROCEEDINGS AND PAPERS OF THE TENTH AULLA CONGRESS. Ed. P. Dane. [Auckland]: Australasian Universities Language and Literature Association, [1966], pp. 202-13; rpt. in ESSAYS ON NEW ZEALAND LITERATURE. Ed. Wystan Curnow. Auckland: Heinemann Educational Books, 1973, pp. 1-15.

The poets are D'Arcy Cresswell, A.R.D. Fairburn, and Geoffrey de Montalk.

Chan, Stephen, "Poetry Outside the Political Condition." ISLANDS, 4 (Summer 1975), 447-50.

A comment on poetry and politics in New Zealand, prompted by the judge's report on a political poetry competition published in the Spring 1975 issue.

Copland, R.A. "Nature and the Writer: Early Poetry." In NEW ZEALAND'S NATURE HERITAGE. Ed. Ray Knox. Hong Kong: Hamlyns, [1974-76], pp. 2357-63.

______. "Nature and the Writer: Later Poetry." In NEW ZEALAND'S NATURE HERITAGE. Ed. Ray Knox. Hong Kong: Hamlyns, [1974-76], pp. 2419-25.

Curnow, Allen. "Aspects of New Zealand Poetry." MEANJIN PAPERS, 2 (Summer 1943), 20-26.

______. "Distraction and Definition: Centripetal Directions in New Zealand Poetry." In NATIONAL IDENTITY: PAPERS DELIVERED AT THE COMMONWEALTH LITERATURE CONFERENCE, UNIVERSITY OF QUEENSLAND, 1968. Ed. K.L. Goodwin. London: Heinemann Educational Books, 1970, pp. 170-86.

The most recent of Curnow's essays, in which he argues that "the evasion, or ignorance of, one's place and circumstances, has been the cause of more bad writing than even the most chauvinistic obsession with them."

Doyle, Charles. "Making It with the Muse." In CONSPECTUS 1964. Auckland University Literary Society. Auckland, 1965, pp. 1-13.

A discussion of a number of poets, most of whom began writing after 1950.

______. SMALL PROPHETS AND QUICK RETURNS: REFLECTIONS ON NEW ZEALAND POETRY. Auckland: New Zealand Publishing Society, 1966.

Edmond, Murray. "The Idea of the Poet." CAVE, no. 4 (November 1973), 29-39.

Fairburn, A.R.D. "Poetry in New Zealand." YEAR BOOK OF THE ARTS, 1 (1945), 123-28. Rpt. in his THE WOMAN PROBLEM AND OTHER PROSE. Ed. Denis Glover and Geoffrey Fairburn. Auckland: Blackwood & Janet Paul, 1967, pp. 131-35.

An essay on the relationship between the poet and society.

Frean, R.G. "Cautious Measure of the Kiwi Muse." NEW ZEALAND LISTENER, 19 April 1971, p. 15.

A survey of New Zealand poetry made on the basis of recent anthologies.

French, Phyllis Ann. "Twelve Women Poets of New Zealand: Imperatives of Shape and Growth." Thesis, University of Texas, 1967.

> The poets discussed are Blanche Baughan, Ursula Bethell, Eileen Duggan, Katherine Mansfield, Robin Hyde, Jessie Mackay, Gloria Rawlinson, Ruth Gilbert, Ruth France, Mary Smithyman (Stanley), Ruth Dallas, and Fleur Adcock.

Gager, Owen. "How Outer is the Edge?" ARGOT, no. 20 (July 1969), 18-22.

> An attack on the insularity of New Zealand poets and readers.

Glover, Denis. "Poets and Poetry in the Welfare State." NEW ZEALAND LISTENER, 27 October 1961, p. 11.

> A light-hearted but, at the same time, serious essay.

Glover, Rupert. "The Poet in New Zealand and the New Zealand Poetic." NEW ZEALAND MONTHLY REVIEW, 6 (May 1965), 20-22.

Gordon, Ian. "Hope for New Zealand Poetry." NEW ZEALAND LISTENER, 12 November 1943, pp. 10-11.

> A talk on the poets of the previous ten years.

Gurr, A.J. "The Two Realities of New Zealand Poetry." JOURNAL OF COMMONWEALTH LITERATURE, no. 1 (September 1965), 122-34. Rpt. in READINGS IN COMMONWEALTH LITERATURE. Ed. William Walsh. Oxford: Clarendon Press, 1973, pp. 100-113.

> Although the common division of New Zealand poets into two warring factions led by Curnow and Johnson was always unreal, this article is nevertheless a useful discussion, especially of the implications of Curnow's poetry. Peter Alcock took issue with Gurr's article in a letter in no. 3 (July 1967), pp. 107-10.

Hart-Smith, W. "Poetry in New Zealand." YEAR BOOK OF THE ARTS, 3 (1947), 145-47.

> An Australian view.

Innes, M.A. "Where Are Our Poets?" TOMORROW, 29 August 1934, p. 17.

> A brief note on poets like Allen Curnow and A.R.D. Fairburn, whom Innes found to be writing convincingly about contemporary social conditions.

Johnson, Louis. "Poetry Since the War." In NEW ZEALAND'S HERITAGE. Ed. Ray Knox. Wellington: Paul Hamlyn, [1971-73], pp. 2762-66, 2797-800.

______. "The Shadow of Conservatism (Prospects for a Young Poet)." SALIENT (Literary Issue), September 1953 [pp. 10-11].

______. "The Tasman's Other Side." POETRY AUSTRALIA, no. 44 (1972), 45-52.

An article mainly on the poetry of R.A.K. Mason, Denis Glover, Charles Doyle, and Richard Packer.

Kingsbury, Anthony L. "Poetry in New Zealand 1850-1930." Thesis, University of Auckland, 1968.

McKay, Frank. NEW ZEALAND POETRY: AN INTRODUCTION THROUGH THE DISCUSSION OF SELECTED POEMS. Wellington: Price Milburn, [1970].

A school textbook.

Maxwell-Mahon, W.B. "Life without Prufrock: A Study in Current New Zealand Poetry." UNISA ENGLISH STUDIES (Pretoria), 2 (1969), 68-79.

Mitcalfe, Barry. "Of Writers (Teachers and Others)." NATIONAL EDUCATION, 33 (December 1951), 430-31.

An article on the Wellington Teachers' Training College group of poets.

Moody, D. "Poets without a Tradition." BLACKFRIARS, 38 (July-August 1957), 331-36.

Comments on Australian and New Zealand poetry.

Mountjoy, Zenocrate. "Modern New Zealand Poetry." NATIONAL EDUCATION, 29 (December 1947), 372-73.

Mulgan, Alan. "Our First Anthologists." NEW ZEALAND LISTENER, 6 September 1957, p. 18.

A note on Alexander and Currie's NEW ZEALAND VERSE (1906), see p. 44.

Oliver, W.H. POETRY IN NEW ZEALAND. [Wellington]: School Publications Branch, Dept. of Education, 1960.

A post-primary school bulletin in which Oliver quotes and discusses poems under a variety of topic headings.

______. POETRY IN NEW ZEALAND. Wellington: Council of Adult Education, Victoria University of Wellington, 1966.

These six lectures, prepared for an adult education discussion course, make an excellent introduction for the student of New Zealand poetry.

Parmée, Frederick C. "View to the Horizon: An Article Concerned with the Problems and Prospects of a New Zealand Poetry for the Nineteen-Eighties." NEW QUARTERLY CAVE, 2, no. 3 (1977), 207-09.

Parr, Chris. " 'The Numbed Poetic': A Critique of Contemporary New Zealand Poetry." PILGRIMS OF TH ARTS, 2 (June 1977), 97-106.

Paterson, Alistair. "Poetry in Transition: Notes on Trends and Influences in New Zealand Verse." LANDFALL, 30 (March 1976), 76-85.

Paul, Blackwood. "Our Poets' Progress." ART IN NEW ZEALAND, 3 (March 1931), 181-89.

Paul laments the "gentlemanly" verse of the past, but sees hope in the precepts of D'Arcy Cresswell and in the practice of Geoffrey de Montalk (a poet now little remembered).

Reid, John C. "Note on New Zealand Poetry." AMERICAN POETRY MAGAZINE, 36 (August 1955), 11-12.

Roddick, Alan. "The Mountains in New Zealand Poetry." NEW ZEALAND ALPINE JOURNAL, 25 (1972), 106-10.

Seymour, R. "Notes on OUTRIGGER's Special Collection on and by Women Poets: A Sociological, Literary and Feminist Perspective." OUTRIGGER, no. 6 (1975), 1-16.

An extensive analysis of the work on and by women writers published in OUTRIGGER nos. 3 and 4. It is followed by a largely dissenting comment from Lauris Edmond.

Shapcott, Thomas. "New Zealand Poetry Now." AUSTRALIAN BOOK REVIEW, 11 (July 1973), 95-97.

An essay based on the publications of the Caveman Press.

Smithyman, C.B.K. "Reflections of Social Attitudes in 'Epic' Poetry of the Drawing-Room, in Pre-1900 New Zealand." UNIVERSITY OF AUCKLAND HISTORICAL SOCIETY ANNUAL, 1967, pp. 28-41.

Smithyman, Kendrick. "Post-War New Zealand Poetry. 1. The Sublime and the Romantic. 2. The Road to Academe. 3. The Clayless Climate. 4. The True Voice of Feeling." MATE, no. 8 (December 1961), 27-36; no. 9 (May 1962), 34-44; no. 10 (December 1962), 29-42; no. 11 (July 1963), 31-48.

These essays formed the basis of the author's A WAY OF SAYING (see below). The fourth essay was reprinted as "Wellington and the Fifties: The True Voice of Feeling" in ESSAYS ON NEW ZEALAND LITERATURE, ed. Wystan Curnow (Auckland: Heinemann Educational Books, 1973), pp. 29-42.

______. A WAY OF SAYING: A STUDY OF NEW ZEALAND POETRY. Auckland: Collins, 1965.

A fascinating and provocative personal view of New Zealand poetry from the 1930s on. The book's packed and disjointed nature is not helped by the lack of chapter headings and index.

Sturm, Terry. "New Zealand Poetry and the Depression." JOURNAL OF COMMONWEALTH LITERATURE, no. 2 (December 1966), 124-37; rpt. in ESSAYS ON NEW ZEALAND LITERATURE. Ed. Wystan Curnow. Auckland: Heinemann Educational Books, 1973, pp. 16-28.

______. "Problems of Cultural Dependence in New Zealand and Australian Poetry." Thesis, University of Leeds, 1967.

Wells, Henry W. "Poetry in New Zealand." VOICES (Vinelhaven, Maine), no. 133 (1948), 38-41.

Whalley, G. "Celebration and Elegy in New Zealand Verse." QUEEN'S QUARTERLY, 74 (Winter 1967), 738-53.

C. FICTION

Alcock, Peter. "Sexual Inadequacy in the New Zealand Novel." QUADRANT, 11 (January-February 1967), 22-26.

Andrews, Isobel. "Short Story Writers--A One-Way Street." NEW ZEALAND LISTENER, 23 June 1950, p. 8.

Isobel Andrews comments on the failure of short-story writers to reflect life as experienced by the majority of New Zealanders.

Ballantyne, David. "The International Symposium on the Short Story: New Zealand." KENYON REVIEW, 32 (1970), 97-104.

Observations on the writing and publishing of short stories in New Zealand.

Baxter, J.C. "The New Zealand National Character as Exemplified by Three Novelists." Thesis, University of New Zealand, 1952.

The novelists discussed are Frank Sargeson, John Mulgan, and Dan Davin.

Brooke, Richard. "A Look at the Myth; Or, The Bourgeois Crock at the End of the Rainbow." FRONTIERS (Christchurch), 2, no. 1 [1969], 5-10.

A jaundiced view of New Zealand fiction.

Chapman, Robert. "Fiction and the Social Pattern: Some Implications of Recent New Zealand Writing." LANDFALL, 7 (March 1953), 26-58; rpt. in ESSAYS ON NEW ZEALAND LITERATURE. Ed. Wystan Curnow. Auckland: Heinemann Educational Books, 1973, pp. 71-98.

A seminal essay on the way writers of fiction have reflected changing social and especially family patterns and, at the same time, have highlighted "the distortions produced by an irrelevant puritanism of misplaced demands and guilts."

Copland, R.A. "Nature and the Writer: Later Prose." In NEW ZEALAND'S NATURE HERITAGE. Ed. Ray Knox. Hong Kong: Hamlyns, [1974-76], pp. 2406-12.

Includes some discussion of natural description in fiction.

Davin, Dan. "The New Zealand Novel." JOURNAL OF THE ROYAL SOCIETY OF ARTS, 110 (July 1962), 586-98.

An attempt to define what is specifically New Zealand in the New Zealand novel.

De Lautour, Christopher R. "New Zealand and the Novels, 1945-60: An Examination of the Use of Background in the Novels Set in New Zealand in this Period." Thesis, University of Otago, 1963.

Evans, Patrick. "The Provincial Dilemma." LANDFALL, 30 (March 1976), 25-36; (September 1976), 246-58; 31 (March 1977), 9-22.

Three articles on novelists' attempts "to find and distinguish those elements in our way of life so worthy and abiding that their translation into literature will make the world into New Zealand."

Franklin, Harvey. "Time, Place and People: A Geographical Projection of the New Zealand Novel." NEW ZEALAND LISTENER, 7 March 1958, p. 6.

A perhaps not remarkably percipient forecast that middle-class urban novels would soon appear--as indeed they have.

Gordon, Ian. WRITING IN NEW ZEALAND: NO. 5, THE NOVEL 1860-90. [Wellington]: Dept. of Education, [1947].

A post-primary bulletin containing brief critical discussion and extracts from several novels.

Grant, A.K. "An Inquiry into the Construction and Classification of the New Zealand Short Story." NEW ZEALAND LISTENER, 27 October 1973, pp. 26-27.

A whimsical but telling classification of New Zealand short stories.

Gries, Joan C. "An Outline of Prose Fiction in New Zealand." Thesis, University of New Zealand, 1951.

Hankin, Cherry. "New Zealand Women Novelists: Their Attitudes toward Life in a Developing Society." WORLD LITERATURE WRITTEN IN ENGLISH, 14 (April 1975), 144-67.

The author finds a "deepening pessimism" in novels of the last hundred years which she believes reflects an "increasing confusion about the role, the status, and the rights of women within New Zealand society."

______, ed. CRITICAL ESSAYS ON THE NEW ZEALAND NOVEL. Auckland: Heinemann Educational Books, 1976.

Essays on nine major novels.

Hilliard, Noel. "Authorship in New Zealand." In THE CHANGING SHAPE OF BOOKS. New Zealand Book Council. [Wellington, 1973], pp. 1-10.

Personal reflections on writing and publishing fiction in New Zealand.

Holcroft, M.H. "Back Streets of Utopia: Interim Report on the New Zealand Short Story." NEW ZEALAND LISTENER, 27 October 1950, pp. 6-7.

An analysis of the settings and themes of fifty short stories submitted to the LISTENER over a period of a few months.

Jones, Lawrence. "The Persistence of Realism: Dan Davin, Noel Hilliard and Recent New Zealand Short Stories." ISLANDS, 6 (Winter 1977), 182-200.

Lee, Edmund. "On Writing the Great New Zealand Novel." ARENA, no. 35 (1953), 11-13.

McCormick, E.H. WRITING IN NEW ZEALAND: THE LATER NOVEL. [Wellington]: School Publications Branch, Dept. of Education, [1947].

A post-primary school bulletin containing a short historical essay on novels published after 1890, with numerous short illustrative extracts.

McEldowney, Dennis. "The Colonial Novel." In NEW ZEALAND'S HERITAGE. Ed. Ray Knox. Wellington: Paul Hamlyn, [1971-73], pp. 1205-10.

______. "The Maori-European Wars in Fiction." In NEW ZEALAND'S HERITAGE. Ed. Ray Knox. Wellington: Paul Hamlyn, [1971-73], pp. 1149-53.

Maxwell, J.C. "New Zealand Fiction." NOTES AND QUERIES, 218 (September 1973), 322-23.

> A note on textual errors and misprints in the first five novels published in the Auckland University Press's "New Zealand Fiction" series.

Mulgan, Alan. "Difficulties of the New Zealand Novelist." ART IN NEW ZEALAND, 1 (December 1928), 115-17.

> Mulgan argues that a great New Zealand novel will be about New Zealand life, but admits that neither New Zealanders nor the British are much interested in anything so unexciting.

______. "The New Zealand Novel." In ANNALS OF NEW ZEALAND LITERATURE. Ed. J.C. Andersen. [Wellington]: New Zealand Authors' Week Committee, 1936, pp. 9-11.

"Myths in Antipodean Writing." TIMES LITERARY SUPPLEMENT, 14 June 1963, p. 420.

> A comparison of Australian and New Zealand writing based on a number of recent collections of short stories.

O'Brien, E.J. "A Critical Study of Selected Short Stories Written in New Zealand since 1930." Thesis, University of New Zealand, 1949.

Parsonage, J.S. "An Introduction to New Zealand Fiction." LIBRARY WORLD, 65 (July 1963), 9-16.

Pearson, W.H. "Attitudes to the Maori in Some Pakeha Fiction." JOURNAL OF THE POLYNESIAN SOCIETY, 67 (September 1958), 211-38; rpt. in his FRETFUL SLEEPERS AND OTHER ESSAYS. Auckland: Heinemann Educational Books, 1974, pp. 46-71.

> This is briefer than his later article on a similar topic (see p. 24), but Pearson here covers fiction from the earliest novels on. In its reprinted form, the essay lacks its original bibliography.

Reid, Ian. "The Influence of the Depression on Australian and New Zealand Fiction 1930-1950." Thesis, University of Adelaide, 1970.

______. "'The Woman Problem' in Some Australian and New Zealand Novels." SOUTHERN REVIEW (Adelaide), 7 (1974), 187-204.

Deals with fiction between 1936 and 1944. Robin Hyde's THE GODWITS FLY is the only New Zealand novel discussed.

Reid, John C. NEW ZEALANDERS AT WAR IN FICTION. Auckland: New Zealand Publishing Society, 1966.

Rhodes, H. Winston. NEW ZEALAND FICTION SINCE 1945: A CRITICAL SURVEY OF RECENT NOVELS AND SHORT STORIES. Dunedin: John McIndoe, 1968.

A brief survey of twenty-five writers.

______. NEW ZEALAND NOVELS: A THEMATIC APPROACH. Wellington: Price Milburn, 1969.

Though written for schools, and provided with questions for discussion, this excellent little book is of value to more than its intended audience.

______. "New Zealand Writing: A Decade and Its Promise." NEW ZEALAND BOOK WORLD, no. 5 (October 1973), 10-12.

A survey of the previous ten years' fiction.

______. "Two Views: The Short Story in New Zealand." LANDFALL, 21 (March 1967), 84-89.

A valuable essay, prompted by the publication of C.K. Stead's NEW ZEALAND SHORT STORIES: SECOND SERIES (1966), in which Rhodes reflects on the nature and shortcomings of such anthologies. The other "view," a more conventional review, was contributed by Terry Sturm.

Roberts, Heather. "Mother, Wife and Mistress: Women Characters in the New Zealand Novel from 1920 to 1940." LANDFALL, 29 (September 1975), 233-47.

Sargeson, Frank. "A Book of Stories." LANDFALL, 8 (March 1954), 22-26.

A note on the isolation of New Zealand authors, as represented in Dan Davin's edition of NEW ZEALAND SHORT STORIES (1953)--see p. 50.

Smith, E.M. A HISTORY OF NEW ZEALAND FICTION FROM 1862 TO THE PRESENT TIME WITH SOME ACCOUNT OF ITS RELATION TO THE NATIONAL LIFE AND CHARACTER. Wellington: Reed, 1939.

Still a usefully full survey of New Zealand's early (but on the whole uninteresting) fiction.

Stevens, Joan. "The Family in New Zealand Fiction." In THE NEW ZEALAND FAMILY AND CHILD DEVELOPMENT. Association for the Study of Childhood. Wellington: Price Milburn, 1969, pp. 21-24.

A summary of one of the Association's 1968 lectures.

______. "Fiction Since 1945." In NEW ZEALAND'S HERITAGE. Ed. Ray Knox. Wellington: Paul Hamlyn, [1971-73], pp. 2817-22, 2847-52.

______. "New Zealand Fiction Since 1945." ASIAN PACIFIC QUARTERLY, 5 (Autumn 1973), 20-29.

______. THE NEW ZEALAND NOVEL 1860-1965. 2nd rev. ed. Wellington: Reed, 1966.

Although this book remains too evidently based on notes for an adult education course, it is especially useful as a guide to early and to minor fiction, and for general reference.

______. NEW ZEALAND SHORT STORIES: A SURVEY WITH NOTES FOR DISCUSSION. Wellington: Price Milburn, 1968.

A useful introductory analysis of the short story, with a discussion of four different examples. Written for schools.

Wall, Nancy. "The Representation of the Maori in Pakeha Fiction." Thesis, University of Otago, 1963.

D. DRAMA

Barker, Ronald H. "Reflections on the New Zealand Theatre." THEATRE 60, no. 6 (1962), 15-17.

Reflections on the lack of New Zealand plays.

Baxter, James K. "Some Notes on Drama." ACT, no. 3 (July-September 1967), 20-22.

Notes on the language of drama, and on Baxter's own experience of writing plays.

Billing, Diane (Farmer). "Growing Child." NEW ZEALAND LISTENER, 19 February 1965, pp. 3, 13.

Notes on some contemporary dramatists.

Dunmore, John. "A Plea for the Playwright." LANDFALL, 11 (December 1957), 314-17.

Chiefly on the inadequacy of playwriting competitions as a means of fostering New Zealand drama.

Lloyd, Victor S. "The Place of Drama in New Zealand Literature." In ANNALS OF NEW ZEALAND LITERATURE. Ed. J.C. Andersen. [Wellington]: New Zealand Authors' Week Committee, 1936, pp. 13-16.

McNaughton, Howard. "Dramatising the Undramatic: A Survey of Play-Writing in New Zealand." EDUCATION, 23, no. 1 (1974), 9-15.

McNaughton concentrates on the work of Bruce Mason and Alistair Campbell. A bibliography of plays published between 1945 and 1973 is included.

______. "An Examination of New Zealand Drama, with Special Emphasis on the Period since 1944." Thesis, University of Canterbury, 1975.

Mason, Bruce. NEW ZEALAND DRAMA: A PARADE OF FORMS AND A HISTORY. Wellington: Price Milburn, 1973.

A varied book, written for schools, which includes a section on the place of theatres and drama in New Zealand society, and a critical analysis of the author's own play THE POHUTUKAWA TREE (see p. 165).

Mason, Bruce, and John Pocock. THEATRE IN DANGER: A CORRESPONDENCE. Hamilton: Paul's Book Arcade, 1957.

This exchange of letters includes discussion of the problems of writing plays in New Zealand.

Musgrove, Sydney. "Dramen auf Neuseelaendischen Buehnen" [Plays on the New Zealand stage]. INSTITUT FUER AUSLANDSBESIEHUNGEN, STUTTGART. MITTEILUNGEN, 6 (January-February 1956), 29-30.

Nelson, Erle. "Maoridom and Theatre." TE AO HOU, 8 (June 1960), 15-16.

______. "Towards a New Zealand Drama." LANDFALL, 17 (June 1963), 122-34.

An article on the way drama should evince a social conscience in its depiction of contemporary society. Nelson gives particular attention to Maori society and to Maori-European relations.

Robinson, Roger. "The Publication of New Zealand Drama." LANDFALL, 29 (December 1975), 271-81.

Thompson, Mervyn. "Downstage, Educationalists and the New Zealand Drama." LANDFALL, 29 (December 1975), 320-25.

An essay on the hostility which Thompson had experienced, especially from universities, towards New Zealand drama.

Wylie, Cathy. "A Survey of N.Z. Playwrights." ACT, no. 18 (December 1972), 4-6.

A brief discussion of some "recently written plays."

Chapter 3
ANTHOLOGIES

Anthologies can offer a good guide to a society's attitude to imaginative literature, both to the degree of its interest and to its taste, and this despite the fact that even the better ones will usually reflect at the same time their compilers' predilections. They also offer a convenient sampling of a country's lesser writers. Elsewhere in this bibliography, the choice of authors has been limited by the space available. It is in these anthologies that minor, and sometimes very minor, authors can be represented. The following list is an inclusive one. It attempts to cover all collections of previously published work, as well as most which print work for the first time. It excludes most, though not all, collections published by student and writers' groups, but does include anthologies of poems written by school children. New Zealand verse often used to be included in anthologies of Australian verse--AUSTRALIAN BALLADS AND RHYMES edited by D.B.W. Sladen (London: Walter Scott, 1888) seems to have been the first--but the New Zealand verse was not usually distinguished from the Australian. Of this kind of anthology, only those of Serle (see under the year 1927,) and of Murdoch and Mulgan (see under the year 1950, p. 49) are included here.

It is important to note that the anthologies which follow are listed chronologically so that the progression of the genre can be seen from a historical perspective.

LITERARY FOUNDLINGS: VERSE AND PROSE COLLECTED IN CANTERBURY, N.Z. Christchurch: The TIMES office, 1864.

> The anonymous editor had the good luck to be able to include an essay by Samuel Butler (who was on the point of leaving Canterbury to return to England), though neither he nor the other contributors are named.

THE BOOK OF CANTERBURY RHYMES. Christchurch: Ward & Reeves, 1866. Rev. and enl. ed., as CANTERBURY RHYMES. Ed. W.P. Reeves. Christchurch: LYTTELTON TIMES Co., 1883.

> Mostly humorous verse on matters of topical interest collected from local newspapers. The contributors to the first edition are identified by initials only.

Anthologies

Alpers, O.T.J. THE JUBILEE BOOK OF CANTERBURY RHYMES. Christchurch: Whitcombe & Tombs, 1900.

A representative selection of poems written during the first fifty years of settlement, chosen often "for their topical interest" as much as for their poetical value. The nineteenth-century anthologies were all from Christchurch, which perhaps reflected that city's conception of the place of poetry in polite "English" society. Much verse was published in wealthier Dunedin in the later nineteenth century, but in separate volumes by independent poets of (usually) Scottish origin.

Alexander, W.F., and A.E. Currie. NEW ZEALAND VERSE. London: Walter Scott Publishing Co., 1906. Rev. and enl. ed., as A TREASURY OF NEW ZEALAND VERSE. Christchurch: Whitcombe & Tombs, 1926.

This was the first (and it remains the only) fully representative and well-considered anthology of nineteenth-century New Zealand verse. Poems and extracts by over fifty authors are arranged by subject--emigration, the landscape, the cities, Maori life and legend, lyric poems of love and death. In a sober introduction, the editors note the supremacy of Alfred Domett's poetical powers, the abundance of landscape poetry, the rarity of verse about back-country farming, and the absence of poems about freezing-works (New Zealand slaughterhouses) or "the results of Universal Franchise and Industrial Arbitration." This is the poetry of immigrants, of men and women who set their knowledge of English poetry to the job of describing a new country. The second, only slightly enlarged, edition omits the introduction.

Mackay, Jessie. NEW ZEALAND RHYMES OLD AND NEW. Christchurch: Whitcombe & Tombs, [1907?].

A small booklet specifically designed as a gift to be sent "home" to England; "prominence has been given to the early links binding New Zealand art and sentiment to those of the beloved Motherland."

De la Mare, F.A., and Siegfried Eichelbaum. THE OLD CLAY PATCH: A COLLECTION OF VERSES WRITTEN IN AND AROUND VICTORIA UNIVERSITY COLLEGE. Christchurch: Whitcombe & Tombs, 1910. 2nd rev. ed. 1920. 3rd rev. ed. Wellington: New Zealand University Press, 1949.

Verse by writers who were students at (or had other links with) Victoria University College. The second and third editions selected from the first and also added much that was new. The third edition was edited by a committee of which the two original editors were members.

Shrimpton, A.W. COUNTESS OF LIVERPOOL'S GIFT BOOK OF ART AND LITERATURE. Christchurch: Whitcombe & Tombs, 1915.

A sumptuously presented collection of essays, stories, and poems, which was sold for the benefit of sick and wounded New Zealand soldiers in the First World War.

Alpers, O.T.J. COLLEGE RHYMES: AN ANTHOLOGY OF VERSE WRITTEN BY MEMBERS OF CANTERBURY COLLEGE 1873-1923. Christchurch: Whitcombe & Tombs, 1923.

The introduction by the editor outlines the dramatic and literary activities of students during the first fifty years of Canterbury University College.

Lawlor, Pat. MAORI TALES: A COLLECTION OF OVER ONE HUNDRED STORIES. Introd. Dick Harris. Sydney: New Century Press, 1926.

A rather dispiriting collection of jests and brief humorous tales supposedly illustrative of the blended "guile and simplicity" of the Maori.

Serle, Percival. AN AUSTRALASIAN ANTHOLOGY. London: Collins, 1927. 2nd ed. 1929. 3rd enl. ed. Sydney: Collins, 1946.

The New Zealand poets included in the third edition are still few and unnotable, but unlike those in the earlier Murdoch anthologies (see under the year 1950, p. 49), they are identifiable as New Zealanders in the index of authors.

Gillespie, Oliver N. NEW ZEALAND SHORT STORIES. London: Dent, 1930.

This was the first anthology of New Zealand short stories. The editor was conscious of having an English audience, restricted his choice to stories which were descriptive of New Zealand, and felt it necessary to explain in his preface the lack of "any national outlook or distinctive atmosphere." It is indicative of the meagre outlets for stories before 1930 that half of the thirty-two stories come from the Sydney weekly BULLETIN and the Christchurch daily SUN.

Pope, Quentin. KOWHAI GOLD: AN ANTHOLOGY OF CONTEMPORARY NEW ZEALAND VERSE. London: Dent; New York: Dutton, 1930.

This anthology covers the poorest years for New Zealand verse (its contents were mostly written between 1915 and 1930), and the name "Kowhai Gold" has become notorious. Few poets of the time escaped an unreal, because unexperienced, conception of the "Home Country," England, and this in turn rendered sentimental their view of their own land and people.

Marris, C.A. NEW ZEALAND BEST POEMS, 1932- . Wellington: Harry H. Tombs, 1932-43.

This series of annual booklets, with the anthology LYRIC POEMS of 1944 which rounded it off, was the last substantial fling of that early twentieth-century attitude to versifying which encouraged jejune lyrics written in a pale, unreal, literary idiom.

Lloyd, Victor S. SEVEN ONE-ACT PLAYS. Wellington: Radio Publishing Company of New Zealand for "The New Zealand Radio Record" under the auspices of The British Drama League, New Zealand Branch, 1933.

Despite the imprint, these were not radio plays. They were published for the use of amateur dramatic societies, and the collection includes the winners of a competition which drew over seventy entries. Lloyd published a similar collection in 1934, two collections in 1935, and a further volume in 1936, the last three volumes being published by National Magazines under the auspices of The British Drama League, New Zealand Branch. The New Zealand Branch of the British Drama League was founded in 1932. Only one further collection was issued under its auspices (see under the year 1964, p. 52).

John o' Dreams (pseud.). GIFT BOOK OF NEW ZEALAND VERSE. Wellington: New Zealand Radio Publishing Co., [1934?].

Verse by little-remembered poets which was first published in the NEW ZEALAND RADIO RECORD, where Helen Longford ran a literary page under the pseudonym of John o' Dreams.

Milner, Ian, and Denis Glover. NEW POEMS. Christchurch: Caxton Club Press, 1934.

A small collection by ten writers, most of them university students, whose work, the editors believed, broke with "that unfortunate tradition in which any sentimental rhapsodising . . . seems to pass for poetry." The poets represented included some who were to be among the finest of the next two or three decades: Charles Brasch, Allen Curnow, A.R.D. Fairburn, Denis Glover, and R.A.K. Mason.

KAURI WHISPERS: AN ANTHOLOGY BY NEW ZEALAND AUTHORS. Auckland: Kington Publishing Co., [1935?].

A collection of conventional poems descriptive of places and of nature.

Kington, John. PATAKA (TREASURE HOUSE): SELECTED SHORT STORIES BY NEW ZEALAND AUTHORS. Auckland: K System Publishing Dept., [1936].

A generally slighter collection than either Gillespie's (p. 45) or Allen's (p. 47).

Lawrence, Warwick. YOURS AND MINE: STORIES BY YOUNG NEW ZEALANDERS. New Plymouth: Thomas Avery, 1936.

Stories for children by young but adult authors, including Robin Hyde and Ngaio Marsh.

MANUKA BLOSSOMS: AN ANTHOLOGY BY NEW ZEALAND AUTHORS. Auckland: K System Publishing Dept., [1936].

A companion volume to KAURI WHISPERS (see under the year 1935, above).

Murray-Oliver, A.. AN ANTHOLOGY OF HIGH SCHOOL VERSE: A DECADE OF VERSE BY BOYS OF THE CHRISTCHURCH BOYS' HIGH SCHOOL, 1926-1935. Christchurch: By the editor, 1936.

The earliest example of a book of verse by school children, and one that was to have an increasing number of successors.

Rhodes, H. Winston, and Denis Glover. VERSE ALIVE. Christchurch: Caxton, 1936.

Verse by a number of poets, including Denis Glover, Allen Curnow, and A.R.D. Fairburn, first published in the periodical TOMORROW (see p. 216). VERSE ALIVE, NUMBER TWO was published in 1937.

A CAXTON MISCELLANY OF POEMS, VERSE, ETC. Christchurch: Caxton, 1937.

Fifteen typographically pleasing pages of verse by six poets, including Allen Curnow, A.R.D. Fairburn, and Denis Glover.

[Dept. of Education. Correspondence School.] CORRESPONDENCE SCHOOL BOOK OF VERSE--1937. Foreword by Eileen Duggan. [Wellington: 1937.]

A selection from the previous ten years' work of pupils ranging from the primers to form six.

Longford, Helen. HERE ARE VERSES. Wellington: South's Book Depot, [1937].

Minor magazine poetry. The collection includes several prose poems.

Allen, C.R. TALES BY NEW ZEALANDERS. Foreword by Sir Hugh Walpole. London: British Authors' Press, [1938].

Twenty-six stories by as many authors, a few of whom are remembered as poets or novelists, but none of whom is today read for his or her short stories. They offer a fair example of the kind of story published in, and therefore written for, newspapers and weeklies in the twenties and thirties.

Hoggard, Noel F. CENTENNIAL MISCELLANY: AN ANTHOLOGY OF SHORT STORIES AND VERSE. Wellington: Handcraft Press, 1939.

Of the thirteen authors, only C.R. Allen and J.R. Hervey are at all remembered.

Lawlor, Pat. WELLINGTON IN VERSE AND PICTURE. [Wellington: Ferguson & Osborn, 1939.] 2nd ed. Wellington: Reed, 1955.

LADY NEWALL'S NEW ZEALAND GIFT BOOK. Wellington: P.E.N. (New Zealand Centre), 1943.

A varied collection of essays, stories, poems, and paintings edited by a committee of seven and published to raise money for the benefit of men and women serving in the Second World War.

Mills, Thomas L. VERSE BY NEW ZEALAND CHILDREN. Wellington: Progressive Publishing Society, 1943.

Verse by children aged eleven to seventeen, originally collected for the use of teachers.

Marris, C.A. LYRIC POEMS, 1928-1942. Wellington: Harry H. Tombs, [1944?].

An anthology drawn almost exclusively from NEW ZEALAND BEST POEMS (see under the year 1932, p. 45) and ART IN NEW ZEALAND (see p. 216).

Curnow, Allen. A BOOK OF NEW ZEALAND VERSE 1923-1945. Christchurch: Caxton, 1945. Enl. ed. (1923-1951), 1951.

The most influential anthology, both for its verse and for its introduction, in the history of New Zealand poetry. It broke with earlier anthologies by printing fuller selections by fewer poets, and deliberately looked for a pattern, some common denominator, in the new verse that had been written since the Depression (few of the poems were more than fifteen years old). What was undoubtedly true was that this verse was written by New Zealanders, not English immigrants, and for New Zealand not English readers. Curnow found that many poems were based on a sense of the insecurity and rootlessness of New Zealanders in these islands. But what, more precisely, the pattern was which Curnow perceived, and whether or not it was really there, are questions which were much discussed. They were reopened on the publication of Curnow's Penguin anthology in 1960; see below under that date, p. 51, for some reviews which treat the whole matter.

Sargeson, Frank. SPEAKING FOR OURSELVES. Christchurch: Caxton, 1945.

The first collection of stories by writers who show themselves to be at home in their own country, who write for their fellow countrymen and do not exploit the exoticism of New Zealand for the benefit of English readers.

[Glover, Denis.] BOOK, no. 9 (July 1947).

A short-story number of the Caxton Press miscellany; a brief collection of verse is also included.

McCormick, E.H. WRITING IN NEW ZEALAND: NO. 4, POETRY. Wellington: Dept. of Education, 1947.

One of the first group of post-primary school bulletins. It prints a short selection of poems from Charles Bowen to Denis Glover, with a translation of a Maori lament by Te Ihu-nui-o-Tonga.

WRITING IN NEW ZEALAND: NO. 3, THE SHORT STORY. [Wellington]: Dept. of Education, [1947].

A post-primary school bulletin. A brief introduction is followed by two stories, by Alice F. Webb and Frank Sargeson.

Martin, Geoffrey L. VOICES I: NEW SHORT STORIES BY MODERN NEW ZEALAND WRITERS. Auckland: Colenso Press, 1948.

A collection of five stories by journalists.

Currie, A.E. A CENTENNIAL TREASURY OF OTAGO VERSE. Christchurch: Caxton, 1949.

Otago, together with Southland, is one of the more distinctive provincial districts, both geographically and in the Scottish origins of its early settlers. The verse in this collection, representing the work of fifty writers, is chosen as much for its Otago flavor as for its absolute poetic merit.

Murdoch, Walter, and Alan Mulgan. A BOOK OF AUSTRALIAN AND NEW ZEALAND VERSE. 4th ed. Melbourne: Oxford University Press, 1950.

This was a collection previously known as THE OXFORD BOOK OF AUSTRALASIAN VERSE and, later, as A BOOK OF AUSTRALASIAN VERSE, edited by Walter Murdoch. The fourth edition was the first to include a representative and separate selection of New Zealand verse; this section of the book was prepared by Alan Mulgan. Earlier editions did not identify the origin of the few selections of New Zealand verse they included.

Woodhouse, Airini E. NEW ZEALAND FARM AND STATION VERSE 1850-1950. Introd. L.J. Wild. Christchurch: Whitcombe & Tombs, 1950.

This is verse, of the kind which Alexander and Currie found so rare, describing rural and especially sheep-farming life. It is chosen principally on the criteria of sincerity and firsthand knowledge.

Johnson, Louis. NEW ZEALAND POETRY YEARBOOK. 11 vols. Christchurch: Pegasus, 1951-64.

Although this series of annual publications was established, in the eyes at least of some of its earlier contributors, to provide an outlet for those who felt the periodical LANDFALL perpetuated a "Curnow-Holcroft" myth (see above, p. 48, under Curnow for the year 1945), Johnson in fact proved eclectically inclusive in his choice. He argued in the third volume that it "is both the strength and weakness of POETRY YEARBOOK that its purpose is revelatory rather than definitive--to show, year by year, that which is growing rather than that which is fully-formed." Each issue carried an introductory essay, usually written by the editor. Three of the volumes covered a two-year period.

Rawlinson, Gloria, and W. Hart-Smith. JINDYWOROBAK ANTHOLOGY, 1951. Melbourne: Jindyworobak, 1952.

For the 1951 issue of this annual Australian anthology of verse, two New Zealand editors prepared a "Trans-Tasman Issue" in which about a third of the poems represent recent work from New Zealand. In a brief introduction the editors note that the common reading of each other country's poets is now rare. Australasian anthologies have become a thing of the past.

Stevens, Joan. WRITING IN NEW ZEALAND: CONTEMPORARY VERSE. Wellington: School Publications Branch, Dept. of Education, 1952.

A post-primary school bulletin: thirty-two pages of verse written during the previous twenty years.

Thompson, Robert. 13 NEW ZEALAND POETS: AN ANTHOLOGY OF VERSE. Wellington: Handcraft Press, 1952.

The poets were mostly in their twenties and thirties.

Davin, Dan. NEW ZEALAND SHORT STORIES. London: Oxford University Press, 1953; rpt. Wellington: Oxford University Press, 1973.

The first anthology to display the strength of the New Zealand short story; admittedly, two-thirds of the thirty-three stories were published after 1937. It is an excellent selection and its continuing popularity is well merited. It has been followed by similar anthologies of more recent stories edited by C.K. Stead (1966) and Vincent O'Sullivan (1975).

POEMS. [Christchurch]: THE OUTLOOK, 1953.

An anthology drawn from the January-June issues of the official organ of the Presbyterian Church of New Zealand, during which period it was edited by Jonathan Bennett.

Chapman, Robert, and Jonathan Bennett. AN ANTHOLOGY OF NEW ZEALAND VERSE. London: Oxford University Press, 1956.

The first comprehensive selection of New Zealand poetry since the Alexander and Currie anthology of 1926 (see p. 44). The fact, however, that four-fifths of the poetry here was written in the three decades after 1926 indicates the way New Zealand poetry established its independence and integrity during that period. Although--indeed probably because--the selection of poems is less tendentious than that in Curnow's Penguin anthology (see the year 1960, below), it did not prove nearly as popular. The introduction is by Robert Chapman. See Lawrence Baigent's review in LANDFALL, 10 (September 1956), 249-53.

Joseph, M.K. WRITING IN NEW ZEALAND: THE NEW ZEALAND SHORT STORY. 2 vols. Wellington: School Publications Branch, Dept. of Education, 1956.

Two post-primary school bulletins.

Curnow, Allen. THE PENGUIN BOOK OF NEW ZEALAND VERSE. Harmondsworth, Middlesex: Penguin, 1960; rpt. Auckland: Blackwood and Janet Paul, 1966.

This anthology is less satisfyingly unified than the one Curnow edited for Caxton in 1945--recent developments were not readily accommodated within his earlier view of the true strengths of New Zealand verse. Under the Penguin imprint however this collection, with its greatly developed and completely recast version of the 1945 introduction, has reached more readers than any anthology before or since. See A.W. Stockwell's review in LANDFALL, 15 (June 1961), 173-77; E.A. Horsman's review "The Anthologist as the Letter C" in COMMENT, 2 (Autumn 1961), 40-42; and Ian Reid's article "Curnow and the Penguins" in COMMENT, 8 (April 1967), 31-33.

Oliver, W.H. WRITING IN NEW ZEALAND: POETRY IN NEW ZEALAND. Wellington: School Publications Branch, Dept. of Education, 1960.

A post-primary school bulletin in which Oliver writes about New Zealand poetry, quoting many poems in full.

NEW AUTHORS SHORT STORY ONE. London: New Authors, 1961.

Three of the four contributors were New Zealanders--Maurice Duggan, Maurice Gee, and C.K. Stead--and the volume provided a notable example of the country's skill in this art form.

Reid, John C. THE KIWI LAUGHS: AN ANTHOLOGY OF NEW ZEALAND PROSE HUMOUR. Wellington: Reed, 1961.

The kiwi is sometimes thought to be a bird not much given to laughter, at least in prose; these gleanings show the bird is not entirely humorless.

Anthologies

Brasch, Charles. LANDFALL COUNTRY: WORK FROM LANDFALL, 1947-61. Christchurch: Caxton, 1962.

An excellent and generous selection of poems, short stories, and essays.

Thomson, John N. FIVE NEW ZEALAND PLAYS. Auckland: Collins, 1962.

A selection of previously unpublished one-act plays, the earliest dating from the late thirties.

British Drama League, New Zealand Branch. THREE PLAYS BY NEW ZEALANDERS. Foreword by Bruce Mason. Wellington: Price Milburn, 1964.

Selected from "plays entered in the League's One Act Playwriting Competition during recent years."

Smart, Peter. DISCOVERING NEW ZEALAND WRITING: AN ANTHOLOGY FOR THIRD, FOURTH, AND FIFTH FORMS. Wellington: Reed, 1964.

_____. EXPLORING NEW ZEALAND WRITING: AN ANTHOLOGY FOR SENIOR STUDENTS. Wellington: Reed, 1964.

Doyle, Charles. RECENT POETRY IN NEW ZEALAND. Auckland: Collins, 1965.

Generous selections from thirteen poets, nearly all of whom established their reputations in the fifties. All but two of them contribute brief essays on poetry, and on their own experience of writing poetry.

Jackson, MacDonald P. POETRY AUSTRALIA, no. 9 (April 1966).

This issue, for which Jackson was guest editor, is devoted to recent New Zealand poetry.

Lewis, Richard. THE WIND AND THE RAIN: A BOOK OF POEMS BY SCHOOLCHILDREN. Wellington: School Publications Branch, Dept. of Education, 1966.

A bulletin for schools which originated as a New Zealand Broadcasting Corporation television programme. The poems are by primary-school children, and the bulletin is extensively illustrated with photographs.

Stead, C.K. NEW ZEALAND SHORT STORIES: SECOND SERIES. London: Oxford University Press, 1966; rpt. Wellington: Oxford University Press, 1976.

A selection of stories, first published between 1948 and 1965, which supplements Davin's 1953 anthology (see p. 50).

Bailey, Rona, and Herbert Roth. SHANTIES BY THE WAY: A SELECTION OF NEW ZEALAND POPULAR SONGS AND BALLADS. Christchurch: Whitcombe & Tombs, 1967.

Orbell, Margaret. CONTEMPORARY MAORI WRITING. Wellington: Reed, 1970.

> This collection of prose stories, with a few poems, illustrates the work of "the first generation of Maori writers to make much use of literary forms that are European in origin."

O'Sullivan, Vincent. AN ANTHOLOGY OF TWENTIETH CENTURY NEW ZEALAND POETRY. London: Oxford University Press, 1970. Enl. ed. Wellington: Oxford University Press, 1976.

> The major current representative anthology.

Hogan, Helen M. NOWHERE FAR FROM THE SEA: AN ANTHOLOGY OF NEW ZEALAND POEMS FOR SECONDARY SCHOOL STUDENTS. Christchurch: Whitcombe & Tombs, 1971.

> Over two hundred poems arranged under a variety of subject headings.

McKay, Frank. POETRY NEW ZEALAND. 3 vols. Christchurch: Pegasus, 1971-76.

> Intended as a biennial successor to NEW ZEALAND POETRY YEARBOOK (1951-64), see p. 49. Only three volumes were published.

Jones, Kevin, and Brent Southgate. REVIEW: 1888-1971: A RETROSPECTIVE ANTHOLOGY OF THE LITERARY REVIEW. [Dunedin]: Bibliography Room, University of Otago, 1972.

> A selection from the OTAGO UNIVERSITY REVIEW, more recently called REVIEW.

Baysting, Arthur. THE YOUNG NEW ZEALAND POETS. Afterword by Kendrick Smithyman. Auckland: Heinemann Educational Books, 1973.

> All but one of the nineteen poets represented were born between 1940 and 1950; very few of them had published more than one volume of their own verse when this book was compiled. A valuable anthology.

Bell, Terry. REFLECTIONS: VOICES FROM PAREMOREMO. [Auckland]: Abelard Press, 1973.

> Prose and verse written by inmates of the country's newest maximum security prison.

Bolton, John. TIMBER, TUSSOCK, & RUSHING RIVERS: POEMS FOR CHILDREN BY WRITERS IN NEW ZEALAND. Dunedin: Dunedin Teachers College, 1973.

Poems "likely to appeal somewhere within the age limits of five and twelve."

Gadd, Bernard. MY NEW ZEALAND: SENIOR. Auckland: Longman Paul, 1973.

Eighteen stories chosen for senior schoolchildren. All but two of the stories were first published during the previous decade.

Hogan, Helen M. MY POEM IS A BUBBLE: AN ANTHOLOGY OF RECENT POEMS BY NEW ZEALAND SECONDARY SCHOOL PUPILS. Christchurch: Whitcombe & Tombs, 1973.

Similar collections have been edited by Helen Hogan each year since 1973.

Jones, Gwenyth. THESE ISLANDS: A COLLECTION OF NEW ZEALAND VERSE FOR YOUNG PEOPLE. Auckland: Longman Paul, 1973.

Simple poems, mostly by well-known poets, arranged under a variety of subject headings.

Meikle, Phoebe. SHORT STORIES BY NEW ZEALANDERS ONE, TWO and THREE. 3 vols. Auckland: Longman Paul, 1972-74.

These collections were prepared, with notes and questions, for secondary-school pupils. ONE is a general collection of stories by seventeen authors first published between 1937 and 1972. TWO is a collection of stories about (and mostly by) non-English New Zealanders (i.e. people of Polynesian or Continental descent). THREE (first published as SHORT STORIES BY NEW ZEALANDERS in 1970) prints stories by Frank Sargeson, Dan Davin, A.P. Gaskell, and Maurice Duggan.

O'Sullivan, Vincent. NEW ZEALAND POETRY IN THE SIXTIES. Wellington: School Publications Branch, Dept. of Education, 1973.

A bulletin for schools. It includes a critical essay as well as a twenty-one page selection of poems.

Dudding, Robin. ISLANDS, 3 (Autumn 1974): entire issue.

This issue of ISLANDS was "an anthology of contemporary New Zealand fiction."

Gadd, Bernard. MY NEW ZEALAND: JUNIOR. Auckland: Longman Paul, 1974.

Nineteen short stories, the earliest of which date from 1947.

McNaughton, Howard. CONTEMPORARY NEW ZEALAND PLAYS. Wellington: Oxford University Press, 1974.

This volume includes four plays, one each by Alistair Campbell, James K. Baxter, Edward Bowman, and Bruce Mason. It also has an introduction, notes by various writers, and bibliographies.

McQueen, Harvey, and Lois Cox. TEN MODERN NEW ZEALAND POETS. Auckland: Longman Paul, 1974.

Generous selections with excellent brief biographical and critical introductions; the poets include Hone Tuwhare, Alistair Campbell, James K. Baxter, and Fleur Adcock. Though two of the poets were born as long ago as 1919 and 1922, the verse included is all post-1945.

Winans, A.D. SECOND COMING: SPECIAL NEW ZEALAND ANTHOLOGY. San Francisco: Second Coming Press, 1974.

A special issue (vol. 3, nos. 1-2) of the periodical SECOND COMING. New Zealand poets have for some time been influenced more by American poets than by poets of other countries, but this is the first anthology of New Zealand verse published specifically for American readers.

Dudding, Robin. ISLANDS, 4 (Winter 1975): entire issue.

This issue was subtitled "An Anthology of Short Stories."

O'Sullivan, Vincent. NEW ZEALAND SHORT STORIES: THIRD SERIES. Wellington: Oxford University Press, 1975.

Twenty-seven stories, nearly all first published during the previous decade. This collection supplements the anthologies of Davin (1953) and Stead (1966)--see pp. 50 and 52.

Fox, A.G., and John Gibb. THE LOST YEARS WERE TOO LONG: A CHRISTIAN ARTS POETRY COLLECTION. Mosgiel, Otago: Christian Arts, 1976.

Meikle, Phoebe. TEN MODERN NEW ZEALAND STORY WRITERS: LONGER STORIES AND LINKED STORIES. Auckland: Longman Paul, 1976.

Thompson, Robert, and Helen Shaw. POEMS BY SEVERAL HANDS: TO THE MEMORY OF NOEL FARR HOGGARD. [Moerewa, North Auckland]: Pompallier Press, 1976.

A small collection by eight contributors to ARENA.

Anthologies

Bertram, James. NEW ZEALAND LOVE POEMS. Dunedin: McIndoe, 1977.

Catley, Christine Cole. SHIRLEY TEMPLE IS A WIFE AND MOTHER: 34 STORIES BY 22 NEW ZEALANDERS. Whatamongo Bay, Marlborough: Cape Catley, 1977.

Most of the stories "are by women, about women."

Ensing, Riemke. PRIVATE GARDENS: AN ANTHOLOGY OF NEW ZEALAND WOMEN POETS. Dunedin: Caveman Press, 1977.

Manhire, Bill. N.Z. LISTENER SHORT STORIES. Wellington: Methuen New Zealand, 1977.

Chosen from stories first published in the NEW ZEALAND LISTENER (see p. 216) between 1941 and 1976.

Chapter 4
INDIVIDUAL AUTHORS

For each author in this chapter material is arranged in the following order:

Bibliography

Collected Works

Biography, Journals and Letters, and Autobiography

Primary Works

- Poetry
- Fiction
- Drama
- Prose

Criticism

Under "Criticism" the arrangement is alphabetical by author, but within all the other sections a chronological order has been adopted. An author's work in nonfiction, whether books or articles, has been included under "Other Prose" if it has any relevance to the author's poetry, fiction, or drama. Biographical material other than in book form appears under "Other Prose" if autobiographical, and under "Criticism" if by other writers. For authors who have not written fiction or drama, "Prose" is substituted for "Other Prose" as a heading. Interviews will be found in the "Criticism" sections under the name of the author interviewed. Extended reviews have sometimes been included among the critical material, particularly when little other critical writing on an author's work has been published. Occasionally the heading "Miscellaneous" has been used for primary works containing more than one genre--for example, Glover's or Satchell's two collections of verse and prose.

ADCOCK, KAREN FLEUR (1934-)

Fleur Adcock was born in Auckland, and studied classics at Victoria University of Wellington. She was for a time married to Alistair Campbell, and later to Barry Crump, both New Zealand writers. After four years as a librarian in Dunedin and Wellington she left New Zealand to pursue her career in London. (She had already lived in England as a girl during the Second World War.) "New Zealand," she has written, "is too far from Europe, and too culturally isolated for my temperament"; but like other expatriate writers she still occasionally returns to New Zealand family memories in her poems.

POETRY

THE EYE OF THE HURRICANE: POEMS. Wellington: Reed, 1964.

TIGERS. London: Oxford University Press, 1967.

HIGH TIDE IN THE GARDEN. London: Oxford University Press, 1971.

THE SCENIC ROUTE. London: Oxford University Press, 1974.

PROSE

A STUDY OF ANCIENT ROME. Wellington: School Publications Branch, Dept. of Education, 1967.

A post-primary school bulletin.

"Women As Poets." In POETRY DIMENSION 2. Ed. Dannie Abse. London: Robson Books and Sphere Books, 1974, pp. 229-33.

Adcock, Karen Fleur

CRITICISM

Abse, Dannie. "Fleur Adcock." In CORGI MODERN POETS IN FOCUS 5. Ed. Dannie Abse. London: Corgi Books, 1973, pp. 101-07.

Abse's introduction to a selection of Fleur Adcock's poems is followed by a two-page account by Adcock of her evolution as a writer of poetry.

Bertram, James. "Review of EYE OF THE HURRICANE." LANDFALL, 18 (December 1964), 369-72.

McGill, David. "Fastidiously Fleur." NEW ZEALAND LISTENER, 13 March 1976, p. 29.

An article based on an interview.

Stead, C.K. "Review of HIGH TIDE IN THE GARDEN." LANDFALL, 25 (December 1971), 457-63.

ASHTON-WARNER, SYLVIA CONSTANCE (1908-)

Sylvia Ashton-Warner--her married name is Henderson--is equally well-known as a novelist and as an educationalist. She attended a number of schools in small North Island towns as a girl, and went on to spend many years teaching in more remote country schools where the children were mostly Maori. Out of this experience she developed ideas on how to teach young children, being particularly successful with their reading. Her ideas at first received little sympathy from the educational authorities, but her reputation began to spread, particularly in America, where she later became professor of education at a teaching centre in Colorado. Her autobiographical works and some of her fiction are based on her teaching experiences. In both kinds of writing, despite the occasionally embarrassing lack of stylistic control, she will often carry the reader with her as a result of her passionate concern with human relationships. Sylvia Ashton-Warner has also written short stories, and has published many articles, not listed here, of an educational nature.

FICTION

SPINSTER. London: Secker & Warburg, 1958; New York: Simon & Schuster, 1959; rpt. Harmondsworth, Middlesex: Penguin Books, 1961; London and Auckland: Heinemann, 1972.

> A series of stories and articles, trial runs for SPINSTER, was published under the title of "The New Race" in NEW ZEALAND PARENT AND CHILD, 7, nos. 2-6 (1959).

INCENSE TO IDOLS. London: Secker & Warburg; New York: Simon & Schuster, 1960.

BELL CALL. New York: Simon & Schuster, [1964]; London: Hale; [Christchurch]: Whitcombe & Tombs, 1971.

GREENSTONE. New York: Simon & Schuster, [1966]; [Christchurch]: Whitcombe & Tombs; London: Secker & Warburg, [1967].

THREE. London: Hale; [Christchurch]: Whitcombe & Tombs, 1971; New York: Knopf, 1973.

OTHER PROSE

TEACHER. London: Secker & Warburg; New York: Simon & Schuster, 1963; rpt. New York: Bantam Books, 1965; Harmondsworth, Middlesex: Penguin Books, 1966.

MYSELF. New York: Simon & Schuster, [1967]; [Christchurch]: Whitcombe & Tombs, [1968]; London: Secker & Warburg, 1968.

SPEARPOINT: "TEACHER" IN AMERICA. New York: Knopf, 1972; rpt. New York: Vintage Books, 1974; as "TEACHER" IN AMERICA. London: Cassell, 1974.

This book, like TEACHER and MYSELF, describes some of the author's teaching experiences; all three might best be described as "creative documentary."

"Yo Ho!" EDUCATION, 25, no. 2 (1976), 16.

An article about her childhood reading.

CRITICISM

McEldowney, Dennis. "Sylvia Ashton-Warner: A Problem of Grounding." LANDFALL, 23 (September 1969), 230-45.

BAXTER, JAMES KEIR (1926-72)

James K. Baxter's mother came from an academic family and was a Cambridge graduate; his father was a self-taught farmer of Highland descent. His poetry is marked by a familiarity with literature and mythology, and by an independent spirit which never allowed him to accept the material values and emotional inhibitions of his society. Apart from a brief spell in England when a boy and another later in India on a UNESCO grant, Baxter spent his life in New Zealand, uneasily working for a university degree, training as a teacher, writing for the School Publications Branch of the Department of Education, or taking on a series of less demanding jobs which gave him time to write. But poetry was always at the centre of his early life, and from the beginning he wrote with an extraordinary facility. About 1957, he shook himself free of the grip of alcoholism and joined the Catholic Church. In his last years, though never ceasing to write, he devoted much of his time to helping drug addicts, and founded a commune at the remote inland settlement of Jerusalem. He was clearly the most important poet of his generation, and is one of the finest in New Zealand's history.

Many of Baxter's poems were circulated in typescript or cyclostyled form and some have not been otherwise published. Only those broadsheets and folders which were printed are included here. His collected poetry is to be published by Oxford University Press, Wellington, in 1980.

BIBLIOGRAPHY

Hughes, P.H. "An Annotated Bibliography of Selected Works by, and about, James K. Baxter Published between 1944-1975." Bibliographical exercise, Library School, Wellington, 1975.

> A bibliography of Baxter's books and separately published poems. All poems are indexed by title and first line. Also listed are critical articles and reviews, excellently annotated.

COLLECTED WORKS

CHOSEN POEMS. Bombay: Konkan Institute of Arts and Sciences, 1958.

A SELECTION OF POETRY. [Wellington]: Poetry Magazine, 1964.

Published as a supplement to POETRY MAGAZINE for distribution among schools.

THE ROCK WOMAN: SELECTED POEMS. London: Oxford University Press, 1969.

This selection of fifty-three poems, although weighted with poems of a religious nature, is still the only one to draw on a full range of Baxter's verse.

POETRY

BEYOND THE PALISADE. Christchurch: Caxton, 1944.

BLOW, WIND OF FRUITFULNESS. Christchurch: Caxton, 1948.

HART CRANE: A POEM. Sumner (Christchurch): Catspaw Press, 1948.

RAPUNZEL: A FANTASIA FOR SIX VOICES. [Wellington: By the author, 1948].

CHARM FOR HILARY. [Christchurch: By the author, 1949].

POEMS UNPLEASANT. With Louis Johnson and Anton Vogt. Christchurch: Pegasus Press, 1952.

THE FALLEN HOUSE. Christchurch: Caxton, 1953.

TRAVELLER'S LITANY. Wellington: Handcraft Press, 1955.

THE IRON BREADBOARD: STUDIES IN NEW ZEALAND WRITING. Wellington: Mermaid Press, 1957.

Parodies of a number of New Zealand poets, including Baxter himself.

THE NIGHT SHIFT: POEMS ON ASPECTS OF LOVE. With Charles Doyle, Louis Johnson, and Kendrick Smithyman. Wellington: Capricorn Press, 1957.

IN FIRES OF NO RETURN: POEMS. London: Oxford University Press, 1958.

BALLAD OF CALVARY STREET. [Wellington: By the author, 1960].

HOWRAH BRIDGE AND OTHER POEMS. London: Oxford University Press, 1961.

A BUCKET OF BLOOD FOR A DOLLAR. [Christchurch: John Summers Bookshop, 1965].

THE OLD EARTH CLOSET. [Wellington: Wai-te-ata Press, 1965].

PIG ISLAND LETTERS. London: Oxford University Press, 1966.

A DEATH SONG FOR MR MOULDYBROKE. [Christchurch: Caxton, 1967].

THE LION SKIN. Dunedin: Bibliography Room, University of Otago, 1967.

A SMALL ODE ON MIXED FLATTING. [Christchurch: Caxton, 1967].

BALLAD OF THE STONEGUT SUGAR WORKS. [Auckland?: By the author, 1969].

JERUSALEM SONNETS: POEMS FOR COLIN DURNING. Dunedin: Bibliography Room, University of Otago, 1970; rpt. Wellington: Price Milburn, 1975.

THE JUNKIES AND THE FUZZ. Wellington: Wai-te-ata Press, 1970.

JERUSALEM BLUES 2. [Plimmerton]: Bottle Press, [1971].

JERUSALEM DAYBOOK. Wellington: Price Milburn, 1971.

Includes passages of prose.

AUTUMN TESTAMENT. Wellington: Price Milburn, 1972.

Includes passages of prose.

FOUR GOD SONGS. Karori (Wellington): Futuna Press, [1972].

LETTER TO PETER OLDS. Dunedin: Caveman Press, 1972.

STONEGUT SUGAR WORKS, JUNKIES & THE FUZZ, ODE TO AUCKLAND, & OTHER POEMS. Dunedin: Caveman Press, 1972.

RUNES. London: Oxford University Press, 1973.

TWO OBSCENE POEMS. Introd. Max Harris. Adelaide: Mary Martin Books, [1973?].

THE LABYRINTH: SOME UNCOLLECTED POEMS, 1944-72. Wellington: Oxford University Press, 1974.

THE TREE HOUSE, AND OTHER POEMS FOR CHILDREN. Wellington: Price Milburn, 1974.

THE BONE CHANTER: UNPUBLISHED POEMS 1945-1972. Ed. and introd. J.E. Weir. Wellington: Oxford University Press, [1976].

THE HOLY LIFE AND DEATH OF CONCRETE GRADY: VARIOUS UNCOLLECTED AND UNPUBLISHED POEMS. Ed. and introd. J.E. Weir. Wellington: Oxford University Press, [1976].

DRAMA

TWO PLAYS: THE WIDE OPEN CAGE AND JACK WINTER'S DREAM. Hastings: Capricorn Press, 1959.

THE DEVIL AND MR MULCAHY [AND] THE BAND ROTUNDA. Auckland: Heinemann Educational Books, 1971.

THE SORE-FOOTED MAN [AND] THE TEMPTATIONS OF OEDIPUS. Auckland: Heinemann Educational Books, 1971.

"Three Mimes." LANDFALL, 29 (December 1975), 328-33.

OTHER PROSE

"Poetry in New Zealand." YEAR BOOK OF THE ARTS, 2 (1946), 111-14.

RECENT TRENDS IN NEW ZEALAND POETRY. Christchurch: Caxton, 1951.

"Early New Zealand [and] Modern New Zealand Poetry." In ADULT EDUCATION DISCUSSION COURSE: NEW ZEALAND LITERATURE. Adult Education Dept., Victoria University College. Wellington: 1953.

"Notes towards an Aesthetic." SALIENT (Literary Issue), September 1953, [pp. 28-31].

"On the Side of Life." NEW ZEALAND POETRY YEARBOOK, 4 (1954), 23-26.

Reflections on writing prompted by a questionnaire.

THE FIRE AND THE ANVIL: NOTES ON MODERN POETRY. Wellington: New Zealand University Press, 1955.

"The World of the Creative Artist." SALIENT (Literary Issue), September 1955, pp. 20-26.

THE COASTER. Wellington: School Publications Branch, Dept. of Education, 1959.

This, and OIL and THE TRAWLER (see below), were primary school bulletins.

OIL. Wellington: School Publications Branch, Dept. of Education, 1959.

"Essay on the Higher Learning." SPIKE, 1961, pp. 61-64.

Baxter's educational experiences.

NEW ZEALAND IN COLOUR. Wellington: Reed, 1961.

The text, by Baxter, accompanied photographs by Kenneth and Jean Bigwood.

THE TRAWLER. Wellington: School Publications Branch, Dept. of Education, 1961.

"Notes Made in Winter." NEW ZEALAND POETRY YEARBOOK, 10 (1961-62), 13-15.

An attack on the "disease of formalism" which Baxter found in New Zealand poetry.

"Writing and Existence." EDUCATION, 12 (August 1963), 16-19.

"Beginnings." LANDFALL, 19 (September 1965), 237-42.

An autobiographical essay.

"Conversation about Writing." NEW ZEALAND MONTHLY REVIEW, 6 (September 1965), 28.

"With Stubble and Overcoat." NEW ZEALAND LISTENER, 26 November 1965, p. 25.

Baxter on his youthful reading.

"Recollections of School Days." NEW ZEALAND MONTHLY REVIEW, 6 (March 1966), 17-19.

"SHOTS AROUND THE TARGET": AN ARTS FESTIVAL TALK. [Palmerston North?: New Zealand Arts Festival Committee?, 1966].

Includes some passages of verse.

ASPECTS OF POETRY IN NEW ZEALAND. Christchurch: Caxton, 1967.

THE MAN ON THE HORSE. Dunedin: University of Otago Press, 1967.

Four lectures on poetry and an autobiographical essay.

"Some Notes on Drama." ACT, no. 3 (July-September 1967), 20-22.

"About the Globe Theatre." In ROSALIE AND PATRIC CAREY PRESENT THE GLOBE THEATRE 1968. Globe Theatre, [Dunedin]: 1968.

"The Burns Fellowship." LANDFALL, 22 (September 1968), 243-47.

THE FLOWERING CROSS. Dunedin: New Zealand Tablet, [1970].

Essays on social and religious subjects originally published in the NEW ZEALAND TABLET.

"Letter to a Catholic Poet." DIALECTIC, no. 6 (August 1970), 23-27.

Some discussion followed in the next issue.

SIX FACES OF LOVE. [Wellington]: Futuna Press, [1972].

Consists of "Essays on Christian Love."

A WALKING STICK FOR AN OLD MAN. Wellington: CMW Print, [1972].

Personal reflections on race relations in New Zealand.

THOUGHTS ABOUT THE HOLY SPIRIT. Karori (Wellington): Futuna Press, 1973.

Includes a number of religious poems.

CRITICISM

Baxter, James K. "Drama Among the Faceless." NEW ZEALAND LISTENER, 7 February 1969, p. 9.

Baxter interviewed by Arthur Baysting about his plays and about drama in New Zealand.

______. "An Interview with James K. Baxter." LANDFALL, 28 (September 1974), 241-50.

Transcript of a recorded interview by J.E. Weir.

______. "James K. Baxter: Worksheets." MALAHAT REVIEW, 5 (January 1968), 114-17.

Four versions illustrating the evolution of the poem "The Jar."

______. "The Jerusalem Experience." NEW ZEALAND LISTENER, 18 October 1971, p. 19.

Baxter interviewed by Ian Hay-Campbell.

Bertram, James. "Poet of Extremes." NEW ZEALAND LISTENER, 20 November 1972, p. 12.

______. "Two New Zealand Poets." EDUCATION, 2 (September 1949), 59-61.

Broughton, W.S. "A Discursive Essay about Jerusalem." WORLD LITERATURE WRITTEN IN ENGLISH, 14 (April 1975), 69-90.

A discussion of Baxter's verse in the light of his social and religious activities, especially during his last years.

______. "Some Considerations of the Verse of James K. Baxter." NUCLEUS (Auckland), no. 4 (August 1961), 24-40.

Campbell, Alistair. "Impressions of the Earlier Baxter." LANDFALL, 27 (September 1973), 179-84.

______. "James K. Baxter: The Earlier Poems." In NEW ZEALAND'S HERITAGE. Ed. Ray Knox. Wellington: Paul Hamlyn, [1971-73], pp. 2561-66.

Chapman, Robert. "Review of THE FALLEN HOUSE." LANDFALL, 7 (September 1953), 209-14.

An excellent analysis of the first full flowering of Baxter's poetical powers.

Davidson, John. "Catullus, Horace and Baxter." ISLANDS, 5 (Autumn 1976), 86-94.

______. "James K. Baxter and the Classics." ISLANDS, 4 (Summer 1975), 451-64.

Doyle, Charles. JAMES K. BAXTER. Boston: Twayne, [1976].

The fullest examination of Baxter's life and writing, with a useful bibliography.

______. "James K. Baxter: In Quest of the Just City." ARIEL, 5 (July 1974), 81-98.

Edmond, Lauris. "James K. Baxter: Poet of Responsibility." AFFAIRS, (February 1973), 9-11.

Hart-Smith, W. "The Poetry of James K. Baxter." MEANJIN, 11 (Summer 1952), 382-90.

"Jack Winter's Dream." NEW ZEALAND LISTENER, 19 September 1958, pp. 8-9.

A discussion, by Baxter and others, of the first radio production. Edited anonymously.

Lawson, D.W. "Greek Myth in Four Plays by James K. Baxter." Thesis, University of Otago, 1974.

Leeming, Owen. "And the Clay Man? Reflections on 'The Rock Woman.'" LANDFALL, 25 (March 1971), 9-19.

A provocative essay suggesting that Baxter's Catholicism limited rather than strengthened his poetic abilities. Correspondence by J.E. Weir, Baxter, and Leeming appeared in the June 1971 issue.

McNaughton, Howard. "Baxter as Dramatist." ISLANDS, 2 (Winter 1973), 184-92.

Interesting for its discussion of the unpublished plays for stage and radio.

Moody, D. "For James K. Baxter." MEANJIN, 32 (June 1973), 219-24.

O'Sullivan, Vincent. "After Culloden: Remarks on the Early and Middle Poetry of James K. Baxter." ISLANDS, 2 (Autumn 1973), 19-30.

An excellent essay on the elements of myth in Baxter, who is said to be "a poet who believed that metaphor was truth, and that the poetic mode finally is inseparable from a socially dramatic one."

______. JAMES K. BAXTER. Wellington: Oxford University Press, [1976].

The best short study.

Paisley, John. "The Double Vision: Local and Universal in the Work of Two New Zealand Poets." Thesis, University of Otago, 1966.

______. "James K. Baxter: Poet & Student." REVIEW (Dunedin), 1963, pp. 74-78.

Pearson, W.H., and Peter Olds. "Two Personal Memories of James K. Baxter." ISLANDS, 2 (Autumn 1973), 2-7.

Shadbolt, Maurice. "James K. Baxter." In his LOVE AND LEGEND: SOME 20TH CENTURY NEW ZEALANDERS. Auckland: Hodder & Stoughton, 1976, pp. 167-79.

Simpson, Tony. "Baxter at Jerusalem." CAVE, no. 2 (August 1972), 28-35.

Smith, H.W. "Baxter's Theatre: A Critical Appraisal." In JAMES K. BAXTER FESTIVAL 1973: FOUR PLAYS, pp. 3-5, 12-13, 16. Manaaki Society, Wellington: [1973].

A balanced and valuable discussion of Baxter's attempts to solve the problems of poetic drama.

______. "James K. Baxter: The Poet as Playwright." LANDFALL, 22 (March 1968), 56-62.

Enthusiastic exegesis.

Stead, C.K. "Towards Jerusalem: The Later Poetry of James K. Baxter." ISLANDS, 2 (Autumn 1973), 7-18.

At first glance slight and impressionistic, but really a warm and sensitive introduction to the later poems.

Turner, B. "The Forest of a Man: James Keir Baxter, 1926-72." LIPSYNC, no. 2 (December 1972), 1-3.

Walker, D.C. "Baxter's Notebook." LANDFALL, 25 (March 1971), 20-24.

An article on the Jerusalem sonnets.

Weir, J.E. "The Green Inn--Some Reflections on the Poetry of James K. Baxter." COMMENT, 10 (April 1970), 22-28.

______. "Man without a Mask: A Study of the Poetry of James K. Baxter." Thesis, University of Canterbury, 1968.

______. THE POETRY OF JAMES K. BAXTER. Wellington: Oxford University Press, 1970.

A compact little monograph, which looks at the poetry from several thematic viewpoints. Its date precluded consideration of the final developments of Baxter's poetic career.

______. "A Voice for the Living: James K. Baxter 1926-72." EDUCATION, 22, no. 1 (1973), 27-30.

BETHELL, MARY URSULA (1874-1945)

Ursula Bethell's father was an early immigrant who had farmed in Canterbury for over twenty years before marrying. Ursula was born during a lengthy honeymoon in England, but grew up in Rangiora, a little north of Christchurch; her life was in fact to be spent equally between New Zealand and England. She completed her secondary education in Oxford and Geneva and later studied painting and music in Germany. But this she gave up for religious and social work among the poor in South London. Further travel between New Zealand and England followed, and then in 1924 she came to Christchurch for good. With a close friend, Effie Pollen, she settled in a cottage on a hill above the city, with a garden and a fine view across the plains to the Southern Alps. Here she began to write, at the age of fifty, the poetry which made her one of the finest New Zealand poets of her time, combining description of her garden and of the Canterbury landscape with universal religious themes. She wrote little more after her friend Effie died in 1934.

COLLECTED WORKS

COLLECTED POEMS. Christchurch: Caxton, 1950.

> In this book are reprinted the poems in the volumes of 1929, 1936, and 1939, with a few additional uncollected poems. The book does not include any work from THE GLAD RETURNING or THE HAUNTED GALLERY (see the note on Robert Erwin's article under "Criticism" below).

POETRY

FROM A GARDEN IN THE ANTIPODES. London: Sidgwick & Jackson, 1929.

TIME AND PLACE. Christchurch: Caxton, 1936.

DAY AND NIGHT: POEMS 1924-35. Christchurch: Caxton, 1939.

CRITICISM

Baigent, Lawrence. "The Poetry of Ursula Bethell." LANDFALL, 5 (March 1951), 23-30.

A knowledgeable and just discussion.

Erwin, Robert. "Ursula Bethell and Evelyn Hayes: A Misattribution?" LANDFALL, 31 (June 1977), 156-62.

Evelyn Hayes was the pseudonym used by Ursula Bethell when she published FROM A GARDEN IN THE ANTIPODES. But Erwin shows there is no positive evidence at all for the attribution to Ursula Bethell of two volumes sometimes listed as hers. The books are THE GLAD RETURNING AND OTHER POEMS, by Evelyn Hayes (London: A.H. Stockwell, [1932?]); and THE HAUNTED GALLERY AND OTHER POEMS, by Evelyn Hayes (London: A.H. Stockwell, [1932?]).

Grave, S.A. "The Image of New Zealand in the Poetry of Ursula Bethell." MEANJIN, 13 (Spring 1954), 381-88.

Grave relates Ursula Bethell's response to New Zealand landscape to her experience of Christian belief and of English cultural traditions in a new country.

Holcroft, M.H. MARY URSULA BETHELL. Wellington: Oxford University Press, 1975.

A biographical as much as a critical study, but nevertheless richly informative for the reader of the poetry.

Morton, J.M. "The Poetry of Ursula Bethell." Thesis, University of New Zealand, 1949.

Shaw, Helen. "I Am the Dark: The Poetry of Ursula Bethell." ARACHNE, no. 3 (December 1951), 25-29.

Somerset, H.C.D., et al. "Ursula Bethell: Some Personal Memories." LANDFALL, 2 (December 1948), 275-96.

Biographical reminiscences and critical comments by H.C.D. Somerset, D'Arcy Cresswell, M.H. Holcroft, John Summers, and L.G. Whitehead.

BRASCH, CHARLES ORWELL (1909-73)

Born into an established Otago family of businessmen, some of whom, on his mother's side, were also highly cultured, Charles Brasch decided, to his father's intense disappointment, not to enter business but to become a writer, a poet. Without obvious gifts of easy lyricism, he slowly but with persistent technical development earned himself at last a secure place among his more precocious contemporaries. After reading history at Oxford he travelled widely in Europe, and worked for the Foreign Office in London during the Second World War. He returned then to New Zealand, which he had come to recognize as home. Family money allowed him to devote much of his energy and a discriminating taste to the fostering of the arts, especially literature and painting. He became the founding editor of the quarterly LANDFALL, the first important literary periodical to survive for more than a year or two, saying that his society would never know what to think and believe "until it is revealed to itself in works of art of its own begetting: works that will at length shape for it in its own terms the cloudy architecture of reality whose defining confirms man in his home on earth."

POETRY

THE LAND AND THE PEOPLE AND OTHER POEMS. Christchurch: Caxton, 1939.

DISPUTED GROUND: POEMS 1939-45. Christchurch: Caxton, 1948.

THE ESTATE AND OTHER POEMS. Christchurch: Caxton, 1957.

OCTONARY. Dunedin: Press Room, University of Otago, 1963.
Some of these poems were subsequently published in AMBULANDO.

AMBULANDO. Christchurch: Caxton, 1964.

OUT OF THE NOTHING OF WORDS. Dunedin: 1964.

TWICE SIXTY. Wellington: Wai-te-ata Press, 1966.

BLACK ROSE. New Delhi: Nagmani, 1967.

Translations by Brasch of poems by the Punjabi writer Amrita Pritam.

NOT FAR OFF. Christchurch: Caxton, 1969.

NORTH-EAST AND SOUTH-WEST: WINDWORDS FOR MARY AT EIGHTY. Dunedin: 1970.

GEDICHTE AUS NEUSEELAND. Dunedin: McIndoe, 1970.

Poems in German by Hilde Zisserman with translations by Brasch.

POEMS BY ESENIN. Wellington: Wai-te-ata Press, 1970.

Translations by Brasch and Peter Soskice.

HOME GROUND. Ed. Alan Roddick. Christchurch: Caxton, 1974.

DRAMA

THE QUEST: WORDS FOR A MIME PLAY. London: The Compass Players, 1946.

PROSE

LANDFALL COUNTRY: WORK FROM LANDFALL, 1947-1961. Ed. Charles Brasch. Christchurch: Caxton, 1962.

"Writer and Reader." NEW ZEALAND MONTHLY REVIEW, 5 (February 1965), 18-19.

PRESENT COMPANY: REFLECTIONS ON THE ARTS. Auckland: Blackwood & Janet Paul, 1966.

"One January." ISLANDS, 2 (Spring 1973), 253-61.

An extract from a diary of 1940.

SUCH SEPARATE CREATURES: STORIES. Christchurch: Caxton, 1973.

Short stories by James Courage, ed. and intro. by Charles Brasch.

HALLENSTEINS--THE FIRST CENTURY, 1873-1973. With C.R. Nicolson. Dunedin: Hallenstein Bros., 1973.

CRITICISM

Bertram, James. CHARLES BRASCH. Wellington: Oxford University Press, [1976].

A fine biographical and literary study written by a lifelong friend.

______. "Charles Brasch: Last Landfall." NEW ZEALAND LISTENER, 11 June 1973, pp. 12-13.

______. "Two New Zealand Poets." EDUCATION, 2 (July 1949), 56-59.

Brasch, Charles. "Conversation with Charles Brasch." LANDFALL, 25 (December 1971), 344-72.

In this interview with Ian Milner, Brasch talked about his poetry and, at considerable length, about the establishing and running of LANDFALL.

Daalder, Joost. "'Disputed Ground' in the Poetry of Charles Brasch." LANDFALL, 26 (September 1972), 247-54.

De Beer, Mary, et al. "Charles Brasch 1909-73: Tributes and Memories from his Friends." ISLANDS, 2 (Spring 1973), 233-53.

The other contributors are Dora and Esmond de Beer, James Bertram, Jack Bennett, John Crockett, M.T. Woollaston, Denis Glover, Ruth Dallas, Douglas Lilburn, W.H. Oliver, Ian Milner, and Janet Frame.

McCormick, E.H. "Charles Brasch, Editor of 'Landfall.'" SOUTHERLY, 33 (1973), 432-39.

O'Sullivan, Vincent. "'Brief Permitted Morning'--Notes on the Poetry of Charles Brasch." LANDFALL, 23 (December 1969), 338-53.

O'Sullivan finds in AMBULANDO (p. 75) and NOT FAR OFF (p. 76) the lesson that "to know reality at its best, is not to be free of limitations, but to be free in one's awareness of them," and rereads the earlier volumes of poetry with fresh insight. "Brasch," he says, "has chosen to write poetry which exposes himself, raw. It is grave poetry, and courageous."

Paisley, D.J. "The Double Vision: Local and Universal in the Work of Two New Zealand Poets." Thesis, University of Otago, 1966.

Rhodes, H. Winston. "Charles Brasch: Editor and Poet, 1909-1973." MEANJIN, 32 (September 1973), 314-15.

Wedde, Ian. "Captivating Invitation: Getting On to Charles Brasch's 'Home Ground.'" ISLANDS, 4 (Spring 1975), 315-27.

A complex, philosophical discussion which sees in the sequence "Home Ground" the final achieving of a balance in the relationship of art and life which had been constantly sought throughout Brasch's poetic career.

CAMPBELL, ALISTAIR TE ARIKI (1925-)

Alistair Campbell was born in Rarotonga in the Cook Islands. His Polynesian mother and his Scottish father both died when he was young and he and his brothers and sister were sent to his father's home town of Dunedin in 1933 where for the rest of his school years he lived in an orphanage. He finished his B.A. at Victoria University of Wellington, taught for a short time, and then took a job as an editor in the School Publications Branch of the Department of Education. He is now editor for the Council for Educational Research. Alistair Campbell has not been a voluminous poet, and despite the unprecedented success of his first volume he has published new verse only occasionally since.

POETRY

MINE EYES DAZZLE: POEMS 1947-49. Christchurch: Pegasus, 1950. As MINE EYES DAZZLE. Introd. James K. Baxter. Christchurch: Pegasus, 1951; rev. ed. 1956.

SANCTUARY OF SPIRITS: POEMS. Wellington: Wai-te-ata Press, 1963.

WILD HONEY. London: Oxford University Press, 1964.

Includes most of the poems in the two preceding titles and some new work.

BLUE RAIN: POEMS. Wellington: Wai-te-ata Press, 1967.

DRINKING HORN. [Paremata, Wellington]: Bottle Press, [1970].

WALK THE BLACK PATH. [Paremata, Wellington]: Bottle Press, [1971].

KAPITI: SELECTED POEMS, 1947-71. Christchurch: Pegasus, 1972.

DREAMS, YELLOW LIONS. Martinborough: Alister Taylor, 1975.

FICTION

THE HAPPY SUMMER. Christchurch: Whitcombe & Tombs, 1961; rpt. Wellington: Price Milburn, 1975.

A children's story reprinted from the SCHOOL JOURNAL.

DRAMA

"When the Bough Breaks." ACT, [no. 11] (July-September 1970), supplementary pages. Rev. version in CONTEMPORARY NEW ZEALAND PLAYS. Ed. Howard McNaughton. Wellington: Oxford University Press, 1974.

"The Suicide: A Radio Play." LANDFALL, 28 (December 1974), 307-25.

OTHER PROSE

THE FRUIT FARM. Wellington: School Publications Branch, Dept. of Education, 1953; rev. ed. 1970.

A primary school bulletin. This and the following two books are documentary stories for children.

THE MILK WE DRINK. Wellington: Milk Publicity Council of New Zealand, [1962].

OUR DAILY MILK. Wellington: Milk Publicity Council of New Zealand, [1962].

"Glover and Georgianism." COMMENT, 6 (October-November 1964), 23-33.

NEW ZEALAND: A BOOK FOR CHILDREN. Wellington: School Publications Branch, Dept. of Education, 1967.

A bulletin for schools.

MAORI LEGENDS. Wellington: Seven Seas Publishing Pty., 1969.

"Some myths and legends of the Maori people, retold by Alistair Campbell."

"James K. Baxter: The Earlier Poems." In NEW ZEALAND'S HERITAGE. Ed. Ray Knox. Wellington: Paul Hamlyn, [1971-73], pp. 2561-66.

"Te Rauparaha--'The Old Sarpent.'" In NEW ZEALAND'S HERITAGE. Ed. Ray Knox. Wellington: Paul Hamlyn, [1971-73], pp. 314-18.

"Return to Rarotonga." NEW ZEALAND LISTENER, 3 July 1976, pp. 24-25.

This and the next six articles are all autobiographical.

"Wild Honey." NEW ZEALAND LISTENER, 4 September 1976, pp. 38-39.

Reflections on a poetry reading tour of the South Island.

"An Orphan in the '30s." NEW ZEALAND LISTENER, 30 October 1976, pp. 16-17.

"Playground of the '30s." NEW ZEALAND LISTENER, 5 February 1977, pp. 22-23.

"Growing Pains in the War Years." NEW ZEALAND LISTENER, 23 April 1977, pp. 18-19.

"The Owl in the Trees." NEW ZEALAND LISTENER, 25 June 1977, pp. 28-29.

"What Shall I Do for Pretty Girls?" NEW ZEALAND LISTENER, 15 October 1977, pp. 20-21, 66-68.

"Alistair Campbell on THE WATER BABIES." EDUCATION, 26, no. 8 (1977), 24-25.

Campbell recalls his childhood discovery of Kingsley's story.

CRITICISM

Bertram, James. "Review of WILD HONEY." COMMENT, 6 (January-February 1965), 42-44.

WILD HONEY was virtually Campbell's "Selected Poems" up till 1964, and this review traces the growth of his poetry from its beginnings. Bertram suggests that Lorca's notion of "duende" offers a key to Campbell's power, and that formal analysis is out of place. Of the poetry he comments, "When it has 'duende' the dark sounds compel, and it works on us irresistibly."

Campbell, Alistair. "Inside the Outsider." NEW ZEALAND LISTENER, 15 April 1965, p. 5.

Campbell interviewed by Diane Billing.

______. "The Plays of Alistair Campbell." LANDFALL, 28 (March 1974), 55-68.

In this interview with Howard McNaughton, Campbell talks in frank detail about the origins and meaning of his plays.

Gunby, David. "Alistair Campbell's 'Mine Eyes Dazzle': An Anatomy of Success." LANDFALL, 23 (March 1969), 34-50.

This essay is chiefly concerned to sharpen or qualify points made by earlier reviewers of Campbell's poetry.

McCracken, Jill. "'Some People Regard Me As a Poet.'" NEW ZEALAND LISTENER, 17 July 1972, pp. 12-13.

McNaughton, Howard. "'The Suicide'--The Evolution of a Technique." LANDFALL, 28 (December 1974), 305-07.

COURAGE, JAMES (1905-63)

James Courage was brought up on his father's Canterbury sheep station, but lived in England from the age of twenty except for a period of convalescence in New Zealand in the early 1930s. The subjects of his New Zealand novels and stories were drawn from the predominantly rural Canterbury family life he had known as a child. His first and his last two novels have English settings.

FICTION

ONE HOUSE. London: Gollancz, 1933.

THE FIFTH CHILD. London: Constable, 1948.

DESIRE WITHOUT CONTENT. London: Constable, 1950.

FIRES IN THE DISTANCE. London: Constable, 1952.

THE YOUNG HAVE SECRETS. London: Jonathan Cape, 1954.

THE CALL HOME. London: Jonathan Cape, 1956.

A WAY OF LOVE. London: Jonathan Cape; New York: Putnam, 1959.

THE VISIT TO PENMORTEN. London: Jonathan Cape, 1961.

SUCH SEPARATE CREATURES: STORIES. Ed. and intro. Charles Brasch. Christchurch: Caxton, 1973.

CRITICISM

Copland, R.A. "The New Zealand Novels of James Courage." LANDFALL, 18 (September 1964), 235-49.

Copland argues that in writing about the psychology of family relationships in the still very English homesteads of Canterbury, Courage borrows English fictional forms which often dull the edge of his personal perceptions.

Wilson, Phillip. "Expatriate Novelist." NEW ZEALAND LISTENER, 21 November 1952, pp. 12-13.

_____. "James Courage: A Recollection." LANDFALL, 18 (September 1964), 234-35.

CRESSWELL, WALTER D'ARCY (1896-1960)

D'Arcy Cresswell left Christchurch to complete architectural studies in London but, with an unswerving faith in his vocation as a poet, was to spend most of his life in an impoverished state. He succeeded in publishing relatively little verse after about 1932, and is remembered more for his autobiography in which he records his attempts to live a poet's life, writing in a strangely mannered but often compelling style and with an unembarrassed candour. It is for this frank self-revelation rather than his poetry or his eccentric views on modern civilization that he remains interesting. Two series of poetry pamphlets, mostly single-leaf poems, were printed for Cresswell, one in the 1920s and the other in 1950. Details are not listed here but can be found in the NEW ZEALAND NATIONAL BIBLIOGRAPHY (see p. 2).

AUTOBIOGRAPHY AND LETTERS

THE POET'S PROGRESS. London: Faber, 1930.

PRESENT WITHOUT LEAVE. London: Cassell, 1939.

> Six extracts from an uncompleted third volume of Cresswell's autobiography appeared under the general title of "The Poet's Progress" in the NEW ZEALAND LISTENER between 17 February and 31 March 1950.

THE LETTERS OF D'ARCY CRESSWELL. Selected and edited by Helen Shaw. Christchurch: University of Canterbury, 1971.

POETRY

POEMS (1921-1927). London: Wells Gardner, Darton & Co., 1928.

TIME LAGS ABED. London: 1930.

THE BAY OF BISCAY. London: 1931.

THE POET TO HIS VERSE. London: 1931.

POEMS 1924-1931. London: Bodley Head, [1932?].

LYTTELTON HARBOUR. [Auckland]: Unicorn Press, 1936.

A PIOUS ODE: COMMEMORATING THE 21ST ANNIVERSARY OF THE INDUSTRIOUS COMPANY OF E. WALTER GEORGE LTD. [London: The Company, 1947].

TWELVE POEMS. [Germany]: Spiegel-Verlag, 1947.

THE VOYAGE OF THE HURUNUI: A BALLAD. Christchurch: Caxton, 1956.

POEMS FOR POPPYCOCK. London: Trireme Press, 1957.

POETRY AND CYPRUS. London: Trireme Press, 1957.

LEANDER: AN ELEGY. London: Trireme Press, 1958.

MORE POEMS FOR POPPYCOCK. London: Trireme Press, 1959.

THEY WHEN IN IRONS. London: Trireme Press, [1959?].

ZANDVOORTER PRELUDES, 1. London: Trireme Press, 1959.

SONNETS, PUBLISHED AND FROM MANUSCRIPTS. Selected by Helen Shaw. Christchurch: Nag's Head Press, 1976.

DRAMA

THE FOREST: A COMEDY IN THREE ACTS. Auckland: Pelorus Press, 1952.

A play in verse.

PROSE

MODERN POETRY AND THE IDEAL. Auckland: Griffin Press, 1934.

EENA DEENA DYNAMO. Christchurch: Caxton, 1936.

A brief summary of his "Thesis" (see the annotation to Finlayson's book under "Criticism" below).

MARGARET McMILLAN: A MEMOIR. Foreword by J.B. Priestley. London: Hutchinson, [1948].

INSPIRATION. [London?]: Poetry Pamphlets, 1950.

"The First Wasp." In THE PURITAN AND THE WAIF: A SYMPOSIUM OF CRITICAL ESSAYS ON THE WORK OF FRANK SARGESON. Ed. Helen Shaw. Auckland: H.L. Hofmann, 1954, pp. 1-6.

CRITICISM

BROUGHTON, W.S. "Problems and Responses of Three New Zealand Poets in the 1920s." In PROCEEDINGS AND PAPERS OF THE TENTH AULLA CONGRESS. Ed. P. Dane. [Auckland]: Australasian Universities Language and Literature Association, [1966], pp. 202-13. Rpt. in ESSAYS ON NEW ZEALAND LITERATURE. Ed. Wystan Curnow. Auckland: Heinemann Educational Books, 1973, pp. 1-15.

______. "W. D'Arcy Cresswell, A.R.D. Fairburn, R.A.K. Mason: An Examination of Certain Aspects of Their Lives and Works." Thesis, University of Auckland, 1968.

Carrington, C.E., et al. "D'Arcy Cresswell, By His Friends." LANDFALL, 14 (December 1960), 341-61.

The other contributors are Oliver Duff, Denis Glover, Frank Sargeson, Roderick Finlayson, Antony Alpers, and Ormond Wilson.

Chapman, Robert. "The Work of D'Arcy Cresswell." IMAGE (Auckland), no. 7 (August 1960), 1-3.

Cresswell, D'Arcy. "Poet's Progress Report." NEW ZEALAND LISTENER, 10 February 1950, p. 6.

Cresswell interviewed by Phillip Wilson.

Finlayson, Roderick. D'ARCY CRESSWELL. New York: Twayne, 1972.

Finlayson writes in full sympathy with Cresswell's lifelong attack on the modern scientific interpretation of the universe and discusses his unpublished "A Thesis on the Mechanism of Spirit or Poetic Intention in Man." He gives equal attention to the whole range of Cresswell's work, regarding him as something of a prophet.

Holcroft, M.H. "A Professional Expatriate." In NEW ZEALAND'S HERITAGE. Ed. Ray Knox. Wellington: Paul Hamlyn, [1971-73], pp. 2210-12.

Rhodes, H. Winston. "The Autobiography of an Unjustified Poet." NEW ZEALAND LIBRARIES, 10 (November 1947), 206-10.

An admirably balanced essay on the two volumes of autobiography.

CURNOW, THOMAS ALLEN MONRO (1911-)

Allen Curnow spent his boyhood at vicarages in Canterbury before finding a menial newspaper job at the beginning of the Depression. A scholarship to St. John's (Anglican theological) College in Auckland enabled him to attend university there at the same time, but in 1935 he went back to the Christchurch daily newspaper, THE PRESS, working there until 1950 when he joined the staff of the English Department at the University of Auckland. Most of his poetry was written during his newspaper years, though there have been two small recent volumes. Allen Curnow, besides being one of the most important poets of his time, is also an accomplished verse satirist, and under the name of Whim-wham has, since the thirties, commented regularly on matters of current interest.

BIBLIOGRAPHY

Graham, Theresa. "A Bibliography of Works by & on Allen Curnow." Bibliographical exercise, Library School, Wellington, 1976.

A fully annotated bibliography. It includes a generous selection of reviews of Curnow's work.

COLLECTED WORKS

A SMALL ROOM WITH LARGE WINDOWS: SELECTED POEMS. London: Oxford University Press, 1962.

COLLECTED POEMS 1933-1973. Wellington: Reed, 1974.

POETRY

VALLEY OF DECISION: POEMS. Auckland: Auckland University College Students' Association Press, 1933.

Curnow, Thomas Allen Monro

THREE POEMS. Christchurch: Caxton Club Press, 1935.

ANOTHER ARGO. With A.R.D. Fairburn and Denis Glover. Christchurch: Caxton Club Press, 1935.

ENEMIES: POEMS 1934-36. Christchurch: Caxton, 1937.

NOT IN NARROW SEAS: POEMS WITH PROSE. Christchurch: Caxton, 1939.

A PRESENT FOR HITLER AND OTHER VERSES. By Whim-wham [pseud.]. [Christchurch]: Caxton, [1940].

ISLAND AND TIME. Christchurch: Caxton, 1941.

RECENT POEMS. With A.R.D. Fairburn, Denis Glover, and R.A.K. Mason. Christchurch: Caxton, 1941.

WHIM-WHAM: VERSES 1941-1942. By Whim-wham [pseud.]. Christchurch: Caxton, 1942.

WHIM-WHAM, 1943. By Whim-wham [pseud.]. Wellington: Progressive Publishing Society, 1943.

SAILING OR DROWNING: POEMS. Wellington: Progressive Publishing Society, [1944].

A BOOK OF NEW ZEALAND VERSE 1923-45. Ed. and intro. Allen Curnow. Christchurch: Caxton, 1945. Enl. ed., as A BOOK OF NEW ZEALAND VERSE 1923-50. Christchurch: Caxton, 1951.

POEMS: JACK WITHOUT MAGIC. Christchurch: Caxton, 1946.

AT DEAD LOW WATER AND SONNETS. Christchurch: Caxton, 1949.

THE HUCKSTERS & THE UNIVERSITY. [Auckland]: Pilgrim Press, 1957.

POEMS 1949-57. Wellington: Mermaid Press, 1957.

MR HUCKSTER OF 1958. [Auckland]: Pilgrim Press, 1958.

THE BEST OF WHIM-WHAM. By Whim-wham [pseud.]. Hamilton: Paul's Book Arcade, 1959.

LANDFALL IN UNKNOWN SEAS. Wellington: Government Printer, [1959].

Separate reprinting of a poem first published in 1943.

ON THE TOUR: VERWOERD BE OUR VATCHWOERD, OR, GOD AMEND NEW ZEALAND. [Auckland]: Pilgrim Press, 1960.

THE PENGUIN BOOK OF NEW ZEALAND VERSE. Ed. and intro. Allen Curnow. Harmondsworth, Middlesex: Penguin Books, 1960; rpt. Auckland: Blackwood & Janet Paul, 1966.

WHIM WHAM LAND. By Whim-wham [pseud.]. Auckland: Blackwood & Janet Paul, 1967.

TREES, EFFIGIES, MOVING OBJECTS: A SEQUENCE OF POEMS. Wellington: Catspaw Press, 1972.

AN ABOMINABLE TEMPER AND OTHER POEMS. Wellington: Catspaw Press, 1973.

DRAMA

THE AXE: A VERSE TRAGEDY. Christchurch: Caxton, 1949.

Reprinted in the next item.

FOUR PLAYS. Wellington: Reed, 1972.

The titles of these verse plays, written for stage and radio, are "The Axe," "The Overseas Expert," "The Duke's Miracle," and "Resident of Nowhere."

PROSE

See chapter 3 for annotations on Curnow's important introductory essays to A BOOK OF NEW ZEALAND VERSE 1923-45 (1945) and THE PENGUIN BOOK OF NEW ZEALAND VERSE (1960).

POETRY & LANGUAGE. Christchurch: Caxton Club Press, 1935.

"Aspects of New Zealand Poetry." MEANJIN PAPERS, 2 (Summer 1943), 20-26.

"Coal Flat: The Major Scale, the Fine Excess." COMMENT, 5 (October 1963), 39-42.

"New Zealand Literature: The Case for a Working Definition." In THE FUTURE OF NEW ZEALAND. Ed. M.F. Lloyd Prichard. Christchurch: Whitcombe & Tombs for the University of Auckland, 1964, pp. 84-107; rpt. in ESSAYS ON NEW ZEALAND LITERATURE. Ed. Wystan Curnow. Auckland: Heinemann Educational Books, 1973, pp. 139-54.

"Distraction and Definition: Centripetal Directions in New Zealand Poetry." In NATIONAL IDENTITY. Ed. K.L. Goodwin. London: Heinemann Educational Books, 1970, pp. 170-86.

"COAL FLAT Revisited." In CRITICAL ESSAYS ON THE NEW ZEALAND NOVEL. Ed. Cherry Hankin. Auckland: Heinemann Educational Books, 1976, pp. 105-27.

CRITICISM

Curnow, Allen. "Conversation with Allen Curnow." ISLANDS, 2 (Winter 1973), 142-62.

> Allen Curnow here talks to MacDonald P. Jackson with admirable clarity and point about his life, his poetry, his reading, and his views on New Zealand verse.

______. "Poet on His Plays." NEW ZEALAND LISTENER, 7 March 1969, p. 9.

> Curnow interviewed by Arthur Baysting.

Fairburn, A.R.D. "New Zealanders You Should Know: Mr Allen Curnow." ACTION, December 1944, pp. 35-37.

Gurr, A.J. "The Two Realities of New Zealand Poetry." JOURNAL OF COMMONWEALTH LITERATURE, 1 (September 1965), 122-34.

"Poet in a Laboratory." NEW ZEALAND LISTENER, 2 June 1950, p. 7.

> This article was based on an interview with Curnow after his return from his first visit to Britain and the United States.

Stead, C.K. "Allen Curnow's Poetry." LANDFALL, 17 (March 1963), 26-45; rpt. in ESSAYS ON NEW ZEALAND LITERATURE. Ed. Wystan Curnow. Auckland: Heinemann Educational Books, 1973, pp. 54-70.

> Stead places Allen Curnow within the tradition of a broad range of English poets, and supports a closely argued philosophical essay, encompassing such topics as the reconciliation of opposites, and the local and the universal experience, with a number of detailed analyses of individual poems.

Sturm, Terry. "Allen Curnow: Forty Years of Poems." ISLANDS, 4 (Autumn 1975), 68-75.

> This well-informed article, written on the publication of Curnow's COLLECTED POEMS, is based on a long and careful study of the verse. Sturm is especially interested in the relationship between the poet and his poems.

_____. "Fictions and Realities: An Approach to Allen Curnow's TREES, EFFIGIES, MOVING OBJECTS." WORLD LITERATURE WRITTEN IN ENGLISH, 14 (April 1975), 25-49.

DALLAS, RUTH (1919-)

(Pseudonym of Ruth Minnie Mumford)

Ruth Dallas belongs to Southland and Otago. She grew up in Invercargill (her family was of pioneering origins), and has now lived for over twenty years in Dunedin, where for a while she assisted Charles Brasch with the editing of LANDFALL. She has been greatly attracted by Chinese poetry and by Buddhism, two influences evident in her own verse. While at school she regularly wrote poems and stories for a "Children's Page" in the local paper, and has continued writing for children both in the SCHOOL JOURNAL and in the volumes of fiction listed below.

POETRY

THE DEMON LOVER: A BALLAD. [Christchurch]: Caxton, 1948.

COUNTRY ROAD AND OTHER POEMS, 1947-52. Christchurch: Caxton, 1953.

THE TURNING WHEEL: POEMS. [Christchurch]: Caxton, 1961.

EXPERIMENT IN FORM. Dunedin: Press Room, University of Otago, 1964.

Most of these poems were reprinted in DAY BOOK.

DAY BOOK: POEMS OF A YEAR. Christchurch: Caxton, 1966.

SHADOW SHOW: POEMS. Christchurch: Caxton, 1968.

SONG FOR A GUITAR AND OTHER SONGS. Ed. and introd. Charles Brasch. Dunedin: University of Otago Press, 1976.

WALKING ON THE SNOW: POEMS. Christchurch: Caxton, 1976.

FICTION

THE CHILDREN IN THE BUSH. London: Methuen, 1969.

This and the following five books were written for children.

RAGAMUFFIN SCARECROW. [Dunedin]: Bibliography Room, University of Otago, 1969.

A DOG CALLED WIG. London: Methuen, 1970.

THE WILD BOY IN THE BUSH. London: Methuen Children's Books, 1971.

THE BIG FLOOD IN THE BUSH. London: Methuen Children's Books, 1972.

THE HOUSE ON THE CLIFFS. London: Methuen Children's Books; Wellington: Hicks Smith, 1975.

OTHER PROSE

SAWMILLING YESTERDAY. Wellington: School Publications Branch, Dept. of Education, 1958.

A primary school bulletin.

"Beginnings." LANDFALL, 19 (December 1965), 348-58.

An autobiographical essay.

CRITICISM

Bertram, James. "Review of THE TURNING WHEEL." LANDFALL, 16 (June 1962), 188-92.

Dallas, Ruth. "Ruth Dallas: An Interview." REVIEW (Dunedin), (1975), 24-29.

Ruth Dallas interviewed by John Gibb.

Doyle, Charles. "Review of DAY BOOK: POEMS OF A YEAR." LANDFALL, 21 (June 1967), 197-201.

DAVIN, DANIEL MARCUS (1913-)

Dan Davin was born into an Irish-Catholic family in Invercargill, went on a church scholarship to Sacred Heart College, Auckland, and then to the University of Otago, and from there as a Rhodes scholar to Oxford where he read classics. He served with British and New Zealand forces in the Mediterranean during the Second World War, and afterwards joined the Clarendon Press in Oxford, rising to Deputy Secretary to the Delegates. The material of his stories and novels has closely followed his own career, and NOT HERE, NOT NOW concluded a cycle of novels originally planned before the war.

FICTION

CLIFFS OF FALL. London: Nicholson & Watson, 1945.

FOR THE REST OF OUR LIVES. London: Nicholson & Watson, 1947; rpt. Auckland: Blackwood & Janet Paul; London: Michael Joseph, 1965.

THE GORSE BLOOMS PALE. London: Nicholson & Watson, 1947.

Short stories.

ROADS FROM HOME. London: Michael Joseph, 1949; rpt. Ed. and introd. Lawrence Jones. [Auckland]: Auckland University Press; [Wellington]: Oxford University Press, 1976.

SELECTED STORIES. Ed. and introd. Dan Davin. London: Oxford University Press, 1953.

Stories by Katherine Mansfield.

NEW ZEALAND SHORT STORIES. Ed. and introd. Dan Davin. London: Oxford University Press, 1953; rpt. Wellington: Oxford University Press, 1973.

An anthology.

THE SULLEN BELL. London: Michael Joseph, 1956.

ENGLISH SHORT STORIES OF TODAY: SECOND SERIES. Ed. Dan Davin. London: Oxford University Press for the English Association, 1958.

An anthology.

NO REMITTANCE. London: Michael Joseph, 1959.

NOT HERE, NOT NOW. London: Robert Hale; [Christchurch]: Whitcombe & Tombs, 1970.

BRIDES OF PRICE. London: Robert Hale; [Christchurch]: Whitcombe & Tombs, 1972.

BREATHING SPACES. London: Robert Hale; [Christchurch]: Whitcoulls, 1975.

Short stories.

OTHER PROSE

AN INTRODUCTION TO ENGLISH LITERATURE. With John Mulgan. Oxford: Clarendon, 1947.

"This work is largely based on the late Professor Émile Legouis's A SHORT HISTORY OF ENGLISH LITERATURE" (Trans. V.F. Boyson and J. Coulson. Oxford: Clarendon Press, 1934).

CRETE. Wellington: War History Branch, Dept. of Internal Affairs, 1953.

"The Narrative Technique of Frank Sargeson." In THE PURITAN AND THE WAIF: A SYMPOSIUM OF CRITICAL ESSAYS ON THE WORK OF FRANK SARGESON. Ed. Helen Shaw. Auckland: H.L. Hofmann, 1954, pp. 56-71.

WRITING IN NEW ZEALAND: THE NEW ZEALAND NOVEL. With W.K. Davin. 2 vols. Wellington: School Publications Branch, Dept. of Education, 1956.

Post-primary school bulletins.

KATHERINE MANSFIELD IN HER LETTERS. Wellington: School Publications Branch, Dept. of Education, 1959.

A post-primary school bulletin.

"The New Zealand Novel." JOURNAL OF THE ROYAL SOCIETY OF ARTS, 110 (July 1962), 586-98.

A paper read to the society, with the discussion which followed.

"New Zealand Literature." BOOKS (London), no. 367 (September-October 1966), 161-63.

CLOSING TIMES. London: Oxford University Press, 1975.

Recollections of literary friends.

"Dan Davin on 'The Rime of the Ancient Mariner.'" EDUCATION, 25, no. 5 (1976), 27.

Davin recalls his childhood discovery of Coleridge's poem.

CRITICISM

Bertram, James. "Dan Davin: Novelist of Exile." MEANJIN, 32 (June 1973), 148-56.

A chronological survey and a warm estimate of Davin's fiction.

Beveridge, Michael. "Review of NOT HERE, NOT NOW." LANDFALL, 24 (September 1970), 296-302.

A substantial and sympathetic review, beginning with a survey of Davin's earlier novels.

Davin, Dan. "Freedom First for Dan Davin." NEW ZEALAND LISTENER, 17 September 1948, pp. 6-7.

An interview.

______. "Roads Back Home: A Conversation with Dan Davin." NEW ZEALAND LISTENER, 3 April 1959, pp. 6-7.

Davin interviewed by M.H. Holcroft.

______. "Eye of the Expatriate." NEW ZEALAND LISTENER, 12 September 1969, p. 10.

Davin interviewed by Ray Knox.

Jones, Lawrence. "The Persistence of Realism: Dan Davin, Noel Hilliard and Recent New Zealand Short Stories." ISLANDS, 6 (Winter 1977), 182-200.

McCormick, E.H. "Review of CLIFFS OF FALL." NEW ZEALAND LISTENER, 28 September 1945, pp. 14-15.

Rhodes, H. Winston. "Dan Davin's ROADS FROM HOME." In CRITICAL ESSAYS ON THE NEW ZEALAND NOVEL. Ed. Cherry Hankin. Auckland: Heinemann Educational Books, 1976, pp. 73-87.

Wellington, W. "Dan Davin: A Writer with Gusto: A Young New Zealand Novelist Wins Praise." NEW ZEALAND MAGAZINE, 27 (April-May 1948), 14-15.

Whelan, D.B. "Alienation in the Novels of Sargeson and Davin: A Study of Four Novels: I SAW IN MY DREAM; I FOR ONE; CLIFFS OF FALL; ROADS FROM HOME." Thesis, University of Canterbury, 1965.

DUGGAN, EILEEN MAY (1894-1972)

Eileen Duggan grew up in Marlborough, on the edge of the Wairau plains, an area often described in her verse. She took a degree in history and lectured for a time at Victoria University College, but thereafter lived a quiet, retired life. She has been less well-known as a poet than she deserves, partly because her three main collections were published in London, and partly because she did not allow her poems to appear in Allen Curnow's anthologies.

POETRY

POEMS. Dunedin: N.Z. Tablet, [1922].

NEW ZEALAND BIRD SONGS. Wellington: Harry H. Tombs, [1929].
Poems written for children.

POEMS. Introd. Walter de la Mare. London: Allen & Unwin, 1937.

NEW ZEALAND POEMS. London: Allen & Unwin, 1940.

MORE POEMS. London: Allen & Unwin; New York: Macmillan, 1951.

PROSE

"The History of Wellington 1840-1843." Thesis, Victoria University College, 1918.

EPISCOPAL GOLDEN JUBILEE OF HIS GRACE ARCHBISHOP REDWOOD, S.M., 1874-1924. [Wellington: O'Kane and McKenzie], 1924.

"Katherine Mansfield." NEW ZEALAND ARTISTS' ANNUAL, 2, no. 2 (1931), 12.

"A Father's Tribute: Eileen Duggan Writes of Katherine Mansfield." ALL ABOUT BOOKS (Melbourne), 13 November 1933, p. 177.

EPISCOPAL DIAMOND JUBILEE OF HIS GRACE ARCHBISHOP REDWOOD, S.M. 1874-1934. Wellington: McKenzie, Thornton, Cooper, 1934.

McHardy, Emmet C. BLAZING THE TRAIL IN THE SOLOMONS: LETTERS FROM THE NORTH SOLOMONS OF REV. EMMET McHARDY, S.M. Ed. Eileen Duggan. Sydney: Right Rev. T.J. Wade, 1935.

CENTENARY: SISTERS OF MERCY, WELLINGTON: 1861-1961. [Wellington]: n.p., [1961].

"New Zealand." Part 7 of A HISTORY OF IRISH CATHOLICISM. Ed. Patrick J. Corish. Dublin: Gill & Macmillan, 1971.

CRITICISM

Baxter, James K. "Review of MORE POEMS." NEW ZEALAND LISTENER, 13 July 1951, p. 12.

McEldowney, Dennis. "A Visit to Miss Duggan." ISLANDS, 2 (Summer 1973), 423-27.

McKay, Frank. EILEEN DUGGAN. Wellington: Oxford University Press, [1977].

Maher, Kevin. "Poet of 'the Calm Beyond.'" NEW ZEALAND LISTENER, 15 January 1973, pp. 12-13.

Mulgan, Alan. "Eileen Duggan's Country." NEW ZEALAND MAGAZINE, 21 (July-August 1942), 5-8.

______. "A New Zealand Poet for the World." In his GREAT DAYS IN NEW ZEALAND WRITING. Wellington: Reed, 1962, pp. 90-94.

Stevens, Joan. "Review of MORE POEMS." LANDFALL, 6 (March 1952), 77-80.

DUGGAN, MAURICE NOEL (1922-74)

Maurice Duggan left school at fourteen, an out-of-doors boy keen on sport. But a leg infection which led to an amputation turned him into a reader. He proceeded to read widely and tenaciously, and at the age of twenty-five to begin writing meticulously written stories, usually about people who were, like himself, of Irish-Catholic origin. A conscious and exacting craftsman, he wrote slowly and published sparingly.

FICTION

IMMANUEL'S LAND: STORIES. Auckland: Pilgrim Press, 1956.

FALTER TOM AND THE WATER BOY. London: Faber; Hamilton: Paul's Book Arcade; New York: Criterion Books, 1958; Harmondsworth, Middlesex: Kestrel Books with Longman Paul, 1974.

> A story for children first published in the SCHOOL JOURNAL (see p. 215). The text of the American edition differs slightly.

SUMMER IN THE GRAVEL PIT: STORIES. [Hamilton]: Blackwood & Janet Paul; London: Gollancz, 1965; rpt. Auckland: Longman Paul, 1971.

O'LEARY'S ORCHARD AND OTHER STORIES. Christchurch: Caxton, 1970.

THE FABULOUS McFANES AND OTHER CHILDREN'S STORIES. Whatamongo Bay, Marlborough: Cape Catley, [1974].

> Stories first published in the SCHOOL JOURNAL (see p. 215).

OTHER PROSE

"Writers in New Zealand: A Questionnaire: Maurice Duggan." LANDFALL, 14 (March 1960), 50-53.

A more connected and original essay than questionnaires usually elicit.

"A Delight of Books: Children's Book Week 1960." NEW ZEALAND LIBRARIES, 24 (April 1961), 65-67.

"The Burns Fellowship." LANDFALL, 22 (September 1968), 237-39.

"Beginnings." LANDFALL, 20 (December 1966), 331-39; rpt. ISLANDS, 3 (Summer 1974), 342-49.

An autobiographical essay.

CRITICISM

Copland, R.A. "Review of IMMANUEL'S LAND." LANDFALL, 11 (March 1957), 77-80.

Jones, Lawrence. "Review of SUMMER IN THE GRAVEL PIT." LANDFALL, 19 (September 1965), 287-90.

Macalister, Molly. "Maurice Duggan 1922-74." ISLANDS, 3 (Summer 1974), 342.

Sinclair, Keith. "Maurice Duggan 1922-1974." NEW ZEALAND LISTENER, 25 January 1975, p. 22.

Memorial tribute spoken at the University of Auckland.

Sturm, Terry. "The Short Stories of Maurice Duggan." LANDFALL, 25 (March 1971), 50-71.

Surprisingly little has been written about Duggan's stories, given the very high esteem in which they are generally held. Sturm's essay, for all its sensitivity to moral ambivalences, illustrates the difficulty of discussing adequately the allusive richness of Duggan's prose.

FAIRBURN, ARTHUR REX DUGARD (1904-57)

A.R.D. Fairburn was all his life an Aucklander. He was no more than ordinarily able at school, and his working knowledge of a vast spread of subjects came from his later reading and conversation. After a variety of jobs, he held during the last six years of his life a lectureship at the Elam School of Art. Fairburn was a keen sportsman, an endless talker, and an irrepressible controversialist, and his contemporaries found it difficult to separate the poetry from the man they loved. Since his death, his writing has provoked more outspoken disagreement than any other poet's. Fairburn was an indefatigable journalist, reviewer, pamphleteer, and letter-writer. The following list includes, besides his separately published works, the more important of his articles which bear on New Zealand literature. Olive Johnson's admirable bibliography (see below) should be consulted for other items.

BIOGRAPHY

Johnson, Olive. A.R.D. FAIRBURN 1904-1957: A BIBLIOGRAPHY OF HIS PUBLISHED WORK. [Auckland]: University of Auckland, 1958.

> Includes Fairburn's journalism and book reviews. The most thorough bibliography yet published on any New Zealand writer.

COLLECTED WORKS

COLLECTED POEMS. Ed., with foreword by Denis Glover. Christchurch: Pegasus, 1966.

THE WOMAN PROBLEM & OTHER PROSE. Ed. Denis Glover and Geoffrey Fairburn. Auckland: Blackwood & Janet Paul, 1967.

LETTERS

"'Yours Rex': A.R.D. Fairburn, Correspondent." ISLANDS, 4 (Autumn 1975), 58-67.

Seven letters edited by Lauris Edmond, who is preparing Fairburn's "Selected Letters" for publication in 1980.

POETRY

HE SHALL NOT RISE: POEMS. London: Columbia Press, 1930.

THE COUNTY. [London: Lahr], 1931.

ANOTHER ARGO. With Allen Curnow and Denis Glover. Christchurch: Caxton Club Press, 1935.

DOMINION. Christchurch: Caxton, 1938.

ON A BACHELOR BISHOP. [Christchurch: Caxton, 1938].

RECENT POEMS. With Allen Curnow, Denis Glover, and R.A.K. Mason. Christchurch: Caxton, 1941.

POEMS, 1929-1941. Christchurch: Caxton, 1943.

THE RAKEHELLY MAN & OTHER VERSES. Christchurch: Caxton, 1946.

LINES COMPOSED IN THE GLOVER KITCHEN DURING A MEMORABLE VISIT. Sumner, Christchurch: Caxton, 1947.

STRANGE RENDEZVOUS: POEMS 1929-1941 WITH ADDITIONS. Christchurch: Caxton, 1952.

THREE POEMS: DOMINION, THE VOYAGE & TO A FRIEND IN THE WILDERNESS. Wellington: New Zealand University Press, 1952.

THE DISADVANTAGES OF BEING DEAD AND OTHER SHARP VERSES, INCLUDING HORSE PANSIES. Ed., with an afterword by Denis Glover. Wellington: Mermaid Press, 1958.

POETRY HARBINGER. With Denis Glover. Auckland: Pilgrim Press, 1958.

PROSE

"Katherine Mansfield." NEW ZEALAND ARTISTS' ANNUAL, 1, no. 3 (1928), 69, 71.

A warm estimate of Katherine Mansfield's poetry.

"A New Zealand Poet." NEW ZEALAND ARTISTS' ANNUAL, 1, no. 4 (1929), 69.

Article on R.A.K. Mason.

"Some Aspects of N.Z. Art and Letters." ART IN NEW ZEALAND, 6 (June 1934), 213-18.

A DISCUSSION ON COMMUNISM. With S.W. Scott. Introd. Arthur Sewell. [Auckland]: Auckland District Party Committee, Communist Party of New Zealand, [1936 ?].

Text of a radio broadcast.

WHO SAID "RED RUIN"?: AN EXAMINATION OF NEWSPAPER METHODS. Auckland: Griffin Press, [1938].

"THE SKY IS A LIMPET" (A POLLYTICKLE PARROTTY); ALSO FOUR (4) STORIES OR MORAL FEEBLES. Devonport, Auckland: Phillips Press, 1939; rpt. (without the four stories) in THE PRACTICE OF PROSE. By Arthur Sewell. Auckland: Auckland University College, 1942, pp. 99-101; rpt. (complete) Auckland: George Fraser and Harold Innes, 1966.

A satire on the Prime Minister M.J. Savage. All but a few copies of the original edition were withdrawn.

La Rochefoucauld, François, duc de. A PRIMER OF LOVE: A SELECTION FROM THE MAXIMS OF LA ROCHEFOUCAULD. Introd. A.R.D. Fairburn. Wellington: Progressive Publishing Society, 1943.

HANDS OFF THE TOM TOM. Wellington: Progressive Publishing Society, 1944.

"New Zealanders You Should Know: Mr Allen Curnow." ACTION, December 1944, pp. 35-37.

WE NEW ZEALANDERS: AN INFORMAL ESSAY. Wellington: Progressive Publishing Society, 1944.

"Poetry in New Zealand." YEAR BOOK OF THE ARTS IN NEW ZEALAND, 1 (1945), 123-28.

"New Zealand Literature and Reviewing." In NEW ZEALAND LIBRARY ASSOCIATION. PROCEEDINGS OF THE FIFTEENTH CONFERENCE. New Zealand Library Association. Wellington: 1946, pp. 30-33, 42-45.

A paper, with the discussion which followed.

HOW TO RIDE A BICYCLE IN SEVENTEEN LOVELY COLOURS. With the Pelorus Press. Auckland: Pelorus Press, [1947].

"An inconsequential but humorous series of typographically diversified absurdities" (NEW ZEALAND NATIONAL BIBLIOGRAPHY).

"Literature and the Arts." In NEW ZEALAND. Ed. Horace Belshaw. Berkeley: University of California Press, 1947, pp. 241-59.

CRISIS IN THE WINE INDUSTRY. Auckland: Pelorus Press, 1948.

AN ISLAND-MOUNTAIN AND A SHIP. [Auckland: New Zealand Shipping Co., 1949].

"Sketch-Plan for the Great N.Z. Novel." PARSONS PACKET (Wellington), 10 (July-August 1950), 8-9.

A SLIGHT MISUNDERSTANDING. Christchurch: Nag's Head Press, 1968.

CRITICISM

Broughton, W.S. A.R.D. FAIRBURN. Wellington: Reed, 1968.

Written with secondary school pupils in mind.

______. "Lyricism and Belief." DISPUTE, 2 (January-February [1967]), 12-17.

A review of Fairburn's COLLECTED POEMS.

______. "Problems and Responses of Three New Zealand Poets in the 1920s." In PROCEEDINGS AND PAPERS OF THE TENTH AULLA CONGRESS. Ed. P. Dane. [Auckland]: Australasian Universities Language and Literature Association, [1966], pp. 202-13; rpt. in ESSAYS ON NEW ZEALAND LITERATURE. Ed. Wystan Curnow. Auckland: Heinemann Educational Books, 1973, pp. 1-15.

______. "W. D'Arcy Cresswell, A.R.D. Fairburn, R.A.K. Mason: An Examination of Certain Aspects of Their Lives and Works." Thesis, University of Auckland, 1968.

Edmond, Lauris. "The Letters of A.R.D. Fairburn." ISLANDS, 4 (Autumn 1975), 49-57.

Glover, Denis. "A.R.D. Fairburn: Man and Poet." In NEW ZEALAND'S HERITAGE. Ed. Ray Knox. Wellington: Paul Hamlyn, [1971-73], pp. 2673-79.

Hamilton, Ian. "Fairburn and Dr Stead." COMMENT, 8 (September 1967), 36-42.

Although in origin a polemical, point-by-point rejoinder to Stead's essay (see below), Hamilton's article has the positive virtue of placing the poet within his social and geographical environment.

Jackson, MacDonald P. "The Visionary Moment: An Essay on the Poetry of A.R.D. Fairburn." KIWI, August 1961, pp. 22-31.

Johnson, Louis, and Eric Schwimmer. "A.R.D. Fairburn: An Assessment." NUMBERS, 2 (August 1957), 15-24.

This essay is unusual among those published on Fairburn's death in discussing his poetry rather than his personality.

"A Lyrical Clown." NEW ZEALAND LISTENER, 22 September 1967, p. 9.

McLean, J.G. "The Versatile Rex Fairburn." NEW ZEALAND MAGAZINE, 26 (January 1947), 7-8, 10.

McNeish, James. "In the Path of Fairburn's Ghost." NEW ZEALAND LISTENER, 22 September 1967, p. 9.

Mason, R.A.K. REX FAIRBURN. [Dunedin]: Press Room, University of Otago, 1962.

A brief, personal memoir.

O'Sullivan, Vincent. "A.R.D. Fairburn: Definitions of Emptiness." COMMENT, 7 (September 1966), 29-35.

O'Sullivan deftly argues the incompatibility between Fairburn's lyric gifts and his expression in verse of political views, and finds the poet's greatest success in the old demesne of lyric poetry--love and death.

Ross, J.C. "A Study of the Poem 'Dominion' by A.R.D. Fairburn." Thesis, University of Auckland, 1962.

Stead, C.K. "Fairburn." LANDFALL, 20 (December 1966), 367-81.

In analyzing "the doubts, irritations and dislikes" which Fairburn's poems arouse in him, Stead seems more intent on correcting the taste of those who admire the poet than on identifying what strengths Fairburn may have possessed.

FINLAYSON, RODERICK DAVID (1904-)

Roderick Finlayson found his talents equally divided between painting and writing. At technical college, moreover, he had enjoyed working in the forge. On leaving school, he found his work as an architect's draftsman dull and repetitive, and he left Auckland to spend some time in a Maori community. D'Arcy Cresswell encouraged him to discontinue writing his didactic social pieces, for which he had found no publisher, and to use his experience of Maori life in fictional stories. In Giovanni Verga's Sicilian stories, as translated by D.H. Lawrence, Finlayson discovered a society in which he recognized Maori values, and he benefited technically by the example of how to write about such people.

COLLECTED WORKS

BROWN MAN'S BURDEN AND LATER STORIES. Ed. and introd. W.H. Pearson. [Auckland]: Auckland University Press; [Wellington]: Oxford University Press, 1973.

> This volume collects Finlayson's stories of Maori life. There is a full bibliography which includes details of Finlayson's other published stories.

FICTION

BROWN MAN'S BURDEN. Auckland: Unicorn Press, 1938.

> Short stories and sketches.

SWEET BEULAH LAND. Auckland: Griffin Press, 1942.

> Short stories.

TIDAL CREEK. Sydney: Angus & Robertson, 1948.

THE SCHOONER CAME TO ATIA. Auckland: Griffin Press, 1952.

Unused sheets of the original edition were bound with a facsimile paper cover and issued by the Auckland University Press in 1974.

THE SPRINGING FERN. Christchurch: Whitcombe & Tombs, 1965.

This historical novel for children was first published in Wellington by the School Publications Branch, Department of Education, in a series of primary school bulletins with the following titles:

THE COMING OF THE MUSKET. 1955.
THE COMING OF THE PAKEHA. 1956.
THE GOLDEN YEARS. 1956.
THE RETURN OF THE FUGITIVES. 1957.
CHANGES IN THE PA. 1958.
THE NEW HARVEST. 1960.

OTHER LOVERS. Dunedin: McIndoe, 1976.

Three short stories.

OTHER PROSE

OUR LIFE IN THIS LAND. Auckland: Griffin Press, 1940.

THE COMING OF THE MAORI. Wellington: School Publications Branch, Dept. of Education, 1955.

A documentary story for primary schools.

THE MAORIS OF NEW ZEALAND. With Joan Smith. [London]: Oxford University Press, 1958. Published in the United States in PEOPLE OF THE WORLD: ZULUS, SHERPAS, MAORIS, DECCAN INDIANS. By Agnes Jackson, et al. 4 vols. in 1. New York: Henry Z. Walck, 1959.

"Beginnings." LANDFALL, 20 (March 1966), 76-82.

An autobiographical essay.

D'ARCY CRESSWELL. New York: Twayne, 1972.

Annotated under Cresswell entry (see p. 87).

"Roderick Finlayson on THE FOUR MILLION." EDUCATION, 24, no. 4 (1975), 29.

On Finlayson's discovery, as a boy, of the O'Henry stories.

CRITICISM

Finlayson, Roderick. "Return to Harmony." NEW ZEALAND LISTENER, 9 July 1973, pp. 16-17.

Finlayson interviewed by O.E. Middleton.

Muirhead, John. "The Social Thesis and Prose Fiction of Roderick Finlayson." Thesis, Massey University, 1971.

_____. "Narrative Stance in the Early Short Stories of Roderick Finlayson." WORLD LITERATURE WRITTEN IN ENGLISH, 14 (April 1975), 120-43.

Although Muirhead concentrates on Finlayson's narrative technique and on what he learned from Verga, he contrives to write an excellent introduction to Finlayson's work as a whole.

FRAME, JANET (1924-   )
(Pseudonym of Janet Paterson Frame Clutha)

Although Janet Frame has supplied the basic facts about herself and her family readily enough, she has been evasive about further details, even referring to the autobiographical essay "Beginnings" as a story. Her father was a railwayman, and she lived in a number of South Island townships as a girl before the family settled in Oamaru. Her mother wrote stories and poems, her father had artistic interests, and Janet and her sisters wrote and had their work published in local newspapers. Always conscious of a distinct inner life, she finally broke with the outer world soon after training to be a teacher. It was almost a disastrous decision, and for several years she was to stay in a number of hospitals. "I never went insane," she has said, "but my early life was a classic case of someone headed for disaster."

Then she began to draw on her inner experiences for the material of her fiction, writing of the loneliness of the human soul and of the inadequacies of everyday language to convey human experience. Her novels, which have strong links with poetry rather than with traditional fiction, have attracted a small but enthusiastic following in New Zealand, and have been more widely studied in North America and Europe than the work of any other contemporary New Zealand author.

BIBLIOGRAPHY

[Hickman, M.] JANET PATERSON FRAME. [Wellington: Alexander Turnbull Library, 1968.]

> This typescript bibliography was prepared in the Alexander Turnbull Library and a copy is held there. A supplement was completed in March 1971. The bibliography includes details of first publication of stories and poems, and of overseas as well as local reviews, but it is not annotated.

Moir, B.N. "Janet Frame: An Annotated Bibliography of Autobiography and Biography, Commentary by Janet Frame and Criticisms and Reviews of Her Works." Bibliographical exercise, Library School, Wellington, 1975.

Restricted, with only two exceptions, to material published in New Zealand.

Ferrier, Carole, and Michael Coleman. "Janet Frame: A Preliminary Bibliography." HECATE, 3 (July 1977), 88-106.

Includes translations into other languages, individual poems and stories, and reviews and critical articles. Unannotated.

POETRY

THE POCKET MIRROR: POEMS. New York: Braziller; London: W.H. Allen, 1967; Christchurch: Pegasus, 1968.

FICTION

THE LAGOON: STORIES. Christchurch: Caxton, 1951; rev. ed., as THE LAGOON AND OTHER STORIES, Caxton, 1961.

OWLS DO CRY. Christchurch: Pegasus, 1957; New York: Braziller, 1960; London: W.H. Allen, 1961; rpt. Melbourne: Sun Books, 1967.

FACES IN THE WATER. Christchurch: Pegasus; New York: Braziller, 1961; London: W.H. Allen, 1962; rpt. New York: Avon Books, 1971.

THE EDGE OF THE ALPHABET. Christchurch: Pegasus; New York: Braziller; London: W.H. Allen, 1962.

THE RESERVOIR: STORIES AND SKETCHES. New York: Braziller, 1963.

SCENTED GARDENS FOR THE BLIND. Christchurch: Pegasus; London: W.H. Allen, 1963. New York: Braziller, [1964].

SNOWMAN SNOWMAN: FABLES AND FANTASIES. New York: Braziller, 1963.

THE ADAPTABLE MAN. Christchurch: Pegasus; New York: Braziller; London: W.H. Allen, 1965.

THE RESERVOIR AND OTHER STORIES. Christchurch: Pegasus; London: W.H. Allen, [1966].

This volume contains most of the stories published in America in THE RESERVOIR: STORIES AND SKETCHES and SNOWMAN SNOWMAN: FABLES AND FANTASIES (see above).

A STATE OF SIEGE. New York: Braziller, [1966]. Christchurch: Pegasus; London: W.H. Allen, 1967.

THE RAINBIRDS. London: W.H. Allen, 1968. Christchurch: Pegasus, 1969; as YELLOW FLOWERS IN THE ANTIPODEAN ROOM. New York: Braziller, 1969.

MONA MINIM AND THE SMELL OF THE SUN. New York: Braziller, 1969.

A children's story.

INTENSIVE CARE. New York: Braziller; [Toronto]: Doubleday Canada, 1970; Wellington: Reed; London: W.H. Allen, 1971.

DAUGHTER BUFFALO. New York: Braziller; [Toronto]: Doubleday Canada, 1972; Wellington: Reed; London: W.H. Allen, 1973.

OTHER PROSE

"Memory and a Pocketful of Words." TIMES LITERARY SUPPLEMENT, 4 June 1964, p. 487.

"This Desirable Property." NEW ZEALAND LISTENER, 3 July 1964, pp. 12-13.

"Beginnings." LANDFALL, 19 (March 1965), 40-47. CORNHILL, no. 1047 (Spring 1966), 189-97.

An essay about the early reading and writing of Janet Frame and her family.

"The Burns Fellowship." LANDFALL, 22 (September 1968), 241-42.

"Janet Frame on TALES FROM GRIMM." EDUCATION, 24, no. 9 (1975), 27.

Janet Frame's childhood reading of the Grimm stories.

CRITICISM

Alcock, Peter. "Frame's Binomial Fall, or Fire and Four in Waimaru." LANDFALL, 29 (September 1975), 179-87.

______. "A Writer on the Edge: Janet Frame and New Zealand Identity." COMMONWEALTH, 1 (1974-75), 171-75.

Ashcroft, W.D. "Beyond the Alphabet: Janet Frame's OWLS DO CRY." JOURNAL OF COMMONWEALTH LITERATURE, 12 (August 1977), 12-23.

Brame, Gillian R. "A Discussion of Theme and Image in the Major Fiction of Janet Frame." Thesis, University of Auckland, 1965.

Delbaere-Garant, Jeanne. "Beyond the Word: Janet Frame's SCENTED GARDENS FOR THE BLIND." In THE COMMONWEALTH WRITER OVERSEAS: THEMES OF EXILE AND EXPATRIATION. Ed. Alastair Niven. [Brussels]: Didier, [1976], pp. 289-301.

______. "Daphne's Metamorphoses in Janet Frame's Early Novels." ARIEL, 6 (April 1975), 23-37.

______. "Death as the Gateway to Being in Janet Frame's Novels." In COMMONWEALTH LITERATURE AND THE MODERN WORLD. Ed. Hena Maes-Jelenik. Brussels: Didier, 1975, pp. 147-55.

Dupont, Victor. "Editor's Postscript." COMMONWEALTH, 1 (1974-75), 175-76.

______. "Janet Frame's Brave New World: INTENSIVE CARE." In COMMONWEALTH LITERATURE AND THE MODERN WORLD. Ed. Hena Maes-Jelenik. Brussels: Didier, 1975, pp. 157-67.

______. "New Zealand Literature: Janet Frame and the Psychological Novel." In COMMONWEALTH. Ed. Anna Rutherford. [Aarhus, Denmark: Akademisk Boghandel, 1971?], pp. 168-76.

A paper given at the Conference of Commonwealth Literature, Aarhus, 1971.

Edmond, Lauris. "New Zealand Writers: Janet Frame." AFFAIRS, (November 1972), 10-11.

Evans, Patrick. "Alienation and the Imagery of Death: The Novels of Janet Frame." MEANJIN QUARTERLY, 32 (September 1973), 294-303.

______. AN INWARD SUN: THE NOVELS OF JANET FRAME. Wellington: Price Milburn, 1971.

A series of brief chapters, with questions designed for secondary school pupils, on the seven novels from OWLS DO CRY to THE RAINBIRDS, and on imagery and narrative viewpoint.

______. JANET FRAME. Boston: Twayne, [1977].

______. "Janet Frame and the Adaptable Novel." LANDFALL, 25 (December 1971), 448-55.

An essay written to justify the unusual structure of THE ADAPTABLE MAN.

Frame, Janet. "Artists' Retreats." NEW ZEALAND LISTENER, 27 July 1970, p. 13.

An interview with Claire Henderson in which Janet Frame talks about American writers' colonies.

Griffiths, Philip. "Janet Frame's 'Swans.'" WORDS (Wellington), no. 4 (January 1974), 97-108.

Hankin, Cherry. "Language as Theme in 'Owls Do Cry.'" LANDFALL, 28 (June 1974), 91-110; rpt. in CRITICAL ESSAYS ON THE NEW ZEALAND NOVEL. Ed. Cherry Hankin. Auckland: Heinemann Educational Books, 1976, pp. 88-104.

Hyman, Stanley Edgar. "Reason in Madness." In his STANDARDS: A CHRONICLE OF BOOKS FOR OUR TIME. New York: Horizon Press, [1966], pp. 239-43.

An enthusiastic review of SCENTED GARDENS FOR THE BLIND (see p. 116), interesting as the response of an established American reviewer reading Janet Frame for the first time.

Jones, Lawrence. "No Cowslip's Bell in Waimaru: The Personal Vision of 'Owls Do Cry.'" LANDFALL, 24 (September 1970), 280-96.

The first and still the best essay on OWLS DO CRY (see p. 116).

Leiter, Robert. "Reconsideration: The Novels of Janet Frame." NEW REPUBLIC, 31 May 1975, pp. 21-22.

McCracken, Jill. "Janet Frame: It's Time for France." NEW ZEALAND LISTENER, 27 October 1973, pp. 20-21.

Malterre, Monique. "Myths and Esoterics: A Tentative Interpretation of Janet Frame's A STATE OF SIEGE." COMMONWEALTH, 2 (1976), 107-12.

______. "La recherche d'identité dans A STATE OF SIEGE de Janet Frame." ETUDES ANGLAISES, 25 (April-June 1972), 232-44.

Rhodes, H. Winston. "Preludes and Parables: A Reading of Janet Frame's Novels." LANDFALL, 26 (June 1972), 135-46.

Rhodes argues that the parable is the characteristic structural device in Janet Frame's fiction.

Robertson, R.T. "Bird, Hawk, Bogie: Janet Frame, 1952-62." STUDIES IN THE NOVEL, 4 (Summer 1972), 186-99.

Rutherford, Anna. "Janet Frame's Divided and Distinguished Worlds." WORLD LITERATURE WRITTEN IN ENGLISH, 14 (April 1975), 51-68.

Stevens, Joan. "The Art of Janet Frame." NEW ZEALAND LISTENER, 4 May 1970, pp. 13, 52.

Te Awekotuku, Ngahuia. "Janet Frame: Some Themes from Her Novels." Thesis, University of Auckland, 1974.

Williamson, May. "Janet Frame: N.Z. Writer." NORTHLAND, 6 (July 1963), 5-11.

A short account of Janet Frame and her family, written by her cousin.

GEE, MAURICE GOUGH (1931-)

Maurice Gee was brought up in Henderson. It was then a small township in an area of vineyards and orchards and is now a part of the city of Auckland. His mother wrote short stories and his grandfather, a Unitarian minister and a pacifist, published his lectures; but although the family was not without books (his brothers' second names were Emerson and Carlyle), English fiction he had to discover for himself. Gee has not been a prolific writer--until recently writing has had to be a spare time activity--but he has shown a sharp eye for the social changes that have accompanied the kind of development that has overtaken Henderson, and is very good on relationships among middle-aged, suburban New Zealanders.

FICTION

THE BIG SEASON. London: Hutchinson, 1962.

A SPECIAL FLOWER. London: Hutchinson, 1965.

IN MY FATHER'S DEN. London: Faber, 1972; rpt. Wellington: Oxford University Press, 1977.

A GLORIOUS MORNING, COMRADE: STORIES. [Auckland]: Auckland University Press; [Wellington]: Oxford University Press, 1975.

GAMES OF CHOICE. London: Faber, 1976; rpt. Wellington: Oxford University Press, 1977.

OTHER PROSE

"Bertolt Brecht, a Select Bibliography of Writings on His Work for the Theatre." Bibliographical exercise, Library School, Wellington, 1966.

"The Burns Fellowship." LANDFALL, 22 (September 1968), 242-43.

"Maurice Gee on Zane Grey." EDUCATION, 24, no. 8 (1975), 25.

On his childhood reading.

"Beginnings." ISLANDS, 5 (Spring 1976), 284-92.

An autobiographical essay.

CRITICISM

Ewan, John. "Moved To Write." NEW ZEALAND BOOK WORLD, no. 41 (October 1977), 11, 34.

Gee, Maurice. "Maurice Gee." SPLEEN, no. 6 (December 1976), 5-7.

Gee interviewed at length by Ian Wedde.

McEldowney, Dennis. "Review of A SPECIAL FLOWER." LANDFALL, 20 (June 1966), 197-200.

Rhodes, H. Winston. "Review of THE BIG SEASON." COMMENT, 4 (April 1963), 48-49.

Williamson, Jim. "The Potent Beast." ISLANDS, 1 (Spring 1972), 74-79.

A review of IN MY FATHER'S DEN.

GLOVER, DENIS JAMES MATTHEWS (1912-)

Denis Glover's greatest achievement lies in his establishing in the literary consciousness of his country the figures of Harry and Arawata Bill, solitaries who keep in their later years the imaginative freshness of youth. That and the lyrical simplicity of his best work has made him one of the most widely read of New Zealand poets. Another lifelong interest, reflected in many poems, has been the sea. Glover served in the Royal Navy during the Second World War, but his best poems are landscape pieces, especially of the Banks Peninsula region, which are unusual in that they describe sea and land from the point of view of the offshore sailor. His importance to New Zealand literature, however, lies not only in his poetry. In the 1930s he established the Caxton Press which quickly became, through its editorial policy and the quality of its typography, the leading publisher of New Zealand writing.

BIBLIOGRAPHY

Johnson, Olive. DENIS GLOVER: A CATALOGUE OF HIS SEPARATELY-PUBLISHED WORK. Auckland: University of Auckland, 1960.

COLLECTED WORKS

ENTER WITHOUT KNOCKING: SELECTED POEMS. Christchurch: Pegasus, 1964; 2nd enl. ed., 1971.

SHARP EDGE UP: VERSES AND SATIRES. Auckland: Blackwood & Janet Paul, 1968.

AUTOBIOGRAPHY

HOT WATER SAILOR. Wellington: Reed, 1962.

An entertaining sketch of Glover's life, originally published in the NEW ZEALAND LISTENER.

POETRY

NEW POEMS. Ed. Denis Glover and Ian Milner. Christchurch: Caxton Club Press, 1934.

ANOTHER ARGO. With A.R.D. Fairburn and Allen Curnow. Christchurch: Caxton Club Press, 1935.

SHORT REFLECTION ON THE PRESENT STATE OF LITERATURE IN THIS COUNTRY. Christchurch: Caxton Club Press, 1935.

THISTLEDOWN. Christchurch: Caxton Club Press, 1935.

SEVERAL POEMS. Christchurch: Caxton, 1936.

Named on the cover "Six Easy Ways of Dodging Debt Collectors."

VERSE ALIVE. Christchurch: Caxton, 1936.

This and a second volume called VERSE ALIVE 2 (Caxton, 1937) contain verse selected by Denis Glover and H. Winston Rhodes from the periodical TOMORROW.

THE ARRAIGNMENT OF PARIS. Christchurch: Caxton, 1937.

THIRTEEN POEMS. Christchurch: Caxton, 1939.

COLD TONGUE. Christchurch: Caxton, 1940.

RECENT POEMS. With Allen Curnow, A.R.D. Fairburn, and R.A.K. Mason. Christchurch: Caxton, 1941.

THE WIND AND THE SAND: POEMS 1934-44. Christchurch: Caxton, 1945.

SUMMER FLOWERS. Christchurch: Caxton, 1946.

"SINGS HARRY" AND OTHER POEMS. Christchurch: Caxton, 1951.

ARAWATA BILL: A SEQUENCE OF POEMS. Christchurch: Pegasus, 1953.

SINCE THEN. Wellington: Mermaid Press, 1957.

POETRY HARBINGER. With A.R.D. Fairburn. Auckland: Pilgrim Press, 1958.

CROSS CURRENTS. Ed. Denis Glover. Christchurch: Pegasus, 1961.

A selection of loosely shaped "sonnets" by the American poet Merrill Moore.

MYSELF WHEN YOUNG. Christchurch: Nag's Head Press, 1970.

TO A PARTICULAR WOMAN. Christchurch: Nag's Head Press, 1970.

DIARY TO A WOMAN. Wellington: Cats-paw Press, 1971.

WELLINGTON HARBOUR. Wellington: Cats-paw Press, 1974.

CLUTHA: RIVER POEMS. Dunedin: McIndoe, 1977.

COME HIGH WATER. Palmerston North: Dunmore Press, [1977].

FICTION

3 SHORT STORIES. Christchurch: Caxton, 1936.

TILL THE STAR SPEAK. Christchurch: Caxton, 1939.

Short story.

OTHER PROSE

"Pointers to Parnassus: A Consideration of the Morepork and the Muse." TOMORROW, 30 October 1935, pp. 16-18.

D-DAY. Christchurch: Caxton, 1944.

A personal account of Glover's part in the Normandy Invasion of 1944.

BOB LOWRY'S BOOKS. Auckland: Pilgrim Press, 1946.

A CLUTCH OF AUTHORS AND A CLOT. Wellington: The Author, 1960.

"Poets and Poetry in the Welfare State." NEW ZEALAND LISTENER, 27 October 1961, p. 11.

THE WOMAN PROBLEM AND OTHER PROSE. Auckland: Blackwood & Janet Paul, 1967.

Essays by A.R.D. Fairburn selected by Denis Glover and Geoffrey Fairburn.

"A.R.D. Fairburn: Man and Poet." In NEW ZEALAND'S HERITAGE. Ed. Ray Knox. Wellington: Paul Hamlyn, [1971-73], pp. 2673-79.

"A Fly Crawls up the Mountain." NEW ZEALAND ALPINE JOURNAL, 29 (1976), 113-16.

Glover here recalls his youthful climbing experiences.

"Denis Glover on PICKWICK PAPERS." EDUCATION, 26, no. 4 (1977), 19.

Glover's early reading of Dickens.

MISCELLANEOUS

DENIS GLOVER'S BEDSIDE BOOK. Wellington: Reed, 1963.

This and the following title are miscellanies of Glover's verse and prose.

DANCING TO MY TUNE. Wellington: Catspaw Press, 1974.

CRITICISM

Campbell, Alistair. "Glover and Georgianism." COMMENT, 6 (October-November 1964), 23-33.

Campbell identifies Glover's shortcomings by analysing an unsympathetic choice of poems.

Cleveland, L. "The Horizon's Eye: Perspectives on the Poetry of Denis Glover." Wellington: Kiwi Records, 1971.

A pamphlet accompanying the gramophone record "Arawata Bill and Other Verse."

Curnow, Wystan. "Two New Zealand Poets: The 'Man Alone' Theme in the Poetry of Denis Glover and Kendrick Smithyman." QUEEN'S QUARTERLY, 74 (Winter 1967), 726-37.

Glover, Denis. "Denis Glover Talks to Marilyn Duckworth." AFFAIRS, (June 1970), 211-14.

Milner, Ian. "Denis Glover and the Caxton Club." ISLANDS, 4 (Spring 1975), 265-70.

Roddick, Alan. "A Reading of Denis Glover." LANDFALL, 19 (March 1965), 48-58.

Excellent notes from a sensitive reader alert to Glover's real strengths.

Scott, David. "'Sings Harry': A Study of Some Aspects of Denis Glover's Poetry." SALIENT (Literary Issue), July 1952, pp. 28-30.

Thomson, John. DENIS GLOVER. Wellington: Oxford University Press, 1977.

A biographical and critical study based on Glover's manuscript papers.

_____. "Time and Youth in the Poetry of Denis Glover." LANDFALL, 21 (June 1967), 192-97.

HYDE, ROBIN (1906-39)

(Pseudonym of Iris Guiver Wilkinson)

Although born in South Africa, Robin Hyde grew up in Wellington where, while still at school, she first became known for her verse. Ideally, she would have liked to develop her gifts as a poet--she read widely in English verse and had a tenacious memory--but she had her living to earn and was forced into the busy life of journalism and then, after her health had collapsed more than once, into the writing of fiction. Her novels have become better known than her poetry, but she continued writing and developing her verse till her death. Some long, unfinished poems, and many shorter pieces remain unpublished. In 1938 she travelled to China, was in Hsuchowfu when it fell to the Japanese, and endured great hardship before managing to reach Hong Kong. Still ill from a tropical disease, she died in London the following year.

BIBLIOGRAPHY

Walls, Jennifer. "A Bibliography of Robin Hyde (Iris Wilkinson) 1906-39." Bibliographical exercise, Library School, Wellington, 1960.

> This bibliography is limited to Robin Hyde's books, and to that part of her literary work and journalism published in some selected New Zealand periodicals.

Scott, Margaret. "A Supplementary Bibliography of Robin Hyde (Iris G. Wilkinson) 1906-39." Bibliography exercise, Library School, Wellington, 1966.

> An attempt to "bring Miss Walls' bibliography as near as possible to completion." Material in newspapers and overseas journals is included.

POETRY

THE DESOLATE STAR AND OTHER POEMS. Christchurch: Whitcombe & Tombs, [1929].

THE CONQUERORS AND OTHER POEMS. London: Macmillan, 1935.

PERSEPHONE IN WINTER: POEMS. London: Hurst & Blackett, 1937.

HOUSES BY THE SEA, AND THE LATER POEMS. Introd. Gloria Rowlinson. Christchurch: Caxton, 1952.

The long introduction gives an account of Robin Hyde's life and work, and quotes extensively from letters written in China and England.

FICTION

CHECK TO YOUR KING: THE LIFE HISTORY OF CHARLES, BARON DE THIERRY, KING OF NUKAHIVA, SOVEREIGN CHIEF OF NEW ZEALAND. London: Hurst & Blackett, [1936]; rpt. with an introd. by Joan Stevens. Wellington: Reed, 1960; as CHECK TO YOUR KING. Auckland: Golden Press, 1975.

PASSPORT TO HELL. London: Hurst & Blackett, [1936].

WEDNESDAY'S CHILDREN. London: Hurst & Blackett, [1937].

THE GODWITS FLY. London: Hurst & Blackett, [1938]; rpt. Ed. and introd. Gloria Rawlinson. [Auckland]: Auckland University Press; [Wellington]: Oxford University Press, 1970.

NOR THE YEARS CONDEMN. London: Hurst & Blackett, [1938].

A sequel to PASSPORT TO HELL.

OTHER PROSE

JOURNALESE. Auckland: National Printing Co., 1934.

"The Singers of Loneliness." T'IEN HSIA MONTHLY, 7 (August 1938), 9-23.

DRAGON RAMPANT. London: Hurst & Blackett, [1939].

Robin Hyde's experiences in China in 1938.

CRITICISM

Bertram, James. "Robin Hyde: A Reassessment." LANDFALL, 7 (September 1953), 181-91.

An appreciative article on a writer "so peculiarly a product of her time and place, and so clear an example of the colonial dilemma in art and letters." Bertram concentrates on the poems in HOUSES BY THE SEA.

Birbalsingh, Frank. "Robin Hyde." LANDFALL, 31 (December 1977), 362-77.

Lawlor, Pat. "Writers and the Faith." CATHOLIC REVIEW (Auckland), 1 (September 1945), 357-65.

A section devoted to Robin Hyde appears on pages 361-63.

Partridge, Colin J. "Wheel of Words: The Poetic Development of Robin Hyde." JOURNAL OF COMMONWEALTH LITERATURE, no. 5 (July 1968), 92-104.

Rawlinson, Gloria. "Robin Hyde and THE GODWITS FLY." In CRITICAL ESSAYS ON THE NEW ZEALAND NOVEL. Ed. Cherry Hankin. Auckland: Heinemann Educational Books, 1976, pp. 40-59.

Rhodes, H. Winston. "Robin Hyde, Novelist." NEW ZEALAND LIBRARIES, 10 (October 1947), 179-83.

Riddy, Felicity. "Robin Hyde and New Zealand." In THE COMMONWEALTH WRITER OVERSEAS: THEMES OF EXILE AND EXPATRIATION. Ed. Alastair Niven. [Brussels]: Didier, [1976], pp. 185-93.

Sharplin, Janscie E. "The Veil Removed: Reality, Ideality and Dream in the Later Works of Robin Hyde." Thesis, University of Canterbury, 1971.

LEE, JOHN ALEXANDER (1891-)

Something of John A. Lee's life can be learned from those of his novels which are closely based on his own career. As a boy in Dunedin, he knew the hardships of the depression of the 1890s, and as an adolescent the rigours of a reformatory institution from which he escaped to lead a wandering and varied life before enlisting for the First World War. He afterwards became a very successful political speaker, and during the later thirties was an important member of the first Labour government. His SOCIALISM IN NEW ZEALAND appeared in 1938, and he published numerous political pamphlets and speeches. From 1940 to 1947 he edited JOHN A. LEE'S WEEKLY. His fiction, despite its frankly popular prose style, is valued for its fresh and unliterary response to local experience. Only his fictional, semifictional, and autobiographical work is listed here; the difficult task of distinguishing among these categories has not been attempted, hence the combined heading, below, of "Fiction and Other Prose."

BIOGRAPHY

Olssen, Erik. JOHN A. LEE. Dunedin: University of Otago Press, 1977.

A biography devoted to Lee's political career.

FICTION AND OTHER PROSE

CHILDREN OF THE POOR. London: Werner Laurie, 1934; New York: Vanguard Press, [1934]; rpt. London: Bernard Henry; Auckland: N.V. Douglas, 1949; London: May Fair Books, 1963; Christchurch: Whitcombe & Tombs, 1973.

THE HUNTED. London: Werner Laurie, 1936; rpt. London: May Fair Books, 1963; Wellington: Price Milburn, 1975.

CIVILIAN INTO SOLDIER. London: Werner Laurie, 1937; rpt. London: May Fair Books, 1963.

THE YANKS ARE COMING. London: Werner Laurie, 1943.

SHINING WITH THE SHINER. Hamilton: F.W. Mead trading as Bonds Printing Co., 1944; rpt. London: Bernard Henry; Auckland: N.V. Douglas, 1950; London: May Fair Books, 1963.

"Cain and Abel Were Brothers." HERE AND NOW, no. 58 (March 1957), 15-17.

Reminiscences of Burnham Industrial School.

"Children of the Not-So-Poor." NEW ZEALAND LISTENER, 23 September 1960, p. 4.

Lee compares his childhood in 1900 with the typical childhood of 1960.

SIMPLE ON A SOAP-BOX. Auckland: Collins, 1963; rpt. Christchurch: Whitcombe & Tombs, 1975.

SHINER SLATTERY. Auckland: Collins, 1964; rpt. Auckland: Collins Fontana Silver Fern, 1975.

DELINQUENT DAYS. Auckland: Collins, 1967.

"New Zealand Paperbacks: The Need for Better Distribution." COMMENT, 9 (December 1967), 17-19.

Lee's experience of selling paperbacks--especially paperbacks of his own novels.

MUSSOLINI'S MILLIONS. London: Howard Baker, 1970.

FOR MINE IS THE KINGDOM. Martinborough: A. Taylor, 1975.

"Why I Still Jump over the Moon." EDUCATION, 25, no. 6 (1976), 29-30.

Lee recalls the importance of nursery rhymes in his childhood.

SOLDIER. Wellington: Reed, 1976.

EARLY DAYS IN NEW ZEALAND. Martinborough: A. Taylor, 1977.

ROUGHNECKS, ROLLING STONES & ROUSEABOUTS; WITH AN ANTHOLOGY OF EARLY SWAGGER LITERATURE. Christchurch: Whitcoulls, 1977.

CRITICISM

Dupont, Victor. "'For Mine Is the Kingdom': a Book, a Man, an Author." COMMONWEALTH, 2 (1976), 113-33.

Edmond, Lauris. "Last of the Demagogues: On John A. Lee." AFFAIRS, April 1973, pp. 18-21.

Isaac, Peter. "What Keeps Lee Going." NEW ZEALAND BOOK WORLD, no. 27 (August 1976), 6-8.

An article based on an interview.

McEldowney, Dennis. "John A. Lee's CHILDREN OF THE POOR." In CRITICAL ESSAYS ON THE NEW ZEALAND NOVEL. Ed. Cherry Hankin. Auckland: Heinemann Educational Books, 1976, pp. 24-39.

Nicholson, John S. "The Novelist's Pair of Tongs: An Investigation into the Literary Significance of John A. Lee's Novels." Thesis, Massey University, 1970.

______. "Letter to the Editor." LANDFALL, 26 (March 1972), 111.

On the neglect of Lee as a literary figure.

Pouilhes, M.-H., and Victor Dupont. "John A Lee's Novels on Juvenile Delinquency." COMMONWEALTH, 1 (1974-75), 131-48.

Rhodes, H. Winston. "The Novels of John A. Lee." NEW ZEALAND LIBRARIES, 10 (December 1947), 230-35.

Shadbolt, Maurice. "John A. Lee." In his LOVE AND LEGEND: SOME 20TH CENTURY NEW ZEALANDERS. Auckland: Hodder & Stoughton, 1976, pp. 15-27.

Wilmot, Denis. "John A. Lee: M.P. and Man of Letters." NEW ZEALAND MAGAZINE, 22 (July-August 1943), 5-7, 10.

MANDER, MARY JANE (1877-1949)

Jane Mander's youth and early adulthood were spent in various parts of North Auckland. Her social and political ideas, though no doubt maturing previously, were encouraged and developed when, at the age of thirty-five, she enrolled at Columbia University, New York. Her four novels set in New Zealand combine material from both spheres. But her New Zealand readers were shocked by her radical views and especially by her attitudes to sex and marriage. Her last two novels have an American and a European setting respectively. Disappointed at the reception given her books, she published nothing further, although after her return to New Zealand in 1932 she kept in touch with local literary circles until her death.

FICTION

THE STORY OF A NEW ZEALAND RIVER. London: John Lane, The Bodley Head; New York: John Lane, 1920; rpt. [Christchurch]: Whitcombe & Tombs, [1938]; London: Robert Hale; [Christchurch]: Whitcombe & Tombs, [1960]; Christchurch: Whitcombe & Tombs, 1973.

THE PASSIONATE PURITAN. London: John Lane, The Bodley Head; New York: John Lane, 1921.

THE STRANGE ATTRACTION. New York: Dodd, Mead & Co., 1922; London: John Lane, The Bodley Head, [1923].

ALLEN ADAIR. London: Hutchinson, [1925]; rpt. Ed. and introd. Dorothea Turner. [Auckland]: Auckland University Press; [Wellington]: Oxford University Press, 1971.

THE BESIEGING CITY: A NOVEL OF NEW YORK. London: Hutchinson, [1926].

PINS AND PINNACLES. London: Hutchinson, [1928].

OTHER PROSE

"A Diary of Evolution." NEW REPUBLIC, 25 March 1916, pp. 211-12.

An account in note form of a woman's spiritual and political development--probably very largely autobiographical.

"Creative Writing in Australia and New Zealand." LITERARY DIGEST INTERNATIONAL BOOK REVIEW, 1 (May 1923), 32, 63-64.

CRITICISM

Bartley, Joy. "Full, Busy Life: The Varied Career of Jane Mander, New Zealand Authoress." OBSERVER (Auckland), 15 September 1943, p. 21.

[Holcroft, M.H.?] "A New Zealand Writer." NEW ZEALAND LISTENER, 13 January 1950, p. 4.

Mitchell, J.J.M. "Recollections of Jane Mander." NORTHLAND, 4 (April 1961), 20-22.

Mulgan, Alan. "THE STORY OF A NEW ZEALAND RIVER--Jane Mander." In his GREAT DAYS IN NEW ZEALAND WRITING. Wellington: Reed, 1962, pp. 84-89.

Pickmere, Nancy. "Jane Mander in Whangarei." NORTHLAND, 3 (December 1960), 19-20.

Smithyman, Kendrick. "Two Novelists of Northland." In NEW ZEALAND'S HERITAGE. Ed. Ray Knox. Wellington: Paul Hamlyn, [1971-73], pp. 1728-32.

"The Story of a New Zealand River." NEW ZEALAND LISTENER, 12 September 1952, p. 7.

An account of a radio adaptation.

Turner, Dorothea. JANE MANDER. New York: Twayne, [1972].

A well-researched biography which relates Jane Mander's considerable social and political interests to her times and to her fiction.

______. "THE STORY OF A NEW ZEALAND RIVER: Perceptions and Prophecies in an Unfixed Society." In CRITICAL ESSAYS ON THE NEW ZEALAND NOVEL. Ed. Cherry Hankin. Auckland: Heinemann Educational Books, 1976, pp. 1-23.

MANSFIELD, KATHERINE (1888-1923)
(Pseudonym of Kathleen Mansfield Beauchamp, Afterwards Mrs. Middleton Murry)

Katherine Mansfield grew up in Wellington, where her father was to become Chairman of the Bank of New Zealand. After finishing her schooling at Queen's College in London she returned to New Zealand, but in 1908 left for good. In England she became one of a group of literary people including D.H. Lawrence and John Middleton Murry (with whom she lived until 1918, when a divorce from her first husband enabled her to marry him). Growing ill-health forced her to seek a better winter climate in various parts of Europe. She died at the Gurdjieff Institute in Fontainebleau.

Of all New Zealand writers, Katherine Mansfield is easily the most widely read and studied in Europe and America. Indeed, as all her mature work was produced on the other side of the world, where she was one of the avant-garde English writers of the 1910s, it can be disputed whether she should be classed as a New Zealand writer at all. But although she has an indisputable place in the history of the English short story, the importance of her childhood and adolescence, both to herself and as material of her stories, warrants her being considered here as a New Zealand author.

In keeping with the full coverage given to other writers in this chapter, the list of critical material below is as complete as is practicable. However, certain modifications have been introduced. Critical material from the 1920s and 1930s is more selectively chosen than later work; and the inclusion of all critical material, especially studies in French and German, has to a large extent been determined by the availability of books and articles in New Zealand. (Fuller bibliographical lists can be found in the items under "Bibliography" below.) Except in the case of more important items, only one bibliographical citation is given to each critical study; the most recent reprinting of any study is usually given preference, and this means, too, that a reference to an essay collected in book form is generally given rather than one to its first appearance in a periodical.

BIBLIOGRAPHY

Mantz, Ruth Elvish. THE CRITICAL BIBLIOGRAPHY OF KATHERINE MANSFIELD. Introd. J. Middleton Murry. London: Constable, 1931; rpt. New York: Burt Franklin, [1968].

This full bibliographical description of the first editions of the stories in book form also provides details of original periodical publication, and contains a list of uncollected contributions to periodicals as well as details of reviews and essays about her work published up to 1930.

Morris, G.N. "Katherine Mansfield Additions." TIMES LITERARY SUPPLEMENT, 13 July 1940, p. 344.

Bibliographical additions to Ruth Mantz's bibliography.

Lawlor, Pat. MANSFIELDIANA: A BRIEF KATHERINE MANSFIELD BIBLIOGRAPHY. Introd. G.N. Morris. Wellington: Beltane Book Bureau, 1948; rpt. [Folcroft, Pa.]: Folcroft Library Editions, 1971.

Harrison, Elizabeth Mary. "A Bibliography of Works about Katherine Mansfield." Thesis, University of London, 1958.

This very full and useful bibliography includes not only books and periodical articles but also material from newspapers and some unpublished manuscripts.

Walker, Warren S. "Katherine Mansfield." In his TWENTIETH-CENTURY SHORT STORY EXPLICATION. 2nd ed. [Hamden, Conn.]: Shoe String Press, 1967, pp. 465-76.

An inventory of mainly short explications of single passages or stories. Additional items are included in SUPPLEMENT 1 (1970), pp. 170-71.

Bardas, Mary Louise. "The State of Scholarship on Katherine Mansfield, 1950-1970." WORLD LITERATURE WRITTEN IN ENGLISH, 11 (April 1972), 77-93.

This consists chiefly of a bibliography of Katherine Mansfield material, including bibliographies and editions as well as books, theses, and articles about her work. The dates at the head of the prefatory note appear to have no bearing on the bibliography, which includes material dating back to 1921. A corrective note about work done in New Zealand was published anonymously in the TURNBULL LIBRARY RECORD, 5 (October 1972), 51.

"'Katherine Mansfield,' Kathleen Mansfield Beauchamp 1888-1923." In THE NEW CAMBRIDGE BIBLIOGRAPHY OF ENGLISH LITERATURE. Vol. 4. Ed. I.R. Willison. Cambridge: Cambridge University Press, 1972, cols. 653-59.

The most readily available bibliography. Critical study coverage is good, and it is useful for material in languages other than English.

Meyers, Jeffrey. "Katherine Mansfield: A Bibliography of International Criticism, 1921-1977." BULLETIN OF BIBLIOGRAPHY & MAGAZINE NOTES, 34 (April-June 1977), 53-67.

This, the fullest bibliography of criticism available, also attempts a full listing of biographical items. It is strong in both New Zealand and in foreign-language material, but includes much of only marginal interest. Theses and reviews are included, and entries are not annotated.

COLLECTED WORKS

STORIES. Selected by J. Middleton Murry. New York: Knopf, 1930; rpt. with an introduction by Marjorie Kinnan Rawlings. Cleveland: World Publishing Co., [1946].

THE DOLL'S HOUSE AND OTHER STORIES. Hamburg: Albatross Modern Continental Library, 1934.

THE SHORT STORIES OF KATHERINE MANSFIELD. Introd. J. Middleton Murry. New York: Knopf; Toronto: Ryerston Press, 1937.

This collection was the first to gather the stories from the five separate volumes into one book.

COLLECTED STORIES OF KATHERINE MANSFIELD. [London]: Constable, 1945; Toronto: Longmans, 1948.

The standard collection, frequently reprinted. See also THE COMPLETE STORIES, p. 142.

THE DOLL'S HOUSE AND OTHER STORIES. Ed. Henri Kerst. Paris: Didier, 1948.

SELECTED STORIES. Chosen and introd. Dan Davin. London: Oxford University Press, 1953.

Davin's frequently reprinted volume is the best and most readily available selection of Katherine Mansfield's stories.

STORIES. Selected with an introd. Elizabeth Bowen. New York: Vintage Books, 1956.

34 SHORT STORIES. Selected with an introd. Elizabeth Bowen. London: Collins, 1957.

Contains seven more stories than the 1956 American edition.

THE COMPLETE STORIES OF KATHERINE MANSFIELD. Rpt. of COLLECTED STORIES OF KATHERINE MANSFIELD (see p. 141). Auckland: Golden Press in association with Whitcombe & Tombs, 1974.

Reprint of the 1945 Constable edition with the addition of the recently discovered story "Brave Love."

UNDISCOVERED COUNTRY: THE NEW ZEALAND STORIES OF KATHERINE MANSFIELD. Ed. Ian Gordon. London: Longman, 1974.

Using a generous definition of what makes a "New Zealand story," Gordon arranges stories and fragments of stories, irrespective of their date of composition, to indicate the growth of a late-Victorian New Zealand family, while warning against identifying Katherine Mansfield's family too closely in her writing. A final section gathers together stories which defy inclusion in this scheme.

KATHERINE MANSFIELD. Eds. Anthony Adams and Esmor Jones. London: Harrap, 1975.

Selected stories arranged according to themes, with questions for discussion.

JOURNALS

JOURNAL OF KATHERINE MANSFIELD. Ed. and introd. J. Middleton Murry. London: Constable; New York: Knopf, 1927; rpt. New York: McGraw Hill, 1964.

JOURNAL OF KATHERINE MANSFIELD. Ed. J. Middleton Murry. London: Constable, 1954.

Although this is a much enlarged version of the 1927 edition, it is still a compilation of material from various sources, even including, for example, memories of Katherine Mansfield's conversation. She seems never to have kept a true journal--at least, not for more than a very short period at a time. This book is not a complete transcription of all the material available to Murry, and yet it suggests a greater continuity than the original manuscripts warrant.

LETTERS

THE LETTERS OF KATHERINE MANSFIELD. Ed. J. Middleton Murry. 2 vols. London: Constable; Toronto: Macmillan, 1928; New York: Knopf, 1929.

A selection from this edition with the same title was published in 1934 (Hamburg: Albatross).

KATHERINE MANSFIELD'S LETTERS TO JOHN MIDDLETON MURRY, 1913-1922. Ed. J. Middleton Murry. London: Constable; New York: Knopf; Toronto: Longmans, 1951.

In this edition, many passages were included which had been omitted in the 1928 volumes (see p. 142). A complete, scholarly edition of Katherine Mansfield's letters is being prepared for Oxford University Press by Margaret Scott of Wellington, but no probable date of publication can be given.

PASSIONATE PILGRIMAGE: A LOVE AFFAIR IN LETTERS: KATHERINE MANSFIELD'S LETTERS TO JOHN MIDDLETON MURRY FROM THE SOUTH OF FRANCE 1915-1920. Ed. Helen McNeish. Auckland: Hodder & Stoughton; London: Michael Joseph, 1976.

This selection gives a deliberately limited picture of Katherine Mansfield, but the accompanying photographic record is valuable.

THE LETTERS AND JOURNALS OF KATHERINE MANSFIELD: A SELECTION. Ed. C.K. Stead. London: Allen Lane, 1977.

BIOGRAPHY

Mantz, Ruth Elvish, and J. Middleton Murry. THE LIFE OF KATHERINE MANSFIELD. London: Constable, 1933; rpt. [Folcroft, Pa.]: Folcroft Library Editions, 1970.

This biography covers only the early years, up to Katherine Mansfield's first meeting with Murry. It was written mainly by Ruth Elvish Mantz.

Clarke, Isabel C. KATHERINE MANSFIELD: A BIOGRAPHY. Introd. Pat Lawlor. Wellington: Beltane Book Bureau, 1944; rpt. [Folcroft, Pa.]: Folcroft Library Editons, 1970.

Isabel Clarke's short biography was first published in her SIX PORTRAITS (London: Hutchinson, 1935).

Lenoël, Odette. LA VOCATION DE KATHERINE MANSFIELD. Introd. Daniel-Rops. Paris: Albin Michel, [1946].

Merlin, Roland. LE DRAME SECRET DE KATHERINE MANSFIELD. Paris: Editions du Seuil, 1950.

Merlin's book is an extreme version of that unreal view of Katherine Mansfield, long held in France, which stressed her spiritual purity, her unworldliness, and her innocent suffering.

Alpers, Antony. KATHERINE MANSFIELD: A BIOGRAPHY. New York: Knopf, 1953; London: Cape, 1954.

Although fuller details about some part of Katherine Mansfield's life have come to light since this book was written, it remains the standard biography--a sympathetic yet balanced study.

Monnet, Anne-Marie. KATHERINE MANSFIELD. [Paris]: Editions du Temps, [1960].

A romanticised account of Katherine Mansfield's life which willfully ignored readily available evidence.

Baker, Ida C. KATHERINE MANSFIELD: THE MEMORIES OF L.M. Introd. and linking text by Georgina Joysmith. London: Michael Joseph, 1971; New York: Taplinger, 1972.

"L.M." (Ida Baker), Katherine Mansfield's friend and confidante from the age of fifteen, here fills out the story of Katherine Mansfield's life. Her book is especially valuable for the period before the first meeting with Murry, and for the times when Katherine Mansfield was away from him in Europe.

POETRY

POEMS. London: Constable, 1923; New York: Knopf, 1924; 2d ed. London: Constable, 1930; New York: Knopf, 1931.

The second edition contains two additional poems.

TO STANISLAW WYSPIANSKI. London: [Rota], 1938.

This piece, one of Katherine Mansfield's best poems, was not included in POEMS.

FICTION

The five main volumes of stories (IN A GERMAN PENSION, BLISS, THE GARDEN PARTY, THE DOVES' NEST, and SOMETHING CHILDISH) have all been frequently reprinted, and are readily available in the form of the collected works detailed above. Only the first editions of these five volumes are noted here.

IN A GERMAN PENSION. London: Stephen Swift, [1911].

PRELUDE. Richmond: Hogarth Press, [1918].

JE NE PARLE PAS FRANÇAIS. Hampstead: Heron Press, 1919.

BLISS AND OTHER STORIES. London: Constable, 1920; New York: Knopf, 1921.

THE GARDEN PARTY AND OTHER STORIES. London: Constable; New York: Knopf, 1922.

THE DOVES' NEST AND OTHER STORIES. London: Constable; New York: Knopf, 1923.

SOMETHING CHILDISH AND OTHER STORIES. London: Constable; Toronto: Macmillan, 1924; as THE LITTLE GIRL AND OTHER STORIES. New York: Knopf, 1924.

THE ALOE. London: Constable; New York: Knopf, 1930; rpt. New York: H. Fertig, 1974.

> This story is an earlier version of "Prelude."

THE SCRAPBOOK OF KATHERINE MANSFIELD. Ed. J. Middleton Murry. London: Constable, 1939; New York: Knopf, 1940; rpt. New York: H. Fertig, 1974.

> The SCRAPBOOK is a miscellany of unpublished fragments (including some which are journal entries rather than fiction) arranged in chronological order.

OTHER PROSE

REMINISCENCES OF LEONID ANDREYEV. By Maxim Gorky. Trans. by Katherine Mansfield and S.S. Koteliansky. New York: C. Gaige, 1928.

NOVELS AND NOVELISTS. Ed. J. Middleton Murry. London: Constable; New York: Knopf, 1930; rpt. Boston: Beacon Press, 1959.

> A collection of book reviews originally published in the ATHENAEUM (London) in 1919 and 1920.

REMINISCENCES OF TOLSTOY, CHEKHOV AND ANDREEV. By Maxim Gorky. Trans. by Katherine Mansfield, S.S. Koteliansky, and Leonard Woolf. London: Hogarth Press, 1934.

CRITICISM

Aiken, Conrad P. "Katherine Mansfield." In his A REVIEWER'S ABC: COL-

LECTED CRITICISM. New York: Meridian Books, 1958; London: Allen, 1961, pp. 291-99.

Aiken reprints reviews of BLISS, THE GARDEN PARTY, and the JOURNAL, first published in 1921, 1922, and 1927, respectively.

Alcock, Peter. "'An Aloe in the Garden: Something Essentially New Zealand in Miss Mansfield.'" JOURNAL OF COMMONWEALTH LITERATURE, 11 (April 1977), 58-64.

Almedingen, E.M. "Chekov and Katherine Mansfield." TIMES LITERARY SUPPLEMENT, 19 October 1951, p. 661.

In this letter, Almedingen compared, to Katherine Mansfield's disadvantage, similarities between a Chekhov story and her "The Child-Who-Was-Tired." Correspondence about this charge of plagiarism ensued during the following month. See also Schneider, p. 160.

Alpers, Antony. KATHERINE MANSFIELD. [Wellington]: School Publications Branch, Dept. of Education, [1947].

A post-primary school bulletin.

Arland, Marcel. "Katherine Mansfield." In his LA GRACE D'ECRIRE. Paris: Gallimard, 1955, pp. 239-57.

Armstrong, Martin. "The Art of Katherine Mansfield." FORTNIGHTLY REVIEW, 1 March 1923, pp. 484-90.

Armstrong's article is an early example of a perceptive and sensitive analysis of Katherine Mansfield's technique.

Arnoux, Rosemary (Whillans). "Katherine Mansfield as a Writer of Short Stories." Thesis, University of Paris--Sorbonne, 1971.

Listed in Rosemary Arnoux's bibliography are seventeen other post-graduate theses on Katherine Mansfield written at the Sorbonne and held in the library there of the Institut d'Anglais.

Baldeshwiler, Eileen. "Katherine Mansfield's Theory of Fiction." STUDIES IN SHORT FICTION, 7 (Summer 1970), 421-32.

Bates, H.E. "Katherine Mansfield and A.E. Coppard." In his THE MODERN SHORT STORY: A CRITICAL SURVEY. London: Michael Joseph, 1972, pp. 122-47.

Bates's book, in which the chapter on Katherine Mansfield is part of a discussion of the historical development of the short story, was first published in 1941.

Bateson, F.W., and B. Shahevitch. "Katherine Mansfield's 'The Fly': A Critical Exercise." ESSAYS IN CRITICISM, 12 (January 1962), 39-53.

Discussion followed in the July and October issues.

Beachcroft, T.O. "Katherine Mansfield." In his THE MODEST ART: A SURVEY OF THE SHORT-STORY IN ENGLISH. London: Oxford University Press, 1968, pp. 162-75.

_____. "Katherine Mansfield's Encounter with Theocritus." ENGLISH, 23 (Spring 1974), 13-19.

Belitt, Ben. "The Short Stories of Katherine Mansfield." In A PREFACE TO LITERATURE. Ed. Edward Wagenknecht. New York: Holt, [1954], pp. 349-53.

This review of the first American edition of the collected stories was originally published in 1937.

Benet, Mary Kathleen. "Katherine Mansfield & John Middleton Murry." In her WRITERS IN LOVE. New York: Macmillan, 1977, pp. 19-109.

Berkman, Sylvia. KATHERINE MANSFIELD: A CRITICAL STUDY. New Haven: Yale University Press; [Christchurch]: Whitcombe & Tombs, 1951; London: Oxford University Press, 1952; rpt. Hamden, Conn.: Archon Books, 1971.

This sensitive and balanced work is the best biographical-critical study of Katherine Mansfield and her stories. See also Isherwood, p. 153.

Bertram, James. "Le tombeau de Katherine Mansfield." LANDFALL, 6 (September 1952), 193-201.

The article is in English.

Blanchet, André. "Le secret de Katherine Mansfield." In his LA LITTERATURE ET LE SPIRITUEL. Vol. 3. Paris: Aubier, 1962, pp. 71-114.

A romantic--indeed sentimental--essay on Katherine Mansfield's religious unrest. It was first published in 1939.

Bosanquet, Theodora. "Life Should Be Glorious: A New View of Katherine Mansfield As Revealed in Her Stories." NEW ZEALAND MAGAZINE, 26 (January 1947), 17-18.

Bowen, Elizabeth. "Stories By Katherine Mansfield." In her AFTERTHOUGHT: PIECES ABOUT WRITING. London: Longmans, 1962, pp. 53-74.

Elizabeth Bowen's essay was first published in 1956, and was used as a preface to her edition of 34 SHORT STORIES by Katherine Mansfield (see p. 141).

Boyle, Ted E. "The Death of the Boss: Another Look at Katherine Mansfield's 'The Fly.'" MODERN FICTION STUDIES, 11 (Summer 1965), 183-85.

Boyle lists a number of earlier studies and explications of "The Fly."

Brewster, D., and A. Burrell. "Soundings: Fiction of Anton Chekhov and Katherine Mansfield" and "Salvaging the Short Story: Chekhov and Mansfield." In their DEAD RECKONINGS IN FICTION. New York: Longmans, Green, 1924; London: Longmans, 1925, pp. 42-100.

Brophy, Brigid. "Katherine Mansfield." In her DON'T NEVER FORGET. London: Cape, [1966], pp. 255-63.

Brigid Brophy finds anger and hatred to be the key to Mansfield's biographical and literary personality. The article was first published in 1962.

Bullett, G.W. "The Short Story." In his MODERN ENGLISH FICTION. London: H. Jenkins, 1926, pp. 107-20.

"Apart from Mr. de la Mare . . . Katherine Mansfield is the one short story writer of indubitable genius who has appeared during the present century."

Burns, James A.S. "Katherine Mansfield As Literary Critic." EDUCATION, 14 (August 1965), 10-12.

Busch, Frieder. "Katherine Mansfield and Literary Impressionism in France and Germany." ARCADIA (Berlin), 5 (1970), 58-76.

Carco, Francis. MONTMARTRE A VINGT ANS. Paris: Albin Michel, [1938].

In chapter 10, which was first published as two articles in 1933, Carco recalls meeting Katherine Mansfield and Middleton Murry in 1914. Carco was influential in establishing a one-sided view of Katherine Mansfield in France.

Cather, Willa S. "Katherine Mansfield." In her NOT UNDER FORTY. New York: Knopf; London: Cassell, 1936, pp. 139-66.

Partly reprinted in her ON WRITING (New York: Knopf, 1949).

Cazamian, Louis. "D.H. Lawrence and Katherine Mansfield As Letter-Writers." UNIVERSITY OF TORONTO QUARTERLY, 3 (April 1934), 286-307.

Citron, Pierre. "Katherine Mansfield et la France." REVUE DE LITTERATURE COMPAREE, 20 (1940), 173-93.

> Citron surveys the material on Katherine Mansfield that had been published in France.

[Closset, M.] "Katherine Mansfield." By Jean Dominique (pseud.). LE THYRSE (Brussels), 54 (April 1952), 156-68; (May 1952), 197-205; (June 1952), 252-62.

Collins, Joseph. "The Rare Craftmanship of Katherine Mansfield." NEW YORK TIMES BOOK REVIEW, 18 February 1923, p. 7.

______. "Two Literary Ladies of London: Katherine Mansfield and Rebecca West." In his THE DOCTOR LOOKS AT LITERATURE: PSYCHOLOGICAL STUDIES OF LIFE AND LETTERS. New York: George H. Doran; London: Allen & Unwin, [1923], pp. 151-80.

Corin, Fern. "Creation of Atmosphere in Katherine Mansfield's Stories." REVUE DES LANGUES VIVANTES, 22, no. 1 (1956), 65-78.

Cowley, Joy, et al. "Mansfield: How Stands She Today?" NEW ZEALAND LISTENER, 11 October 1968, pp. 8-9.

> Brief comments from Joy Cowley, M.H. Holcroft, Ian Cross, Marilyn Duckworth, Denis Glover, Noel Hilliard, Maurice Shadbolt, and Phillip Wilson on how they viewed Katherine Mansfield in 1968.

Cox, Sidney. "The Fastidiousness of Katherine Mansfield." SEWANEE REVIEW, 39 (April-June 1931), 158-69.

Curnow, Heather. KATHERINE MANSFIELD. Wellington: Reed, 1968.

> A study written "primarily for secondary schools."

Daiches, David. "The Art of Katherine Mansfield." In his NEW LITERARY VALUES. Edinburgh: Oliver & Boyd, 1936, pp. 83-114.

______. "Katherine Mansfield and the Search for Truth." In his THE NOVEL IN THE MODERN WORLD. Chicago: University of Chicago Press, [1939], pp. 65-79.

> This chapter on Katherine Mansfield was not included in Daiches' later revision of his book.

Daly, Saralyn R. KATHERINE MANSFIELD. New York: Twayne, [1965].

> A close study of Katherine Mansfield's stories which has the virtues

and limitations of its type. It is suggestive about individual stories and passages, but leaves no rounded impression of the writer's work as a whole.

Davin, Dan. KATHERINE MANSFIELD IN HER LETTERS. Wellington: School Publications Branch, Dept. of Education, 1959.

A post-primary school bulletin.

Davis, Robert M. "The Unity of 'The Garden Party.'" STUDIES IN SHORT FICTION, 2 (Fall 1964), 61-65.

Dinkins, Paul. "Katherine Mansfield: The Artist As Critic." DESCANT (Fort Worth, Texas), 3 (Fall 1958), 28-33.

_____. "Katherine Mansfield: An Introduction." DESCANT (Fort Worth, Texas), 3 (Fall 1958), 15-19.

_____. "Katherine Mansfield's Childhood: Some Literary Presages." DESCANT (Fort Worth, Texas), 3 (Fall 1958), 20-27.

Drabble, Margaret. "The New Woman of the Twenties: Fifty Years On." HARPERS & QUEEN, June 1973, pp. 106-07, 135.

Duggan, Eileen. "A Father's Tribute." ALL ABOUT BOOKS (Melbourne), 13 November 1933, p. 177.

_____. "Katherine Mansfield." NEW ZEALAND ARTISTS' ANNUAL, 2, no. 2 (1931), 12.

Eustace, C.J. "The Genius: Katherine Mansfield." In his AN INFINITY OF QUESTIONS: A STUDY OF THE RELIGION OF ART AND OF THE ART OF RELIGION IN THE LIVES OF FIVE WOMEN. London: Dennis Dobson; New York: Longmans, 1946, pp. 53-78.

Fairburn, A.R.D. "Katherine Mansfield." NEW ZEALAND ARTISTS' ANNUAL, 1, no. 3 (1928), 69, 71.

A warm estimate of Katherine Mansfield's poetry.

Foot, John. THE EDWARDIANISM OF KATHERINE MANSFIELD. Wellington: Brentwoods Press, 1969.

Freeman, Kathleen. "The Art of Katherine Mansfield." CANADIAN FORUM, 7 (July 1927), 302-08.

Friis, Anne. KATHERINE MANSFIELD: LIFE AND STORIES. Copenhagen: Einar Munksgaard, 1946; rpt. Folcroft, Pa.: Folcroft Library, 1974; [Norwood, Pa.]: Norwood Editions, 1977.

Garlington, Jack. "Katherine Mansfield: The Critical Trend." TWENTIETH CENTURY LITERATURE, 2 (July 1956), 51-61.

______. "An Unattributed Story By Katherine Mansfield?" MODERN LANGUAGE NOTES, 71 (February 1956), 91-93.

The story is "The Meeting of Gwendolen," published in the NEW AGE, 2 November 1911.

Gateau, Andrée-Marie. "Katherine Mansfield impressioniste; ou, quand et comment se déroulent les nouvelles de K. Mansfield." CALIBAN (Toulouse), 6 (January 1969), 33-48.

______. "Poétesse, musicienne et peintre d'un moment éphémère, ou Katherine Mansfield impressioniste." CALIBAN (Toulouse), 5 (January 1968), 93-102.

Gillet, Louis. "'Kass'; ou la jeunesse de Katherine Mansfield." REVUE DES DEUX MONDES, 15 January 1934, pp. 456-68.

______. "Katherine Mansfield." REVUE DES DEUX MONDES, 15 December 1924, pp. 929-42.

______. "Les lettres de Katherine Mansfield." REVUE DES DEUX MONDES, 1 May 1929, pp. 213-27.

Gordon, Ian. "The Banker and the Banker's Daughter." NEW ZEALAND LISTENER, 27 November 1972, pp. 8-9.

Gordon reexamines Katherine Mansfield's relationship with her father and the financial benefits she received from him.

______. "The Editing of Katherine Mansfield's Journal and Scrapbook." LANDFALL, 13 (March 1959), 62-69.

Gordon examines here the manuscript material on which Murry based the SCRAPBOOK and the two editions of the JOURNAL. See also Waldron, p. 162.

______. KATHERINE MANSFIELD. London: Longmans, Green for The British Council and the National Book League, 1954. Rev. ed. London: Longman for the British Council, 1963.

______. "Katherine Mansfield, New Zealander." NEW ZEALAND NEW WRITING, no. 3 (June 1944), 58-63.

______. "Warmth and Hydrangeas: Katherine Mansfield's Wellington Years, 1907-8." NEW ZEALAND LISTENER, 8 May 1976, pp. 22-23.

Guéritte, Madeleine T. "Katherine Mansfield and Music." CHESTERIAN, 18 (1937), 94-99.

Haferkamp, Berta. "Zur Bildersprache Katherine Mansfields." DIE NEUEREN SPRACHEN, 18 (May 1969), 221-39.

On Katherine Mansfield's imagery.

Hagopian, John T. "Capturing Mansfield's 'Fly.'" MODERN FICTION STUDIES, 9 (Winter 1963-64), 385-90.

Halter, Peter. KATHERINE MANSFIELD UND DIE KURZGESCHICHTE. Bern: Francke Verlag, [1972].

On Katherine Mansfield and the short story.

Hamill, Elizabeth. "Katherine Mansfield and Virginia Woolf." In her THESE MODERN WRITERS. Melbourne: Georgian House, 1946, pp. 113-24.

Harper, George McLean. "Katherine Mansfield." QUARTERLY REVIEW, 253 (October 1929), 377-87.

Hawke, Helena. "Katherine Mansfield and Karori." STOCKADE (Wellington), 3 (September 1975), [1-7].

Hayman, Ronald. LITERATURE AND LIVING: A CONSIDERATION OF KATHERINE MANSFIELD & VIRGINIA WOOLF. [London]: Covent Garden Press, 1972.

Hayward, M. "KM--Loved in Letters." NEW ZEALAND BOOK WORLD, no. 29 (October 1976), 18-19.

An article, based on an interview with Helen McNeish, about the origins of PASSIONATE PILGRIMAGE (see p. 143).

Henriot, Emile. "Le souvenir de Katherine Mansfield." In his DE MARIE DE FRANCE A KATHERINE MANSFIELD. Paris: Librairie Plon, [1937], pp. 242-49.

Hoare, Dorothy M. "A Note on Katherine Mansfield." In her SOME STUDIES

IN THE MODERN NOVEL. London: Chatto & Windus, 1938; Litchfield, Conn.: Prospect Press, 1940, pp. 148-54.

Hormasji, Nariman. KATHERINE MANSFIELD: AN APPRAISAL. Foreword by Ian Gordon. Auckland: Collins, 1967.

Hubbell, George Shelton. "Katherine Mansfield and Kezia." SEWANEE REVIEW, 35 (July-September 1927), 325-35.

Hynes, Sam. "Katherine Mansfield: The Defeat of the Personal." SOUTH ATLANTIC QUARTERLY, 52 (October 1953), 555-60.

Isherwood, Christopher. "Katherine Mansfield." In his EXHUMATIONS. London: Methuen, 1966, pp. 64-72.

> Although Isherwood undertook this essay as a review of Sylvia Berkman's book (see p. 147), he includes interesting comment on his own view of Katherine Mansfield's literary personality.

Iversen, Anders. "Life and Letters: Katherine Mansfield Drawing On Kathleen Beauchamp." ENGLISH STUDIES, 52 (February 1971), 44-54.

______. "A Reading of Katherine Mansfield's 'The Garden Party.'" ORBIS LITTERARUM, 23 (1968), 5-34.

Jean-Aubry, J. "Katherine Mansfield." REVUE DE PARIS, 1 November 1931, pp. 57-72.

Justus, James H. "Katherine Mansfield: The Triumph of Egoism." MOSAIC (Winnipeg), 6 (Spring 1973), 13-22.

"Katherine Mansfield's Stories." TIMES LITERARY SUPPLEMENT, 2 March 1946, p. 102.

> A general study written on the publication of the COLLECTED STORIES.

King, Russell S. "Katherine Mansfield As an Expatriate Writer." JOURNAL OF COMMONWEALTH LITERATURE, 8 (June 1973), 97-109.

Kirkwood, Hilda. "Katherine Mansfield." CANADIAN FORUM, 35 (July 1955), 81-82.

Kleine, Don W. "The Chekhovian Source of 'Marriage à la Mode.'" PHILOLOGICAL QUARTERLY, 42 (April 1963), 284-88.

______. "An Eden for Insiders: Katherine Mansfield's New Zealand." COLLEGE ENGLISH, 27 (December 1965), 201-09.

______. "'The Garden Party': A Portrait of the Artist." CRITICISM, 5 (Fall 1963), 360-71.

______. "Katherine Mansfield and the Prisoner of Love." CRITIQUE (Minneapolis), 3 (Winter-Spring 1960), 20-33.

A discussion of "A Man without a Temperament."

Kominars, Sheppard B. "Katherine Mansfield: The Way to Fontainebleau." Thesis, Boston University Graduate School, 1966.

Kranendonk, A.G. van. "Katherine Mansfield." ENGLISH STUDIES, 12 (April 1930), 49-57.

Kurylo, Charanne C. "Chekov and Katherine Mansfield: A Study in Literary Influence." Thesis, University of North Carolina at Chapel Hill, 1974.

Lawlor, Pat. "Collecting Katherine Mansfield." In his BOOKS AND BOOKMEN, NEW ZEALAND AND OVERSEAS. Wellington: Whitcombe & Tombs, 1954, pp. 120-29.

______. "Katherine Mansfield and Wellington." In his MORE WELLINGTON DAYS. Christchurch: Whitcombe & Tombs, 1962, pp. 163-77.

______. THE LONELINESS OF KATHERINE MANSFIELD. Wellington: Beltane Book Bureau, 1950.

This small booklet was prompted by Keith Sinclair's article "Men, Women and Mansfield" (see p. 161).

______. THE MYSTERY OF MAATA: A KATHERINE MANSFIELD NOVEL. Introd. G.H. Scholefield. Wellington: Beltane Book Bureau, 1946.

Lawlor discusses what could then be discovered about this unfinished novel and its heroine. He had not seen any manuscript. Two fragments were later published in the TURNBULL LIBRARY RECORD (see p. 160 under Margaret Scott); and two chapters were bought at auction in 1957 by an unknown buyer, and have not been released.

______. "Wellington and Katherine Mansfield." In his OLD WELLINGTON DAYS. Wellington: Whitcombe & Tombs, 1959, pp. 167-87.

______. "Writers and the Faith." CATHOLIC REVIEW (Auckland), 1 (September 1945), 357-65.

Katherine Mansfield is discussed in a section on pages 357-60.

Lawrence, Margaret. WE WRITE AS WOMEN. London: Michael Joseph, [1937]; as THE SCHOOL OF FEMININITY. New York: Frederick Stokes, 1937.

In short hectic sentences, Mansfield is discussed, and as a woman rather than as a writer, in chapter 13.

Leeming, Owen. "Katherine Mansfield and Her Family." NEW ZEALAND LISTENER, 29 March 1963, p. 4.

______. "Katherine Mansfield in Europe." NEW ZEALAND LISTENER, 11 April 1963, p. 6.

______. "Katherine Mansfield's Rebellion." NEW ZEALAND LISTENER, 5 April 1963, pp. 6-7.

______. "Katherine Mansfield's Sisters." NEW ZEALAND LISTENER, 1 March 1963, p. 4.

McIntosh, A.D. "The New Zealand Background of K.M." ADAM, nos. 370-75 (1972-73), 76-83.

Magalaner, Marvin. THE FICTION OF KATHERINE MANSFIELD. Preface by Harry T. Moore. Carbondale: Southern Illinois University Press; London: Feffer & Simons, [1971].

An attempt at what the author recognizes is the difficult task of "summing up" Katherine Mansfield. A judicious use of her critical comments on literature and of her letters and journals, a close examination of just a few of her best stories, and an unstrained consideration of her imagery enable Magalaner to produce a satisfying result.

Mais, S.P.B. "Katherine Mansfield." In his SOME MODERN AUTHORS. London: Grant Richards; New York: Dodd, Mead, 1923, pp. 108-14.

"The Mansfield Manuscripts." NEW ZEALAND LISTENER, 20 June 1958, p. 4.

A brief account of the manuscripts bought for the Alexander Turnbull Library from Sotheby's, including extracts from Antony Alpers' written assessment of their importance.

Mantz, Ruth Elvish. "K.M.--Fifty Years After." ADAM, nos. 370-75 (1972-73), 117-27.

Mantz here recalls the time she spent with Murry in London in the early thirties, working on her biography of Katherine Mansfield. She comments knowledgeably on the misleading nature of the JOURNAL and on its biographical inadequacies.

Marcel, Gabriel. "Katherine Mansfield." REVUE HEBDOMADAIRE, 11 July 1931, pp. 172-81.

Marion, Bernard. A LA RENCONTRE DE KATHERINE MANSFIELD. [Brussels]: La Sixaine, 1946.

Mason, Bruce. "A Commission Fulfilled." NEW ZEALAND LISTENER, 31 August 1970, pp. 2-3.

An article about Katherine Mansfield's friend, Mrs. E.K. Robison.

Maurois, André. "Katherine Mansfield." In his POINTS OF VIEW FROM KIPLING TO GRAHAM GREENE. Trans. Hamish Miles. New York: Ungar, 1968; London: Muller, 1969, pp. 313-45.

This English translation of Maurois's essay was first published in 1935.

Meyers, Jeffrey. "Katherine Mansfield, Gurdjieff, and Lawrence's MOTHER AND DAUGHTER." TWENTIETH CENTURY LITERATURE, 22 (December 1976), 444-53.

Michel-Michot, Paulette. "Katherine Mansfield's 'The Fly': An Attempt to Capture the Boss." STUDIES IN SHORT FICTION, 11 (Winter 1974), 85-92.

Mills, Tom L. "Katherine Mansfield: How Kathleen Beauchamp Came into Her Own." NEW ZEALAND RAILWAYS MAGAZINE, 8 (September 1933), 6-7.

Milner, Ian. "A Note on Katherine Mansfield." PHOENIX (Auckland), 1 (March 1932), unpaged.

Moore, Virginia. "Katherine Mansfield." In her DISTINGUISHED WOMEN WRITERS. Port Washington, N.Y.: Kennikat Press, 1968, pp. 235-53.

First published in book form in 1934.

Morgan, Patricia A. (Kane). KATHERINE MANSFIELD: FACT AND FICTION IN THE NEW ZEALAND STORIES. [Wellington]: 1972.

In this post-graduate essay, Patricia Morgan identifies, for what it is worth, people and places described in the New Zealand stories.

Morrell, Lady Ottoline. "K.M." In KATHERINE MANSFIELD: AN EXHIBITION. Austin: Humanities Research Center, University of Texas, [1975?], pp. 8-15.

This memoir was written in 1933, but had remained previously unpublished.

Morris, G.N. "The Early Work of Katherine Mansfield." NEW ZEALAND MAGAZINE, 22 (November-December 1943), 23-25.

______. "Her Unlucky Star: Some Thoughts on the Inner Life of Katherine Mansfield." NEW ZEALAND MAGAZINE, 28 (Autumn 1949), 23-24.

______. "Katherine Mansfield: Early London Days." HISTORY AND BIBLIOGRAPHY (Christchurch), 1 (August 1948), 102-05.

______. "Katherine Mansfield in Fiction." NEW ZEALAND MAGAZINE, 22 (May-June 1943), 8-10.

About stories and novels which contain characters based on Katherine Mansfield.

______. "Katherine Mansfield in Ten Languages." NEW ZEALAND MAGAZINE, 23 (May-June 1944), 23-25.

______. "Katherine Mansfield: The Last Ten Years." HISTORY AND BIBLIOGRAPHY (Christchurch), 1 (December 1948), 209-14.

______. "Katherine Mansfield: The New Zealand Period." HISTORY AND BIBLIOGRAPHY (Christchurch), 1 (April 1948), 28-32.

______. "Katherine Mansfield's Wellington." NEW ZEALAND MAGAZINE, 23 (November-December 1944), 27-29.

Morris, Maude E. "Katherine Mansfield's 'At the Bay.'" TURNBULL LIBRARY RECORD, 1 (November 1968), 19-24.

Factual background and early photographs of the setting of the story. Discussion of this article followed in the issues for April and October 1969.

Mortelier, Christiane. "The Genesis and Development of the Katherine Mansfield Legacy in France." AUMLA, no. 34 (November 1970), 252-63.

______. "Un inédit de Katherine Mansfield: 'Toots,' pièce inédite inachevée." ETUDES ANGLAISES, 26 (October-December 1973), 399-404.

Christiane Mortelier's article is followed by a transcription of the unfinished play.

______. "Le talent dramatique de Katherine Mansfield 1916-1917." ETUDES ANGLAISES, 26 (October-December 1973), 385-98.

Muffang, May Lilian. KATHERINE MANSFIELD: SA VIE, SON OEUVRE, SA PERSONNALITE. Paris: Imprimerie A.L.P., 1937.

Mulgan, Alan. "Katherine Mansfield: Double Expatriate." In his GREAT DAYS IN NEW ZEALAND WRITING. Wellington: Reed, 1962, pp. 62-74.

Murry, J. Middleton. BETWEEN TWO WORLDS: AN AUTOBIOGRAPHY. London: Cape, 1935.

Murry ends his story in 1918, the year in which he formally married Katherine Mansfield.

______. "Katherine Mansfield." In his KATHERINE MANSFIELD AND OTHER LITERARY PORTRAITS. London: P. Nevill, 1949, pp. 7-31.

Under the collective title of "Katherine Mansfield," Murry includes three distinct essays: "The Isolation of Katherine Mansfield," "The Letters of Katherine Mansfield," and "Portrait of a Pa-Man."

______. "Katherine Mansfield." In his KATHERINE MANSFIELD AND OTHER LITERARY STUDIES. London: Constable, 1959, pp. 69-93.

______. "Katherine Mansfield, Stendhal and Style." ADELPHI, 1 (September 1923), 342-43.

Nebeker, Helen E. "The Pear Tree: Sexual Implications in Katherine Mansfield's 'Bliss.'" MODERN FICTION STUDIES, 18 (Winter 1972-73), 545-51.

Nelson, Arthur. "Katherine Mansfield: Artist in Miniature." In THE CREATIVE READER. Ed. R.W. Stallman and R.E. Watters. New York: Ronald Press, [1954], pp. 308-12.

An analysis (written by a first-year college student) of "The Daughters of the Late Colonel," originally published in 1941.

[O'Donovan, Michael]. "An Author in Search of a Subject." By Frank O'Connor (pseud.). In his THE LONELY VOICE. London: Macmillan, 1965, pp. 128-42.

O'Donovan analyzes his dissatisfaction with Katherine Mansfield's stories. "There is one quality that is missing . . . and that is heart."

Orage, A.R. "Talks with Katherine Mansfield." In his SELECTED ESSAYS AND CRITICAL WRITINGS. Ed. Herbert Read and Denis Saurat. London: Stanley Nott, 1935, pp. 125-32.

In this report, first published in 1924, Orage records a new attitude to life and literature described to him by Katherine Mansfield shortly before her death.

O'Sullivan, Vincent. KATHERINE MANSFIELD'S NEW ZEALAND. Auckland: Golden Press, 1974; London: Muller, [1975].

A book of early photographs of places in New Zealand connected with Katherine Mansfield.

______. "The Magnetic Chain: Notes and Approaches to K.M." LANDFALL, 29 (June 1975), 95-131.

O'Sullivan, in the belief that there are "many aspects of her [Katherine Mansfield's] work, such as the large question of her reading, and her assumptions about life, which have not yet brought forward much debate," writes usefully about the influence of Wilde and Pater, about the nature of the Joycean epiphanies in her stories, and about her attitude towards sex.

Palmer, Vance. "Katherine Mansfield." MEANJIN, 14 (June 1955), 177-85.

Porter, Katherine Anne. "The Art of Katherine Mansfield." In her THE DAYS BEFORE. New York: Harcourt Brace, [1952]; London: Secker & Warburg, 1953, pp. 82-87.

A short study first published on the appearance of the American edition of the collected stories in 1937.

Pritchett, V.S. "Katherine Mansfield's Short Stories." LISTENER, 4 July 1946, pp. 20-21; rpt. as "Katherine Mansfield and the Short Story." NEW ZEALAND LISTENER, 20 September 1946, pp. 9-11.

______. Review of COLLECTED STORIES. NEW STATESMAN AND NATION, 2 February 1946, p. 87.

Rillo, L.E. KATHERINE MANSFIELD AND VIRGINIA WOOLF. Buenos Aires: Talleres Gráficos Contreras, 1944.

Rohrberger, Mary Helen. THE ART OF KATHERINE MANSFIELD. Ann Arbor, Mich.: University Microfilms International, 1977.

Sargeson, Frank. "The Feminine Tradition: A Talk about Katherine Mansfield." NEW ZEALAND LISTENER, 6 August 1948, pp. 10-12.

[Schiff, S.] "First Meetings with Katherine Mansfield." By Stephen Hudson (pseud.). CORNHILL, 170 (Autumn 1958), 202-12.

Schneider, Elisabeth. "Katherine Mansfield and Chekhov." MODERN LANGUAGE NOTES, 50 (June 1935), 394-97.

Schneider believed "The Child-Who-Was-Tired" to be an unconscious imitation of Chekhov's "Sleepyhead." See p. 146 for a letter by Almedingen on this subject.

Scholefield, G.H. "Katherine Mansfield." In REMINISCENCES AND RECOLLECTIONS. By H. Beauchamp. New Plymouth: Thomas Avery, 1937, pp. 190-217.

Scholefield's chapter is mainly about Mansfield's early life, but it also sketches in her later career from a New Zealand point of view.

Schwendimann, Max A. KATHERINE MANSFIELD: IHR LEBEN IN DARSTELLUNG UND DOKUMENTEN. Munich: Winkler-Verlag, 1967.

A documentary and descriptive biography.

Schwinn, Liesel. "Katherine Mansfield." HOCHLAND (Munich), 53 (1960-61), 333-42.

Scott, Margaret. "The Extant Manuscripts of Katherine Mansfield." ETUDES ANGLAISES, 26 (October-December 1973), 413-19.

______. "Katherine Mansfield." In NEW ZEALAND'S HERITAGE. Ed. Ray Knox. Wellington: Paul Hamlyn, [1971-73], pp. 2175-79.

______. "More Katherine Mansfield Manuscripts." TURNBULL LIBRARY RECORD, 7 (October 1974), 18.

______, ed. "The Unpublished Manuscripts of Katherine Mansfield." 6 parts. TURNBULL LIBRARY RECORD, 3 (March 1970), 4-28; (November 1970), 128-36; 4 (May 1971), 4-20; 5 (May 1972), 19-25; 6 (October 1973), 4-8; 7 (May 1974), 4-14.

In this series, Margaret Scott prints a variety of manuscript fragments, including passages from two unfinished early novels and the unfinished play "Toots."

Sewell, Arthur. KATHERINE MANSFIELD: A CRITICAL ESSAY. Auckland: Unicorn Press, 1936; rpt. Darby, Pa.: Folcroft Library Editions, 1972.

In this short but admirably delicate study, Sewell concentrates on "those trivial little items of experience which no one but a sensitive artist would notice or think worth noticing" and on her search for "a prose which will give the ABSOLUTE form to the idea."

Shadbolt, Maurice. "Katherine Mansfield." In his LOVE AND LEGEND: SOME 20TH CENTURY NEW ZEALANDERS. Auckland: Hodder & Stoughton, 1976, pp. 141-52.

Shanks, Edward. "Katherine Mansfield." LONDON MERCURY, 17 (January 1928), 286-93.

Shaw, Helen. "Katherine Mansfield." MEANJIN, 10 (Summer 1951), 376-82.

______. "Sargeson and Mansfield in Contrast." In THE PURITAN AND THE WAIF: A SYMPOSIUM OF CRITICAL ESSAYS ON THE WORK OF FRANK SARGESON. Ed. Helen Shaw. Auckland: H.L. Hofmann, 1954, pp. 51-55.

Sinclair, Keith. "Men, Women and Mansfield." LANDFALL, 4 (June 1950), 128-38.

Sinclair finds loneliness and isolation to be the condition of most of Katherine Mansfield's characters, a condition which her own tenderness and sympathy for them denies as a general truth of life. See also Lawlor, p. 154.

Squire, J.C. "Miss Mansfield's Stories." In his BOOKS REVIEWED. London: Heinemann, [1922], pp. 9-16.

Squire's notice of BLISS, reprinted in this book, is an example of a good early review.

Stanley, C.W. "The Art of Katherine Mansfield." DALHOUSIE REVIEW, 10 (April 1930), 26-41.

Stone, Jean E. KATHERINE MANSFIELD: PUBLICATIONS IN AUSTRALIA 1907-09; WITH FOUR SKETCHES AND A POEM NOW COLLECTED FOR THE FIRST TIME. Sydney: Wentworth Books, 1977.

Sutherland, Ronald. "Katherine Mansfield: Plagiarist, Disciple or Ardent Admirer?" CRITIQUE (Minneapolis), 5 (1962-63), 58-76.

Sutherland examines the relationship between Mansfield and Chekhov.

Taylor, Donald S., and Daniel A. Weiss. "Crashing the Garden Party." MODERN FICTION STUDIES, 4 (Winter 1958-59), 361-64.

Taylor, Moira. "Untangling the Mansfield Riddles." NEW ZEALAND LISTENER, 29 December 1973, pp. 6-7.

Moira Taylor discusses the issue of ADAM (nos. 370-75) devoted to Mansfieldiana. See also McIntosh (p. 155) and Mantz (p. 155).

Villard, Léonie. "Katherine Mansfield." LES LANGUES MODERNES, 43 (1949), 304-13.

Wadsworth, Celina. "Symbolism in the Short Stories of Katherine Mansfield: An Epiphany of Her Sensitivity to Suffering." Thesis, University of Ottawa, 1969.

Wagenknecht, Edward. "Dickens and Katherine Mansfield." In his DICKENS AND THE SCANDALMONGERS. Norman: University of Oklahoma Press, [1965], pp. 99-108.

An earlier version of this essay was published in 1929.

______. "Katherine Mansfield." ENGLISH JOURNAL, 17 (April 1928), 272-84.

An important early analysis of her stylistic technique.

Waldron, Philip. "Katherine Mansfield's 'Journal.'" TWENTIETH CENTURY LITERATURE, 20 (January 1974), 11-18.

Waldron amplifies Ian Gordon's account (see p. 151) of the distortions Murry introduced into the JOURNAL.

Walker, Warren S. "The Unresolved Conflict in 'The Garden Party.'" MODERN FICTION STUDIES, 3 (Winter 1957-58), 354-58.

Walsh, William. "Katherine Mansfield." In his A MANIFOLD VOICE: STUDIES IN COMMONWEALTH LITERATURE. London: Chatto & Windus, 1970, pp. 154-84.

Walt, James. "Conrad and Katherine Mansfield." CONRADIANA, 4, no. 1 (1972), 41-52.

Ward, Alfred C. "Katherine Mansfield." In his ASPECTS OF THE MODERN SHORT STORY: ENGLISH AND AMERICAN. London: University of London Press, 1924, pp. 283-96.

Whitridge, Arnold. "Katherine Mansfield." SEWANEE REVIEW, 48 (April-June 1940), 256-72.

Wiegelmann, Thea. "Das Weltbild der Katherine Mansfield." Thesis, University of Bonn, 1937.

On how Katherine Mansfield saw her world.

Williams, Orlo. "Review of THE JOURNAL OF KATHERINE MANSFIELD and THE LETTERS OF KATHERINE MANSFIELD." CRITERION, 8 (April 1929), 508-13.

A review commended by Murry.

Willy, Margaret. "Katherine Mansfield." In her THREE WOMAN DIARISTS: CELIA FIENNES, DOROTHY WORDSWORTH, KATHERINE MANSFIELD. London: Longmans, Green for The British Council and the National Book League, 1964, pp. 31-39.

Woolf, Virginia. "A Terribly Sensitive Mind." In her COLLECTED ESSAYS. Vol. 1. London: Hogarth Press, 1966, pp. 356-58.

A review of THE JOURNAL OF KATHERINE MANSFIELD, first published in 1927.

Wright, Celeste T. "Darkness as a Symbol in Katherine Mansfield." MODERN PHILOLOGY, 51 (February 1954), 204-07.

______. "Genesis of a Short Story." PHILOLOGICAL QUARTERLY, 34 (January 1955), 91-96.

An interpretation of "The Fly" based on Katherine Mansfield's supposed relations with her father.

______. "Katherine Mansfield and the Secret Smile." LITERATURE AND PSYCHOLOGY, 5 (Summer 1955), 44-48.

______. "Katherine Mansfield's Boat Image." TWENTIETH CENTURY LITERATURE, 1 (October 1955), 128-32.

______. "Katherine Mansfield's Dog Image." LITERATURE AND PSYCHOLOGY, 10 (Summer 1960), 80-81.

______. "Katherine Mansfield's Father Image." In THE IMAGE OF THE WORK. Ed. B.H. Lehman et al. Berkeley: University of California Press, 1955, pp. 137-55.

"A Writer's Sanctuary: Katherine Mansfield with Her Scrapbook." TIMES LITERARY SUPPLEMENT, 28 October 1939, p. 626.

A review of THE SCRAPBOOK OF KATHERINE MANSFIELD.

Yen, Yuan-shu. "Katherine Mansfield's Use of Point of View." Thesis, University of Wisconsin, 1967.

Zinman, Toby S. "The Snail under the Leaf: Katherine Mansfield's Ironic Vision." Thesis, Temple University, Philadelphia, 1973.

MASON, BRUCE EDWARD GEORGE (1921-)

Bruce Mason has made a highly varied contribution to the cultural life of Wellington and New Zealand. He is one of the country's very few successful playwrights; his solo performances, especially in THE END OF THE GOLDEN WEATHER, have been well received over many years; and he has published articles on the theatre, short stories, and autobiographical sketches. He has been closely involved in the fostering of amateur theatre; and he helped to establish the New Zealand Players Company, and more recently Wellington's professional Downstage Theatre. He edited the periodicals TE AO HOU (see p. 219) and ACT (see p. 220) for a number of years; he has produced opera; and over a long period he has written some of the liveliest and best-informed reviews of music and drama. The exploration of New Zealand's poly-cultural society has been the distinctive theme of several of his plays, of which some are as yet unpublished.

DRAMA

THE POHUTUKAWA TREE. Wellington: Price Milburn, 1960; rev. ed., 1963.

THE END OF THE GOLDEN WEATHER: A VOYAGE INTO A NEW ZEALAND CHILDHOOD. Wellington: Price Milburn, 1962; rev. ed., 1970.

> The revised edition is prefaced with a television script written to celebrate the five-hundredth performance of the play.

WE DON'T WANT YOUR SORT HERE: A COLLECTION OF SONGS, PARODIES AND SKETCHES. Hamilton: Paul's Book Arcade, 1963.

AWATEA. Wellington: Price Milburn, 1969.

ZERO INN. Christchurch: Canterbury Area of the N.Z. Theatre Federation, 1970.

"Hongi." In CONTEMPORARY NEW ZEALAND PLAYS. Ed. Howard McNaughton. Wellington: Oxford University Press, 1974, pp. 132-52.

OTHER PROSE

"Et in Arcadia Ego: A Chapter of Reminiscence." LANDFALL, 9 (December 1955), 294-300.

"The Plays of Claude Evans." LANDFALL, 10 (March 1956), 43-48.

THEATRE IN DANGER: A CORRESPONDENCE. With John Pocock. Hamilton: Paul's Book Arcade, 1957.

> The most considerable and broadly based discussion yet written about New Zealand theatre.

"All in One Basket." NEW ZEALAND LISTENER, 29 July 1960, pp. 4-5.

> Reflections on the experience of touring his one-man show, THE END OF THE GOLDEN WEATHER.

"Beginnings." LANDFALL, 20 (June 1966), 143-49.

> An autobiographical sketch.

"Theatre." In THE PATTERN OF NEW ZEALAND CULTURE. Ed. A.L. McLeod. Ithaca, N.Y.: Cornell University Press; Melbourne: Oxford University Press, 1968, pp. 239-56.

DISCUSSION GUIDE TO BRUCE MASON'S 3-ACT PLAY, "THE POHUTUKAWA TREE." [Wellington]: Price Milburn, [1969].

"The 'Golden Weather' Odyssey." NEW ZEALAND LISTENER, 5 September 1969, p. 13.

"A Commission Fulfilled." NEW ZEALAND LISTENER, 31 August 1970, pp. 2-3.

> An article about Katherine Mansfield's friend, Mrs. E.K. Robison.

"Bruce Mason Talks of His Experiences with the Maori People." AFFAIRS, May 1971, pp. 184-87.

"New Stages in Theatre." In NEW ZEALAND'S HERITAGE. Ed. Ray Knox. Wellington: Paul Hamlyn, [1971-73], pp. 2644-51.

Theatre in New Zealand from 1920 on.

NEW ZEALAND DRAMA: A PARADE OF FORMS AND A HISTORY. Wellington: Price Milburn, 1973.

"Bruce Mason on 'Windsor Castle.'" EDUCATION, 25, no. 8 (1976), 25.

Mason traces his own "florid exuberance" of style to his excited childhood reading of Ainsworth's novel.

CRITICISM

MacLeod, Alexander. "A New Zealand Talent." NEW ZEALAND LISTENER, 24 June 1960, p. 19.

McNaughton, Howard. BRUCE MASON. Wellington: Oxford University Press, [1976].

Includes a bibliography of Mason's work and of the more important reviews of his plays.

Mason, Bruce. "Bruce Mason: Playwright." AFFAIRS, May 1971, pp. 182-84.

Mason interviewed by Marilyn Duckworth.

______. "The Plays of Bruce Mason." LANDFALL, 27 (June 1973), 102-38.

The edited transcript of an interview between Howard McNaughton and Mason.

MASON, RONALD ALLISON KELLS (1905-71)

R.A.K. Mason was born and spent most of his life in Auckland. Although some of the verse in his COLLECTED POEMS was written while he was still at school, he did not shine academically, and it was not until he was twenty-one that he enrolled as a part-time student at the university. He interrupted his study and did not graduate until he was thirty-four, but he had become a keen Latinist, an interest reflected in the manner, and some say in the very prosody, of his verse. His difficulties in getting his verse before the public illustrate the problems then faced by writers in a country that was little interested in cultural matters and was facing a growing economic depression. THE BEGGAR which he published himself did not sell, though it is now recognized as the first sign of a new and original poetic talent. NO NEW THING, a handsomely designed volume, fared little better. Only when the Caxton Press brought out THIS DARK WILL LIGHTEN did Mason's poetry become at all easy to obtain. By this time his poetic inspiration had run dry, and he was putting his efforts into leftwing journalism and Trade Union work. His holding of the Burns Fellowship at the University of Otago in 1962 coincided with the publication of his COLLECTED POEMS, but although he had plans for writing plays and a biography, nothing of this has been published.

BIBLIOGRAPHY

Traue, J.E. A PRELIMINARY CHECKLIST OF WORKS BY AND ABOUT R.A.K. MASON. 2nd rev. checklist. Wellington: 1963.

> A full finding list on which final work was temporarily suspended until Mason's papers, presented to the Hocken Library, could be checked. The list now seems likely to remain in its "preliminary" state. It was issued in only three copies. One is held at the Alexander Turnbull Library, Wellington.

COLLECTED WORKS

COLLECTED POEMS. Introd. Allen Curnow. Christchurch: Pegasus, 1962.

POETRY

THE BEGGAR. Auckland: 1924.

PENNY BROADSHEET. [Auckland: 1925].

NO NEW THING: POEMS, 1924-1929. Auckland: Spearhead Publishers, 1934.

END OF DAY. Christchurch: Caxton, 1936.

RECENT POEMS. With Allen Curnow, A.R.D. Fairburn, and Denis Glover. Christchurch: Caxton, 1941.

THIS DARK WILL LIGHTEN: SELECTED POEMS, 1923-1941. Christchurch: Caxton, 1941.

DRAMA

SQUIRE SPEAKS. Christchurch: Caxton, 1938.

A brief, highly satirical play for radio.

"To Save Democracy." TOMORROW, 27 April 1938, pp. 408-11.

Mason said this was "based on H.E. Holland's Armageddon or Calvary," which was a book attacking the treatment of New Zealand conscientious objectors during the First World War. The piece is really a political essay set out in dramatic form.

CHINA. Auckland: 1943.

"Script . . . for a dance-drama by Margaret Barr."

CHINA DANCES. Dunedin: 1962.

Reprint of CHINA, with two other pieces.

OTHER PROSE

HELP RUSSIA--OR HELP HITLER! Auckland: Aid to Russia Committee, 1941.

FRONTIER FORSAKEN: AN OUTLINE HISTORY OF THE COOK ISLANDS. Auckland: "Challenge," 1947.

Published anonymously.

REX FAIRBURN. [Dunedin]: Press Room, University of Otago, 1962.

A brief memorial tribute to A.R.D. Fairburn.

CRITICISM

Bertram, James. "Death of a Poet." NEW ZEALAND LISTENER, 2 August 1971, p. 9.

Broughton, W.S. "'Sponges Steeped in Vinegar': A Note on the 'Collected Poems' of R.A.K. Mason." EDUCATION, 12 (July 1963), 16-18.

______. "W. D'Arcy Cresswell, A.R.D. Fairburn, R.A.K. Mason: An Examination of Certain Aspects of Their Lives and Works." Thesis, University of Auckland, 1968.

Curnow, Allen. "The Poetry of R.A.K. Mason." BOOK, no. 2 (May 1941), [5-9].

Though Mason's poems lack "explicit reference to the New Zealand scene and people," says Curnow, they "could not have been written . . . by any other than a New Zealander."

Curnow, Allen, et al. "R.A.K. Mason 1905-71: Some Tributes." LANDFALL, 25 (September 1971), 222-42.

The other contributors were Jean Alison, E.M. Blaiklock, Roderick Finlayson, E.H. McCormick, Charles Brasch, James K. Baxter, Frank Sargeson, and Kevin Ireland.

Doyle, Charles. R.A.K. MASON. New York: Twayne, 1970.

The fullest discussion of Mason's verse, exploring themes and literary parallels in great detail. The effect of the poet's work as a whole however remains somewhat elusive.

Fairburn, A.R.D. "A New Zealand Poet." NEW ZEALAND ARTISTS' ANNUAL, 1, no. 4 (1929), 69.

A rather belated comment on THE BEGGAR, noting both Mason's intellectuality and his romantic pessimism.

Mason, R.A.K. "New Zealand's First Wholly Original, Unmistakably Gifted Poet." AFFAIRS, no. 5 (June 1969), 23-25.

This interview with Sam Hunt is of particular interest for Mason's discussion of his own poetry. The title comes from Allen Curnow's article of 1941 (see above).

Savage, Roger. "Review of COLLECTED POEMS." LANDFALL, 17 (September 1963), 286-90.

A substantial attack on the generally favorable view of Mason. Savage finds Mason's ideas immature, his syntax clumsy, and his diction artificially "poetical" in all but a small handful of poems.

Stead, C.K. "R.A.K. Mason's Poetry: Some Random Observations." COMMENT, 4 (July 1963), 34-39.

A sensitive, illuminating analysis. Stead anticipates and comes to grips with some of the problems in evaluating Mason's poetry which are dealt with less sympathetically by Savage (see above).

Weir, J.E. R.A.K. MASON. Wellington: Oxford University Press, [1977].

A systematic examination of the poems.

MULGAN, JOHN ALAN EDWARD (1911-45)

John Mulgan was twenty-seven when he wrote his only novel, MAN ALONE. It is a work to be ranked among the country's very best, and one which by itself earns him a secure place in his country's literary history. It is valued for its account of the New Zealand national character between the two world wars, but it is also a political novel that could only have been written by an observer of European developments in the thirties. Mulgan had joined the Oxford University Press after a brilliant scholastic career at Auckland and Oxford, but on the outbreak of war in 1939 he enlisted and served in the Mediterranean, where he was to die.

AUTOBIOGRAPHY

REPORT ON EXPERIENCE. London: Oxford University Press, 1947; 2nd ed. Auckland: Blackwood & Janet Paul, 1967.

> Incisive reflections on New Zealand and especially English society and politics in the thirties, and on the author's war experience in Egypt and with guerillas in Greece. The second edition includes a letter from the author to his wife in which he said, "It is only the draft and outline of a book I'd like to write."

POETRY

POEMS OF FREEDOM. Ed. John Mulgan. Introd. W.H. Auden. London: Gollancz, 1938.

> Mulgan said this anthology of English verse was "conceived in an effort to represent the liberalism of poetry in its oldest and widest sense."

FICTION

MAN ALONE. London: Selwyn & Blount, [1939]; rpt. Hamilton: Paul's

Book Arcade, 1949; Auckland: Longman Paul, 1970.

OTHER PROSE

THE CONCISE OXFORD DICTIONARY OF ENGLISH LITERATURE. Oxford: Clarendon, 1939.

An abridgement of Sir Paul Harvey's OXFORD COMPANION TO ENGLISH LITERATURE (Oxford: Clarendon Press, 1932).

THE EMIGRANTS: EARLY TRAVELLERS TO THE ANTIPODES. With Hector Bolitho. London: Selwyn & Blount, [1939].

Mulgan wrote the chapters on Charles Armitage Brown, the friend of Keats, and Charles Meryon, a French naval officer.

AN INTRODUCTION TO ENGLISH LITERATURE. With Dan Davin. Oxford: Clarendon, 1947.

This was based on Emile Legouis's A SHORT HISTORY OF ENGLISH LITERATURE (Trans. V.F. Boyson and J. Poulson. Oxford: Clarendon Press, 1934).

CRITICISM

Bertram, James. "John Mulgan in Perspective." COMMENT, 9 (November 1969), 10-14.

About the man, and only indirectly about his books.

Davin, Dan. "Review of REPORT ON EXPERIENCE." LANDFALL, 2 (March 1948), 50-55; rpt. as "John Mulgan" in LANDFALL COUNTRY. Ed. Charles Brasch. Christchurch: Caxton, 1962, pp. 373-78.

Day, Paul. JOHN MULGAN. New York: Twayne, 1968.

A full and knowledgeable literary and biographical study. There is an annotated bibliography.

______. JOHN MULGAN. Wellington: Oxford University Press, [1977].

In Day's second book, the emphasis is more on biography.

______. "Mulgan's MAN ALONE." COMMENT, 6 (August 1965), 15-22; rpt. in CRITICAL ESSAYS ON THE NEW ZEALAND NOVEL. Ed. Cherry Hankin. Auckland: Heinemann Educational Books, 1976, pp. 60-72.

Partridge, Colin. "The Organisation of Courage: John Mulgan's MAN ALONE." COMMONWEALTH, 2 (1976), 98-106.

Scott, Mary. "'Always a New Zealander': Tribute to John Mulgan." NEW ZEALAND LISTENER, 1 June 1945, pp. 14-15.

PEARSON, WILLIAM HARRISON (1922-)

W.H. Pearson grew up on the West Coast, which is the setting of his only novel, COAL FLAT, a work that has established its author's place in New Zealand literature. His interests have included Pacific history, sociology, and race relations. Since 1954 he has been a member of the English department at the University of Auckland.

FICTION

COAL FLAT. Auckland: Paul's Book Arcade; London: Angus & Robertson, 1963; rpt. Auckland: Longman Paul, 1970; London and Auckland: Heinemann, 1976.

COLLECTED STORIES 1935-1963. By Frank Sargeson. Ed. and introd. W.H. Pearson. Preface by E.M. Forster. Auckland: Blackwood & Janet Paul, 1964; rpt. London: MacGibbon & Kee, 1965; enl. ed. as THE STORIES OF FRANK SARGESON. Auckland: Longman Paul, 1973.

> Stories by Frank Sargeson, edited with an excellent introduction, bibliography, and glossary (not included, however in the English edition) by W.H. Pearson. The second New Zealand edition added six new stories, but omitted a short biographical passage and also the introduction and glossary.

BROWN MAN'S BURDEN AND LATER STORIES. Stories by Roderick Finlayson. Ed. and introd., glossary, and bibliog. W.H. Pearson. [Auckland]: Auckland University Press; [Wellington]: Oxford University Press, 1973.

OTHER PROSE

"Attitudes to the Maori in Some Pakeha Fiction." JOURNAL OF THE POLYNESIAN SOCIETY, 67 (September 1958), 211-38; rpt. in his FRETFUL SLEEPERS AND OTHER ESSAYS. Auckland: Heinemann Educational Books, 1974, pp. 46-71.

"The Recognition of Reality." In COMMONWEALTH LITERATURE: UNITY AND DIVERSITY IN A COMMON CULTURE. Ed. John Press. London: Heinemann Educational Books, 1965, pp. 32-47; rpt. in his FRETFUL SLEEPERS AND OTHER ESSAYS. Auckland: Heinemann Educational Books, 1974, pp. 137-50.

"Henry Lawson among Maoris." MEANJIN, 27 (Autumn 1968), 67-73.

HENRY LAWSON AMONG MAORIS. Wellington: Reed; Canberra: Australian National University Press, 1968.

"The Maori and Literature 1938-65." In THE MAORI PEOPLE IN THE NINETEEN-SIXTIES. Ed. Eric Schwimmer. Auckland: Longman Paul, 1968, pp. 217-56; rpt. in ESSAYS ON NEW ZEALAND LITERATURE. Ed. Wystan Curnow. Auckland: Heinemann Educational Books, 1973, pp. 99-138.

"H. Winston Rhodes." LANDFALL, 24 (December 1970), 388-92.

"Henry Lawson in New Zealand." In NEW ZEALAND'S HERITAGE. Ed. Ray Knox. Wellington: Paul Hamlyn, [1971-73], pp. 1649-52.

"Two Personal Memories of James K. Baxter." ISLANDS, 2 (Autumn 1973), 2-5.

The other "memory" was by Peter Olds.

FRETFUL SLEEPERS AND OTHER ESSAYS. Auckland: Heinemann Educational Books, 1974.

The title essay was first published in LANDFALL in 1952.

CRITICISM

Curnow, Allen. "COAL FLAT Revisited." In CRITICAL ESSAYS ON THE NEW ZEALAND NOVEL. Ed. Cherry Hankin. Auckland: Heinemann Educational Books, 1976, pp. 105-27.

_____. "COAL FLAT: The Major Scale, the Fine Excess." COMMENT, 5 (October 1963), 39-42.

COAL FLAT "embodies more human lives, and more of the life in the lives, than any New Zealand novel before it. It is a project in fiction on the major scale. . . ." Curnow's review article drew two extended letters by Kenneth Prebble and P.S. Ardern which were published in the following issue.

Johnston, Stuart. "Review of COAL FLAT." LANDFALL, 17 (September 1963), 298-301.

An interestingly unfavorable review.

Sargeson, Frank. "Conversation in a Train; Or, What Happened to Michael's Boots?" LANDFALL, 21 (December 1967), 352-61.

An imaginary conversation about COAL FLAT.

SARGESON, FRANK (1903-)

Frank Sargeson was born and grew up in Hamilton. He trained as a solicitor but escaped the law offices to travel to England and Europe. The attempt to find a way into the living culture of another land, however, failed; and he abandoned his attempts to write like James Joyce, realizing that "for better or worse, and for life, [he] belonged to the new world." It was another five years after his return before his first story was published, but soon, from a small Auckland bach [a small holiday house] (he has lived in the same spot ever since), came a number of short sketches written in a literary reworking of a simple, recognizably New Zealand idiom. These stories, full of a warmth for the deviancies of the human heart, gradually became more complex, while at the same time Sargeson felt ready to write at novel length, again at first in very simple language but later in novels like MEMOIRS OF A PEON and JOY OF THE WORM with an inimitable comic-macabre invention and ironic sophistication.

BIBLIOGRAPHY

Hayward, J.W. "Frank Sargeson: An Annotated Bibliography: Works and Critical Comment." Bibliographical exercise, Library School, Wellington, 1975.

Cunningham, Kevin. "Frank Sargeson's Critical and Autobiographical Writings: An Annotated Bibliography." Bibliographical exercise, Library School, Wellington, 1977.

COLLECTED WORKS

COLLECTED STORIES, 1935-1963. Introd. W.H. Pearson. Auckland: Blackwood & Janet Paul, 1964; rpt. London: MacGibbon & Kee, 1965; enl. ed. as THE STORIES OF FRANK SARGESON. Auckland: Longman Paul, 1973.

> The 1964 edition contains, in addition to the introduction, a glossary and an excellent bibliography, and also a brief preface by E.M. Forster. The 1965 edition contains only Forster's preface,

renamed "Introduction." The 1973 edition prints only the (updated) bibliography, but includes six further stories.

BIOGRAPHY

McEldowney, Dennis. FRANK SARGESON IN HIS TIME. Dunedin: McIndoe, 1976.

A fine, short, fully illustrated, literary biography.

AUTOBIOGRAPHY

ONCE IS ENOUGH: A MEMOIR. Wellington: Reed; London: Martin, Brian & O'Keeffe, 1973.

MORE THAN ENOUGH: A MEMOIR. Wellington: Reed; London: Martin, Brian & O'Keeffe, 1975.

NEVER ENOUGH!: PLACES AND PEOPLE MAINLY. Wellington: Reed; London: Martin, Brian & O'Keeffe, 1977.

FICTION

CONVERSATION WITH MY UNCLE, AND OTHER SKETCHES. Auckland: Unicorn Press, 1936.

A MAN AND HIS WIFE. Christchurch: Caxton, 1940; rev. ed. Wellington: Progressive Publishing Society, 1944.

Short stories.

WHEN THE WIND BLOWS. Christchurch: Caxton, 1945.

SPEAKING FOR OURSELVES. Ed. Frank Sargeson. Christchurch: Caxton, 1945.

A collection of short stories by New Zealanders.

THAT SUMMER, AND OTHER STORIES. London: John Lehmann, 1946.

I SAW IN MY DREAM. London: John Lehmann, 1949; rpt. ed. and introd. H. Winston Rhodes. [Auckland]: Auckland University Press; [Wellington]: Oxford University Press, 1974.

Includes, as part 1, WHEN THE WIND BLOWS.

I FOR ONE . . . Christchurch: Caxton, 1954.

First published in LANDFALL in 1952.

MEMOIRS OF A PEON. London: MacGibbon & Kee, 1965; rpt. Auckland: Heinemann, 1974.

THE HANGOVER. London: MacGibbon & Kee, 1967.

JOY OF THE WORM. London: MacGibbon & Kee, 1969.

MAN OF ENGLAND NOW; WITH, I FOR ONE . . ., AND, A GAME OF HIDE AND SEEK. Christchurch: Caxton; London: Martin, Brian & O'Keeffe, 1972.

SUNSET VILLAGE. Wellington: Reed; London: Martin, Brian & O'Keeffe, 1976.

DRAMA

WRESTLING WITH THE ANGEL: TWO PLAYS: A TIME FOR SOWING AND THE CRADLE & THE EGG. Christchurch: Caxton, 1964.

OTHER PROSE

"Sherwood Anderson." TOMORROW, 6 November 1935, pp. 14-15.

"The Feminine Tradition: A Talk about Katherine Mansfield." NEW ZEALAND LISTENER, 6 August 1948, pp. 10-12.

"A Book of Stories." LANDFALL, 8 (March 1954), 22-26.

"Shakespeare and the Kiwi." LANDFALL, 18 (March 1964), 49-54.

"Beginnings." LANDFALL, 19 (June 1965), 122-29.

Sargeson's early experiences of writing.

"Greville Texidor 1902-1964." LANDFALL, 19 (June 1965), 135-38.

"Henry Lawson: Some Notes after Re-Reading." LANDFALL, 20 (June 1966), 156-62; rpt. in TRANSITION: AN AUSTRALIAN SOCIETY OF AUTHORS ANTHOLOGY. Comp. Nancy Keesing. Sydney: Angus & Robertson, 1970, pp. 105-11; rpt. in HENRY LAWSON CRITICISM 1894-1971. Ed. Colin Roderick. Sydney: Angus & Robertson, 1972, pp. 420-26.

"An Imaginary Conversation: William Yate and Samuel Butler." LANDFALL, 20 (December 1966), 349-57.

"Conversation in a Train; Or, What Happened to Michael's Boots?" LANDFALL, 21 (December 1967), 352-61.

An imaginary dialogue on the subject of W.H. Pearson's novel COAL FLAT.

"Two Novels by Ronald Hugh Morrieson: An Appreciation." LANDFALL, 25 (June 1971), 133-37.

"Frank Sargeson on THE SWISS FAMILY ROBINSON." EDUCATION, 24, no. 3 (1975), 24.

About his childhood reading.

CRITICISM

Baigent, Lawrence. "Review of I SAW IN MY DREAM." LANDFALL, 4 (June 1950), 157-60.

Chapman, Robert. "Review of THAT SUMMER AND OTHER STORIES." LANDFALL, 1 (September 1947), 218-22.

Copland, R.A. FRANK SARGESON. Wellington: Oxford University Press, [1976].

A sensitive analysis of the fiction.

______. "Frank Sargeson: MEMOIRS OF A PEON." In CRITICAL ESSAYS ON THE NEW ZEALAND NOVEL. Ed. Cherry Hankin. Auckland: Heinemann Educational Books, 1976, pp. 128-39.

______. "The Goodly Roof: Some Comments on the Fiction of Frank Sargeson." LANDFALL, 22 (September 1968), 310-23; rpt. in ESSAYS ON NEW ZEALAND LITERATURE. Ed. Wystan Curnow. Auckland: Heinemann Educational Books, 1973, pp. 43-53.

A fine analysis of the strengths and weaknesses of Sargeson's narrative technique.

Cunningham, Kevin. "The Making of a New Zealander." ISLANDS, 2 (Summer 1973), 410-15.

A review article on ONCE IS ENOUGH--"the only adequate statement of what it means to be an artist in New Zealand."

Dudding, Robin, ed. "In Celebration, for Frank Sargeson at 75." ISLANDS, 6 (Spring 1977), 209-360.

A valuable collection of personal reminiscences about Sargeson, with comments on his work, by a wide variety of writers and friends.

Edmond, Lauris. "Frank Sargeson." EDUCATION, 25, no. 3 (1976), i-iv.

______. "The Later Stories." ISLANDS, 2 (Summer 1973), 415-23.

______. "New Zealand Writers: Frank Sargeson." AFFAIRS, October 1972, pp. 8-9.

Horsman, E.A. "The Art of Frank Sargeson." LANDFALL, 19 (June 1965), 129-34.

Written on the publication of Sargeson's COLLECTED STORIES (see p. 181). Horsman argues that it is "the enacting of a process of discovery . . . which confers value rather than the nature of what is discovered."

Insley, Marie. "Frank Sargeson: The Man and the Writer." NEW ZEALAND MAGAZINE, 29 (January-March 1950), 16-17.

Isaac, Peter. "Sargeson on Success." NEW ZEALAND BOOK WORLD, no. 28 (September 1976), 8-9.

An article based on an interview.

Johnston, C.M. "The Short Stories of Anderson, Hemingway, and Sargeson: A Comparative Analysis of Mode of Regard, Fictional World, Style, and Technique." Thesis, University of Otago, 1970.

McEldowney, Dennis. "Sargeson Again." NEW ZEALAND MONTHLY REVIEW, 6 (June 1965), 21.

New, W.H. "Enclosures: Frank Sargeson's 'I Saw in My Dream.'" WORLD LITERATURE WRITTEN IN ENGLISH, 14 (April 1975), 15-22.

Ower, J.B. "Wizard's Brew: Frank Sargeson's 'Memoirs of a Peon.'" LANDFALL, 26 (December 1972), 308-21.

This article deals with both the psychology of the protagonist and the history of his society. Ower responds to Sargeson's intellectual complexities but misses something of his narrative fun.

Rhodes, H. Winston. FRANK SARGESON. New York: Twayne, 1969.

Rhodes admirably elucidates the solutions Sargeson has found to the problems faced by a novelist in a new country and a new society without indigenous literary traditions.

______. "The Stories of Frank Sargeson." NEW ZEALAND LIBRARIES, 10 (September 1947), 166-70.

"A Sad and Savage World." TIMES LITERARY SUPPLEMENT, 17 June 1965, p. 494.

Sargeson, Frank. "Conversation with Frank Sargeson." LANDFALL, 24 (March 1970), 4-27; (June 1970), 142-60.

A long, informative, and fascinating conversation. The interviewer was Michael Beveridge.

______. "Frank Sargeson." In SPEAKING OF WRITING . . . : SEVENTEEN LEADING WRITERS OF AUSTRALIAN AND NEW ZEALAND FICTION ANSWER QUESTIONS ON THEIR CRAFT. Ed. R.D. Walshe. Sydney: Reed Education, 1975, pp. 78-81.

Brief but valuable answers to a questionnaire.

______. "Pig Islander into French." NEW ZEALAND LISTENER, 20 September 1946, pp. 16-17.

Sargeson interviewed by Jean Bertram on the publication of a French translation of THAT SUMMER.

______. "The Word Is Liberating." NEW ZEALAND LISTENER, 29 March 1975, pp. 28-29.

Sargeson interviewed by Tony Reid.

Shaw, Helen, ed. THE PURITAN AND THE WAIF: A SYMPOSIUM OF CRITICAL ESSAYS ON THE WORK OF FRANK SARGESON. Auckland: H.L. Hofmann, 1954.

The essays included in this volume are as follows:

Allen, Walter. "A note from England."
Baxter, James K. "Back to the Desert."
Cresswell, D'Arcy. "The First Wasp."
Davin, Dan. "The Narrative Technique of Frank Sargeson."
Dawson, E.P. "I Believe."
Rhodes, H. Winston. "The Moral Climate of Sargeson's Stories." Rpt. LANDFALL, 9 (March 1955), 25-41; rpt. in LANDFALL COUNTRY. Ed. Charles Brasch. Christchurch: Caxton, 1962, pp. 412-29.

Schwimmer, Eric. "A Picaresque View of Life."
Shaw, Helen. "Sargeson and Mansfield in Contrast."

Smith, Sidney O. "The World of Frank Sargeson's Novels." Thesis, University of Auckland, 1974.

Whelan, D.B. "Alienation in the Novels of Sargeson and Davin: A Study of Four Novels: I SAW IN MY DREAM; I FOR ONE; CLIFFS OF FALL; ROADS FROM HOME." Thesis, University of Canterbury, 1965.

SATCHELL, WILLIAM (1860-1942)

William Satchell arrived in North Auckland in 1886, and spent six years, before moving to Auckland, in a timber-milling district which was being opened up for farming. His experiences during those years lie behind THE LAND OF THE LOST and THE TOLL OF THE BUSH. The later historical romance, THE GREENSTONE DOOR, based on considerable research into the wars in the Waikato in the middle of the nineteenth century, has become since its reprinting in 1935 Satchell's most popular work. He is now recognized as New Zealand's earliest novelist of any standing.

POETRY

PATRIOTIC AND OTHER POEMS. Auckland: Brett Printing & Publishing Co., 1900.

FICTION

THE LAND OF THE LOST: A TALE OF THE NEW ZEALAND GUM COUNTRY. London: Methuen, 1902; rpt. Auckland: Whitcombe & Tombs; London: Methuen, 1938; as THE LAND OF THE LOST. Ed. and introd. Kendrick Smithyman. [Auckland]: Auckland University Press; [Wellington]: Oxford University Press, 1971.

THE TOLL OF THE BUSH. London: Macmillan, 1905.

THE ELIXIR OF LIFE. London: Chapman & Hall, 1907.

THE GREENSTONE DOOR. London and Toronto: Sidgwick & Jackson; New York: Macmillan, 1914; rpt. Auckland: Whitcombe & Tombs, 1935; London: Sidgwick & Jackson, 1936; London: John Spencer, 1961; Auckland: Golden Press in association with Whitcombe & Tombs, 1973.

MISCELLANEOUS

BEDLAM BALLADS AND STRAITWAISTCOAT STORIES, PART I. By Saml. Cliall White (pseud.). London: W. Satchell, 1883.

No other parts were published.

WILL O' THE WISP AND OTHER TALES IN PROSE AND VERSE. London: W. Satchell, 1883.

Published anonymously.

CRITICISM

Mulgan, Alan. "William Satchell: Story Teller of the Bush and the Gum-Fields." NEW ZEALAND MAGAZINE, 21 (January-February 1942), 3-6.

Smithyman, Kendrick. "Two Novelists of Northland." In NEW ZEALAND'S HERITAGE. Ed. Ray Knox. Wellington: Paul Hamlyn, [1971-73], pp. 1728-32.

Wilson, Phillip. "Behind the Greenstone Door." NEW ZEALAND LISTENER, 23 July 1954, p. 8.

______. THE MAORILANDER: A STUDY OF WILLIAM SATCHELL. Christchurch: Whitcombe & Tombs, 1961.

______. WILLIAM SATCHELL. New York: Twayne, [1968].

"A revision of . . . THE MAORILANDER." This extended study of Satchell and his novels, while not uncritical, tends to overestimate their absolute as compared with their local importance.

SHADBOLT, MAURICE FRANCIS RICHARD (1932-   )

Maurice Shadbolt's original intention was to become a filmmaker, but while he was in London in the late 1950s his first book of short stories was published and was well received. He has since become one of New Zealand's most popular novelists both at home and abroad (his AMONG THE CINDERS sold 150,000 copies in its first ten years), but even with the help of grants, scholarships, and commissions he has been unable to live on his writing without also continuing his freelance journalism. Fiction remains his vocation, however; he is, he has said, "a storyteller who tells stories for the love of telling them, and who uses fictions to describe truth, if that isn't too large a word."

FICTION

THE NEW ZEALANDERS: A SEQUENCE OF STORIES. [Christchurch]: Whitcombe & Tombs, [1959]; London: Gollancz, 1959; New York: Atheneum, 1961; rpt. Christchurch: Whitcombe & Tombs, 1974.

SUMMER FIRES AND WINTER COUNTRY. London: Eyre & Spottiswoode; [Christchurch]: Whitcombe & Tombs, 1963; New York: Atheneum, 1966.

Short stories.

AMONG THE CINDERS. [Christchurch]: Whitcombe & Tombs; London: Eyre & Spottiswoode; New York: Atheneum, 1965; rpt. with introd. Stephen Becker. Christchurch: Whitcoulls, 1975.

THE PRESENCE OF MUSIC: THREE NOVELLAS. London: Cassell, 1967.

THIS SUMMER'S DOLPHIN. London: Cassell; New York: Atheneum, 1969.

AN EAR OF THE DRAGON. London: Cassell, 1971.

STRANGERS AND JOURNEYS. London: Hodder & Stoughton, 1972; New York: St. Martin's Press, [1972]; rpt. London: Coronet Books, 1975.

A TOUCH OF CLAY. London: Hodder & Stoughton, 1974.

DANGER ZONE. London: Hodder & Stoughton, [1975].

OTHER PROSE

NEW ZEALAND: GIFT OF THE SEA. With photos. Brian Brake. Christchurch: Whitcombe & Tombs, 1963; Honolulu: East-West Center Press, 1964; rev. ed. Christchurch: Whitcombe & Tombs, 1973.

"Michael (Renato) Amato, 1928-64." LANDFALL, 18 (September 1964), 250-52.

"Writer Out of Hiding." NEW ZEALAND LISTENER, 21 July 1967, pp. 19-20.

Literary and cultural reflections of a personal nature set down on the publication of PRESENCE OF MUSIC.

"The Burns Fellowship." LANDFALL, 22 (September 1968), 239-41.

ISLES OF THE SOUTH PACIFIC. With Olaf Ruhen. Prepared by the Special Publications Division, National Geographic Society. 2nd ed. Washington, D.C.: National Geographic Society, 1971.

THE SHELL GUIDE TO NEW ZEALAND. Ed. Maurice Shadbolt. Christchurch: Whitcombe & Tombs, 1968; London: Michael Joseph, 1969; 3rd rev. ed. Christchurch: Whitcoulls; London: Michael Joseph, 1976.

"We've Had It Too Easy, Too Long." NEW ZEALAND LISTENER, 27 September 1971, p. 12.

A writer's view of life in New Zealand.

"Hermit of Hawera." NEW ZEALAND LISTENER, 12 February 1973, p. 9.

The "hermit" was the novelist Ronald Morrieson.

"White: Filling the Australian Void." NEW ZEALAND LISTENER, 17 November 1973, p. 11.

An article on Patrick White.

"The Making of a Book." LANDFALL, 27 (December 1973), 275-89.

A lecture given at the University of Canterbury. Although it centers on the three novellas in THE PRESENCE OF MUSIC, it is valuably informative about Shadbolt's literary beliefs and career.

"The Other Side." OVERLAND, no. 58 (Winter 1974), 44-49.

LOVE AND LEGEND: SOME 20TH CENTURY NEW ZEALANDERS. Auckland: Hodder & Stoughton, 1976.

Includes chapters on John A. Lee, Katherine Mansfield, and James K. Baxter.

CRITICISM

Amoamo, Jacqueline. "Maurice Shadbolt: The Beginning Years." NEW ZEALAND LISTENER, 7 August 1972, pp. 8-9.

An account of Shadbolt's first forty years of life, based on an interview.

Arvidson, K.O. "Letter to the Editor." LANDFALL, 25 (December 1971), 469-73.

In this letter, Arvidson explained why he could not review AN EAR OF THE DRAGON, and in so doing reviewed the novel most interestingly.

Copland, R.A. "Review of THE NEW ZEALANDERS." LANDFALL, 14 (March 1960), 87-89.

Hamilton, Ian. "The Amazing Mr Shadbolt." MATE, no. 4 (February 1960), 44-48.

An abrasive attack on both the narrative and the prose style of the stories in THE NEW ZEALANDERS.

Isaac, Peter. "The Great New Zealand Pastime--Knocking." NEW ZEALAND BOOK WORLD, no. 29 (October 1976), 17-18.

Jones, Lawrence. "Ambition and Accomplishment in Maurice Shadbolt's STRANGERS AND JOURNEYS." In CRITICAL ESSAYS ON THE NEW ZEALAND NOVEL. Ed. Cherry Hankin. Auckland: Heinemann Educational Books, 1976, pp. 140-68.

Pearson, W.H. "In the Shadbolt Country." COMMENT, 1 (Autumn 1960), 26-28.

An extended review of THE NEW ZEALANDERS.

Reid, Tony. "Shadbolt Alone." NEW ZEALAND LISTENER, 29 January 1977, p. 24.

Shadbolt, Maurice. "Author Shadbolt's Long Journey." NEW ZEALAND BOOK WORLD, no. 1 (June 1973), 11-12.

Shadbolt talks to Michael King about STRANGERS AND JOURNEYS.

______. "Maurice Shadbolt: Writer." AFFAIRS, February 1971, pp. 18-21.

Shadbolt interviewed by Alister Taylor.

Simpson, Peter. "Shadbolt's First Novel: A Reassessment." LANDFALL, 31 (June 1977), 186-91.

Volkerling, Michael. "Clearing the Ground." ISLANDS, 2 (Spring 1973), 319-25.

A review of STRANGERS AND JOURNEYS.

STEAD, CHRISTIAN KARLSON (1932-)

C.K. Stead is an Auckland poet who is now professor of English at Auckland University. He is probably best known for his one novel, SMITH'S DREAM which is a political thriller, but besides his poetry he has written some good short stories and a number of excellent studies of New Zealand poets. He is not himself a copious writer. His poems come slowly and are thoroughly worked on before publication. He has held a number of awards and fellowships.

POETRY

WHETHER THE WILL IS FREE: POEMS 1954-62. Auckland: Paul's Book Arcade, 1964.

CROSSING THE BAR. [Auckland]: Auckland University Press; [Wellington]: Oxford University Press, 1972.

QUESADA: POEMS, 1972-74. Auckland: The Shed, 1975.

FICTION

NEW ZEALAND SHORT STORIES: SECOND SERIES. Ed. C.K. Stead. London: Oxford University Press, 1966; rpt. Wellington: Oxford University Press, 1976.

SMITH'S DREAM. Auckland: Longman Paul, 1971; rev. ed., 1973.

> In the revised edition, the last few pages are rewritten to give the novel a different ending.

OTHER PROSE

"The Hulk of the World's Between." In DISTANCE LOOKS OUR WAY: THE

EFFECTS OF REMOTENESS ON NEW ZEALAND. Ed. Keith Sinclair. [Auckland]: Paul's Book Arcade for the University of Auckland, 1961, pp. 79-96.

"Allen Curnow's Poetry." LANDFALL, 17 (March 1963), 26-45; rpt. in ESSAYS ON NEW ZEALAND LITERATURE. Ed. Wystan Curnow. Auckland: Heinemann Educational Books, 1973, pp. 54-70.

"R.A.K. Mason's Poetry: Some Random Observations." COMMENT, 4 (July 1963), 34-39.

THE NEW POETIC. London: Hutchinson University Library, 1964. New York: Harper & Row, [1966]; rpt. as THE NEW POETIC: YEATS TO ELIOT. Harmondsworth, Middlesex: Penguin Books, 1967.

"Fairburn." LANDFALL, 20 (December 1966), 371-81.

"Foreword." NEW ZEALAND ARTS FESTIVAL YEARBOOK, 1968, pp. 7-8.

An autobiographical note on the verse Stead wrote when he was a student.

SHAKESPEARE: MEASURE FOR MEASURE: A CASEBOOK. Ed. C.K. Stead. London: Macmillan, 1971.

Critical essays.

"Towards Jerusalem: The Later Poetry of James K. Baxter." ISLANDS, 2 (Autumn 1973), 7-18.

"A Poet's View." ISLANDS, 3 (Spring 1974), 314-25.

THE LETTERS AND JOURNALS OF KATHERINE MANSFIELD: A SELECTION. Ed. C.K. Stead. London: Allen Lane, 1977.

CRITICISM

Bertram, James. "Curbed Romantic." ISLANDS, 1 (Summer 1972), 169-70.

A review of CROSSING THE BAR.

Horsman, E.A. "Review of WHETHER THE WILL IS FREE." LANDFALL, 18 (September 1964), 273-77.

Middleton, O.E. "Writing and Belonging: A Note on C.K. Stead's 'For the Hulk of the World's Between' in the Volume 'Distance Looks Our Way.'" REVIEW (Dunedin), 1971, pp. 45-51.

Robertson, R.T. "The Nightmare of Kiwi Joe: C.K. Stead's Double Novel." ARIEL, 6 (April 1975), 97-110.

Stead, C.K. "Stead: No Stainless Steel Poet." NEW ARGOT, 2 (May 1974), 14-15.

An interview with Stephen Chan.

TUWHARE, HONE (1922-)

Hone Tuwhare was born in North Auckland into a Maori-speaking family, but grew up speaking only English. He has lived most of his life in Auckland, a boilermaker by trade and an active official in trade-union affairs and in Maori social and political organizations. His discovery of his poetic ability was delayed until his mid-thirties, when he was attracted by poets like Neruda, Aragon, Lorca, and R.A.K. Mason. He was one of the best-known poets of the sixties and is certainly the most popular Maori poet writing in English. Although in the later sixties he began to relearn Maori, he has made use of few Maori elements in his verse: he writes, with his own individual voice, in New Zealand's European tradition.

POETRY

NO ORDINARY SUN: POEMS. Foreword by R.A.K. Mason. Auckland: Blackwood & Janet Paul, 1964; rpt. Auckland: Longman Paul, 1969; 3rd ed., rev. and enl. Dunedin: McIndoe, 1977.

COME RAIN HAIL: POEMS. [Dunedin]: Bibliography Room, University of Otago, 1970; rpt. Dunedin: Caveman Press, 1973.

SAP-WOOD & MILK. Dunedin: Caveman Press, [1972].

SOMETHING NOTHING: POEMS. Dunedin: Caveman Press, [1974].

CRITICISM

Crisp, Peter. "Hone Tuwhare: An Appreciation." MULTICULTURAL SCHOOL, no. 4 (1976-77), 32-36.

Elliott, Molly G. "Hone Tuwhare--Poet: A Truly New Zealand Voice." ARTS AND COMMUNITY, 5 (June 1969), 1.

Jackson, MacDonald P. "Review of NO ORDINARY SUN." LANDFALL, 19 (June 1965), 189-93.

Tamplin, Ron. "The Poetry of Hone Tuwhare." NEW QUARTERLY CAVE, 1 (October 1976), 4-12.

Tuwhare, Hone. "Being Purely and Solely Alone, a Bloody Solitary and Pure Artist--That's Crap." NEW ARGOT, 3 (May 1975), 2.

Tuwhare interviewed by Taura Eruera.

______. "Conversation: Taura Speaks with Hone Tuwhare." KORU, 1 (1976), unpaged.

______. "Hone Tuwhare." AFFAIRS, August 1970, pp. 322-25.

Tuwhare interviewed by Jan Coad.

Chapter 5
OTHER AUTHORS

This section, although it is largely devoted to writers who are usually considered of less importance than those of the previous chapter, does also include some who are of greater significance on the strength of one important book only, as well as a number of younger authors who are still establishing their place in the country's literature.

Entries are arranged alphabetically by author's name. As a rule, full details of only one work are given in each entry, but the annotation indicates the range and extent of each author's output and also notes any important secondary material.

Adams, Arthur Henry (1872-1936). THE COLLECTED VERSES OF ARTHUR H. ADAMS. Melbourne: Whitcombe & Tombs, [1913].

> Arthur Adams, while still a young man, left New Zealand for Australia, where the greater part of his literary output was written. This included some fiction and drama, as well as poetry.

Alley, Rewi (1897-). GUNG HO: POEMS. Chosen and ed. H. Winston Rhodes. Christchurch: Caxton, 1948.

> This was the first of numerous volumes of prose and verse giving expression to the author's experiences in China. Most were published in New Zealand. There is a bibliography by A.P.U. Millett ("Rewi Alley: A Preliminary Checklist of Published Books and Pamphlets." In REWI ALLEY SEVENTY FIVE. Secretariat of the National Committee for the Commemoration of Rewi Alley's Seventy Fifth Birthday, [Hamilton, 1972], pp. 17-21); and a biography by W.T.G. Airey (A LEARNER IN CHINA: A LIFE OF REWI ALLEY. Christchurch: Caxton and the Monthly Review Society, 1970). An interview with David Gunby appeared in LANDFALL, 26 (March 1972), 62-86.

Amato, Renato (1928-64). THE FULL CIRCLE OF THE TRAVELLING CUCKOO: STORIES. With a memoir of the author by Maurice Shadbolt. Christchurch: Whitcombe & Tombs, 1967.

Amato was an adolescent in Italy during the Second World War and lived only the last ten years of his life in New Zealand. It was during this time that he wrote these stories.

Anthony, Frank Sheldon (1891-1927). ME AND GUS. Hawera: Hawera Star Publishing Co., 1938; rpt. with his novel GUS TOMLINS as GUS TOMLINS; TOGETHER WITH THE ORIGINAL STORIES OF "ME AND GUS." Ed. and introd. Terry Sturm. [Auckland]: Auckland University Press; [Wellington]: Oxford University Press, 1977.

Frank Anthony's wry, comic stories of a returned dairy-farming soldier became very popular in the 1950s when they were republished in versions adapted by Francis Jackson.

Arvidson, Kenneth Owen John (1938-). RIDING THE PENDULUM: POEMS 1961-69. Wellington: Oxford University Press, 1973.

K.O. Arvidson's only volume of poems.

Ballantyne, David Watt (1924-). THE CUNNINGHAMS. New York: Vanguard, [1948]; rpt. Christchurch: Whitcoulls, 1976.

A novel of family life in a provincial town. David Ballantyne has published other novels as well as a volume of short stories.

Barr, John (1809-89). POEMS AND SONGS DESCRIPTIVE AND SATIRICAL. Edinburgh: John Greig, 1861.

John Barr, writing in the tradition of Burns, recorded in verse the early life of the Scottish settlement of Dunedin.

Baughan, Blanche Edith (1870-1958). SHINGLE-SHORT AND OTHER VERSES. Christchurch: Whitcombe & Tombs, [1908].

Blanche Baughan published several other volumes of verse, and one collection of short stories. Peter Alcock has written of her work in "A True Colonial Voice: Blanche Edith Baughan," LANDFALL, 26 (June 1972), 162-76.

Baysting, Arthur Norman (1947-). OVER THE HORIZON. Auckland: Hurricane House, [1972].

Arthur Baysting, a poet, has also edited THE YOUNG NEW ZEALAND POETS (Auckland: Heinemann Educational Books, 1973).

Billing, Graham John (1936-). FORBUSH AND THE PENGUINS. Wellington: Reed; London: Hodder & Stoughton, 1965.

None of Graham Billing's three later novels has had the success of this story of a man alone in an Antarctic hut.

Bland, Peter Gordon (1934-   ). MY SIDE OF THE STORY: POEMS 1960-1964. Auckland: Mate Books, 1964.

Peter Bland, a British immigrant who has since returned to England, published while living in New Zealand several volumes of poems and also a few plays.

Brathwaite, Errol Freeman (1924-   ). THE FLYING FISH. London and Auckland: Collins, 1964.

The first of a trilogy of novels set during the Taranaki wars of the 1860s. Errol Brathwaite has also written several other novels.

Brunton, Alan (1946-   ). MESSENGERS IN BLACKFACE. London: Amphedesma Press, 1973.

Poet.

Caselberg, John (1927-   ). CHART TO MY COUNTRY: SELECTED PROSE 1947-1971. Dunedin: McIndoe, 1973.

A collection of travel notes, art criticism, and stories. John Caselberg has also published poems.

Challis, Cecil Gordon (1932-   ). BUILDING: POEMS. Christchurch: Caxton, 1963.

Gordon Challis's only volume.

Chamier, George (1842-1915). A SOUTH-SEA SIREN: A NOVEL DESCRIPTIVE OF NEW ZEALAND LIFE IN THE EARLY DAYS. London: Fisher Unwin, 1895.

Chamier wrote two novels. In character they lie near Thomas Love Peacock's and Aldous Huxley's. A SOUTH-SEA SIREN was republished with an introduction by Joan Stevens in 1970 ([Auckland]: Auckland University Press; [Wellington]: Oxford University Press).

Cole, John Reece (1916-   ). IT WAS SO LATE AND OTHER STORIES. Christchurch: Caxton, 1949.

John Reece Cole's only volume of fiction.

Cowley, Cassia Joy (Summers) (1936-   ). OF MEN AND ANGELS. New York: Doubleday, 1972; London: Hodder & Stoughton, 1973.

Joy Cowley is the author of several novels. She writes particularly of women in a modern urban environment. She also writes stories for children.

Cross, Ian Robert (1925-   ). THE GOD BOY. New York: Harcourt, Brace, [1957]; London: Deutsch, 1958; rpt. Christchurch: Whitcombe & Tombs, 1972.

Ian Cross's two following novels did not win the popular success of this work. See Patrick Evans, "The Provincial Dilemma: 1, After THE GOD BOY," LANDFALL, 30 (March 1976), 25-36.

Crump, Barry John (1935-). A GOOD KEEN MAN. Wellington: Reed, 1960.

Barry Crump writes in this and his later books heightened yarns about deer-culling [the systematic shooting of deer by government employees] and other outdoor activities.

Domett, Alfred (1811-87). RANOLF AND AMOHIA: A SOUTH-SEA DAY-DREAM. London: Smith, Elder, 1872.

A second edition with fuller notes and some Maori texts appeared in 1883. This long narrative and reflective poem has not maintained its early success. Domett published several other volumes of verse. See Dennis McEldowney, "The Unbridled Bridal Pair: 'Ranolf and Amohia,'" LANDFALL, 22 (December 1968), 374-83.

Dowling, Basil Cairns (1910-). A DAY'S JOURNEY: POEMS. Christchurch: Caxton, 1941.

The first of a number of volumes of quiet verse by Basil Dowling.

Doyle, Charles Desmond (1928-). A SPLINTER OF GLASS: POEMS 1951-55. Christchurch: Pegasus, 1956.

Other volumes of verse followed. Charles Doyle came to New Zealand in 1951, and now lives in Canada. He has written works of literary criticism, and edited RECENT POETRY IN NEW ZEALAND (Auckland: Collins, 1965).

Duckworth, Marilyn Rose (Adcock) (1935-). A BARBAROUS TONGUE. London: Hutchinson, 1963.

Marilyn Duckworth's fiction is generally set in London; this, one of her better novels, has a New Zealand setting.

Edmond, Murray Donald (1949-). ENTERING THE EYE. Dunedin: Caveman Press, 1973.

Murray Edmond's first volume of poems.

Escott, Cicely Margaret (1908-77). SHOW DOWN. London: Chatto & Windus, 1936. As I TOLD MY LOVE. New York: Norton, [1936].

Two earlier novels by Margaret Escott were set in England. SHOW DOWN was reprinted with an introduction by Robert Goodman in 1973 ([Auckland]: Auckland University Press; [Wellington]: Oxford University Press). See Dennis McEldowney, "Margaret Escott 1908-1977," ISLANDS, 6 (Winter 1977), 124-26.

France, Helena Ruth (1913-68). THE RACE. London: Constable, 1958.

Ruth France published one other novel, and, under the pseudonym of Paul Henderson, two volumes of verse.

Gaskell, A.P., pseud. Alexander Gaskell Pickard (1913-). THE BIG GAME AND OTHER STORIES. Christchurch: Caxton, 1947.

The author's only volume.

Gilbert, Florence Ruth (1917-). LAZARUS AND OTHER POEMS. Wellington: Reed, 1949.

The first of three volumes of verse by Ruth Gilbert.

Grossmann, Edith Howitt (Searle) (1863-1931). THE HEART OF THE BUSH. London: Sands, [1910].

The last and best-known of Edith Grossmann's novels. Most of them reflect her passionate concern for the position of women in her society.

Haley, Harry Russell (1934-). THE WALLED GARDEN. Auckland: Mandrake Root, 1972.

Haley's first volume of poems.

Hall, Roger Leighton (1939-). GLIDE TIME. Wellington: Price Milburn for Victoria University Press, 1977.

The most successful New Zealand play to date.

Hart-Smith, William (1911-). CHRISTOPHER COLUMBUS: A SEQUENCE OF POEMS. Christchurch: Caxton, 1948.

An English immigrant, W. Hart-Smith has lived and published verse in both New Zealand and Australia.

Hervey, John Russell (1889-1958). SELECTED POEMS. Christchurch: Caxton, 1940.

J.R. Harvey published three further volumes of poems.

Hilliard, Noel Harvey (1929-). MAORI GIRL. London: Heinemann, 1960.

Noel Hilliard has published several further novels. His SELECTED STORIES appeared in 1977 (Dunedin: McIndoe). His theme is often that of race relations--the place of the Maori in the European society of New Zealand. See Jeffrey Downs, "Noel Hilliard: A Preliminary Bibliography" (Bibliographical exercise, Library School, Wellington, 1976); and Lawrence Jones, "The Persistence of Realism:

Dan Davin, Noel Hilliard and Recent New Zealand Short Stories," ISLANDS, 6 (Winter 1977), 182-200.

Hodge, Horace Emerton (1903-58). THE WIND AND THE RAIN: A PLAY IN THREE ACTS. London: Gollancz, 1934.

Merton Hodge went to Britain as a medical student and during the thirties had several plays successfully produced (and published) in London. There was at that time no chance of successful professional production in New Zealand. See John Reece Cole, "Merton Hodge, Playwright" in NEW ZEALAND'S HERITAGE (Ed. Ray Knox. Wellington: Paul Hamlyn, [1971-73], pp. 2387-92).

Hunt, Sam (1946-). FROM BOTTLE CREEK. Wellington: Alister Taylor, 1972.

Sam Hunt has been a prolific writer of straightforward lyric poems, and is well known for his public readings of them. See Jill McCracken, "Sam Hunt--Ten Years After," LANDFALL, 27 (September 1973), 221-32, an article which includes extensive comment by Hunt himself.

Ihimaera, Witi Tame (1944-). POUNAMU POUNAMU. Auckland: Heinemann, [1972].

This collection of stories as well as two later novels by Witi Ihimaera, draw on his experience of rural Maori life.

Ireland, Kevin (1933-). FACE TO FACE: TWENTY-FOUR POEMS. Christchurch: Pegasus, 1963.

Kevin Ireland has written three further volumes of wry, deceptively simple poems. He has also published translations of Bulgarian poetry.

Johnson, Louis Albert (1924-). BREAD AND A PENSION: SELECTED POEMS. Christchurch: Pegasus, 1964.

Louis Johnson, author of several volumes of verse, became well known as the most outspoken of those who in the fifties rebelled against what they conceived to be Allen Curnow's provincial doctrines in poetry. In the best of his own verse, this "poet of subtopia," as he has called himself, manages to avoid doctrinaire thinking of his own. Johnson was also important as the editor of NEW ZEALAND POETRY YEARBOOK (see p. 49), and of the periodical NUMBERS (see p. 219).

Joseph, Michael Kennedy (1914-). I'LL SOLDIER NO MORE. London: Gollancz; [Hamilton]: Paul's Book Arcade, 1958.

Poet, literary critic, biographer, novelist, and writer of science fiction--M.K. Joseph brings a distinctive elegance of style to every form. I'LL SOLDIER NO MORE is a quiet novel of experiences behind the lines in the Second World War.

Leeming, Owen (1930-). VENUS IS SETTING: POEMS. Christchurch: Caxton, 1972.

Leeming, best known as a poet, has also written plays for radio and television.

Lord, Robert Needham (1945-). "Meeting Place." ACT, no. 18 (December 1972), 15-29.

During the 1970s, Robert Lord has written and produced a number of short and full-length plays.

Mackay, Jessie (1864-1938). THE SPIRIT OF THE RANGATIRA AND OTHER BALLADS. Melbourne: George Robertson, 1889.

The first of several volumes of verse. Jessie Mackay used a late Victorian verse style to give expression to her country's aspiring nationhood. She also attempted to set down Maori myth in English verse, and wrote a number of poems in Scottish dialect.

McNeish, James Henry Peter (1931-). MACKENZIE. London: Hodder & Stoughton, 1970.

James McNeish's most successful novel.

Manhire, William (1946-). HOW TO TAKE OFF YOUR CLOTHES AT THE PICNIC: POEMS. Wellington: Wai-te-ata Press, 1977.

Bill Manhire is one of the best of the younger poets.

Marsh, Ngaio (1899-). DIED IN THE WOOL. London: Collins for the Crime Club, [1944].

Ngaio Marsh is in one sense New Zealand's most popular writer, but her fiction has very little connection with this country. DIED IN THE WOOL is one of the few of her detective stories to be set in New Zealand. She is also known in New Zealand as a theatre enthusiast and an excellent Shakespearean producer. PLAY PRODUCTION (Wellington: School Publications Branch, Dept. of Education, 1960) is an example of her writing in this field. She has also written BLACK BEECH AND HONEYDEW: AN AUTOBIOGRAPHY (Boston: Little, Brown, [1965]; London: Collins, 1966).

Middleton, Osman Edward Gordon (1925-). SELECTED STORIES. Dunedin: McIndoe, [1975].

O.E. Middleton has published several volumes of short stories.

His autobiographical sketch "Beginnings" appeared in LANDFALL, 21 (March 1967), 53-59. See Jim Williamson, "O.E. Middleton: Not Just a Realist," ISLANDS, 2 (Winter 1973), 172-83.

Mitchell, David Ross (1940-). PIPE DREAMS IN PONSONBY: POEMS. Auckland: Stephen Chan for the Association of Orientally Flavoured Syndics, 1972; rpt. Dunedin: Caveman Press, 1975.

David Mitchell writes verse of an exceptionally lyrical quality.

Morrieson, James Ronald Hugh (1922-72). THE SCARECROW. Sydney: Angus & Robertson, 1963; rpt. Auckland: Heinemann, 1976.

The first and the best of Ronald Hugh Morrieson's several comic-macabre tales of life in country towns. See Frank Sargeson, "Two Novels by Ronald Hugh Morrieson: An Appreciation," LANDFALL, 25 (June 1971), 133-37, and C.K. Stead, "Ronald Hugh Morrieson and the Art of Fiction," LANDFALL, 25 (June 1971), 137-45.

Mulgan, Alan Edward (1881-1962). SPUR OF MORNING. London: Dent, 1934.

Alan Mulgan, a man very conscious of his country's English heritage, was a literary journalist who wrote a wide variety of books. SPUR OF MORNING is a novel set in Auckland in the years after the turn of the century.

Musaphia, Joseph (1935-). MOTHERS AND FATHERS. Sydney: Currency Press; Wellington: Price Milburn, 1977.

The best of Joseph Musaphia's plays for the stage.

Olds, Peter (1944-). LADY MOSS REVIVED: POEMS. Dunedin: Caveman Press, [1972].

Peter Olds has produced several volumes of poems.

O'Sullivan, Vincent Gerard (1937-). REVENANTS. Wellington: Prometheus Books, 1969.

Vincent O'Sullivan is the author of several volumes of poems and is also an important literary critic. He edited AN ANTHOLOGY OF TWENTIETH CENTURY NEW ZEALAND POETRY (2nd ed. Wellington: Oxford University Press, 1976).

Rawlinson, Gloria Jasmine (1918-). OF CLOUDS AND PEBBLES: POEMS. Auckland: Paul's Book Arcade, 1963.

Gloria Rawlinson also published some volumes of verse in the 1930s.

Reeves, William Pember (1857-1932). THE PASSING OF THE FOREST AND OTHER VERSE. London: By the author, 1925.

W.P. Reeves, best remembered as an historian and as a notable minister of labour, published three volumes of verse before the turn of the century. THE PASSING OF THE FOREST reprints his best-known poems.

Roddick, Alan Melven (1937-). THE EYE CORRECTS: POEMS 1955-1965. Auckland: Blackwood & Janet Paul, 1967.

Alan Roddick's only volume.

Scanlan, Nelle Margaret (1882-1968). PENCARROW. London: Jarrolds, 1932.

The first of a series of four novels. Scanlan also wrote many other popular works of light romantic fiction.

Scott, Mary Edith (Clarke) (1888-). ONE OF THE FAMILY. Hamilton: Paul's Book Arcade; Sydney: Angus & Robertson, 1958.

Mary Scott's many light love stories gain from her amused and observant descriptions of farming life.

Shaw, Helen Lilian (Mrs. Hofmann) (1913-). THE ORANGETREE: STORIES. Auckland: Pelorus Press, 1957.

Helen Shaw's only volume of stories. She has also published three small volumes of verse.

Sinclair, Keith (1922-). STRANGERS OR BEASTS: POEMS. Christchurch: Caxton, 1954.

Keith Sinclair, who has published several volumes of verse, is best known as a historian.

Smithyman, William Kendrick (1922-). THE SEAL IN THE DOLPHIN POOL. [Auckland]: Auckland University Press; [Wellington]: Oxford University Press, [1974].

This is the most recent of a number of volumes of compact, close-textured poems. Kendrick Smithyman has also written A WAY OF SAYING: A STUDY OF NEW ZEALAND POETRY (Auckland: Collins, 1965).

Spear, Charles (1910-). TWOPENCE COLOURED: POEMS. Christchurch: Caxton, 1951.

Carefully wrought verse, Parnassian but not solemn. The author's only published poems.

Stewart, Douglas Alexander (1913-). COLLECTED POEMS 1936-1967. Sydney: Angus & Robertson, 1967.

Douglas Stewart has a higher reputation as a poet in Australia, where he has lived and published for some time, than in New Zealand, where he first began writing verse. He has also published plays, including a comedy in verse on a Maori theme.

Vogt, Herlof Anton Herlofsen (1914-). ANTI ALL THAT. Christchurch: Caxton, 1940.

The first of Anton Vogt's several volumes of verse.

Wall, Arnold (1869-1966). BLANK VERSE LYRICS AND OTHER POEMS. London: David Nutt, 1900.

Arnold Wall, best known in New Zealand as an authority on English usage, published volumes of verse throughout his long life. His autobiography is called LONG AND HAPPY (Wellington: Reed, 1965).

Wedde, Ian Curtis (1946-). EARTHLY: SONNETS FOR CARLOS. Akaroa: Amphedesma Press, 1975.

Ian Wedde is one of the best of the younger poets. See Peter Crisp, "Ian Wedde's Poetry: 1971-5," ISLANDS, 5 (Spring 1976), 293-302.

Weir, John Edward (1935-). THE SUDDEN SUN: FIFTY-TWO POEMS. Christchurch: Pegasus, 1963.

The first of J.E. Weir's three volumes of verse.

Wilson, Guthrie Edward Melville (1914-). BRAVE COMPANY. London: Robert Hale, 1951.

This was the first of six novels by Guthrie Wilson, set variously in wartime Italy, Sydney, Australia, and New Zealand.

Wilson, Patrick Seymour (1926-). THE BRIGHT SEA. Christchurch: Pegasus, 1951.

Pat Wilson's main volume of verse.

Wilson, Phillip John (1922-). SOME ARE LUCKY. Wellington: Denis Glover, 1960.

As well as this volume of short stories, Phillip Wilson has published several novels.

Witheford, Hubert (1921-). A NATIVE, PERHAPS BEAUTIFUL. Christchurch: Caxton, 1967.

The last of several volumes of poems.

Wright, David McKee (1869-1928). THE STATION BALLADS AND OTHER VERSES OF DAVID MCKEE WRIGHT. Ed. and introd. Robert Solway. Auckland: John A. Lee, 1945.

David McKee Wright, who published several volumes of poems about the turn of the century, is regarded as the best of the back-country ballad poets. He lived in New Zealand from 1887 to 1910, when he left to pursue a career in literary journalism in Australia.

Chapter 6
PERIODICALS

Only the more important literary magazines are included in this chapter. For a full and well-annotated bibliography which includes minor and short-lived periodicals and other general magazines of only marginal relevance to literature, the reader should consult Iris M. Park, NEW ZEALAND PERIODICALS OF LITERARY INTEREST (Wellington: National Library Service, 1962). Note that some annual publications of the poetry yearbook type have been treated as anthologies and are to be found listed in chapter 3 (see p. 43).

The periodicals below are arranged chronologically. The publisher named is the one given either at the date publication ceased or, in the case of current periodicals, in the year 1977. Editors are identified whenever they are especially associated with the periodical concerned. Articles about individual periodicals, and indexes to them, are detailed in the annotations. For general studies, the reader should turn to chapter 2 (see p. 15) and for subject indexes to chapter 1 (see p. 1).

OTAGO UNIVERSITY REVIEW. Dunedin: Otago University Students' Association, August 1888- . Annual.

> This was issued first as a monthly during the academic session (five numbers per year) and then for a short period semiannually. From the 1920s on it has appeared as an annual. Like all the university magazines it began as a review of university affairs, and though space was occasionally given to literary work it was not until the 1950s that it became predominantly--and then entirely--a literary magazine. The title varied to TWELVEMONTH from 1948 to 1950 and became REVIEW from 1961 on.

THE TRIAD: A MONTHLY MAGAZINE OF MUSIC, SCIENCE & ART. Ed. C.N. Baeyertz to 1925. Sydney: Triad Publishing Co., 1893-1927.

> The publishing history is complicated. During its early and most famous years the magazine was published in Dunedin by Baeyertz himself. The publisher is later variously named and the magazine was published in Wellington and finally, from October 1915, in

Sydney. The New Zealand volume numbering continued concurrently with the new Australian volume numbers until 1926. The subtitle varies.

Baeyertz was a cosmopolitan and his magazine was never restricted to the arts in New Zealand. He was best qualified in music, so literature received less emphasis until an assistant editor, Frank Morton, was appointed. The magazine faltered when Baeyertz left. It revived as the NEW TRIAD for two further years but ceased publishing in 1929. The TRIAD was an extraordinarily lively and well-informed magazine of the arts which succeeded in combining a wide range of intellectual and artistic interests with considerable popular appeal. There was nothing to begin to rival its achievement until the 1940s.

See M.H. Holcroft, "Baeyertz of the Triad," in NEW ZEALAND'S HERITAGE, ed. Ray Knox (Wellington: Paul Hamlyn, [1971-73]), pp. 1924-28; Pat Lawlor, "In the Days of 'The Triad': The Passing of C.N. Baeyertz," NEW ZEALAND MAGAZINE, 22 (September-October 1943), 12-15, and (November-December 1943), 12; and K.K. Ruthven, "Ezra Pound, Alice Kenny & the 'Triad,'" LANDFALL, 23 (March 1969), 73-84.

CANTERBURY UNIVERSITY COLLEGE REVIEW. Christchurch: Canterbury University Students' Association, 1897-1948. Semiannual to 1929, annual from 1930.

Annual issues were unnumbered after 1939 and the magazine was suspended in 1941, 1943, and 1945. Literary work and essays on current affairs began to appear more regularly in the 1930s.

THE NEW ZEALAND ILLUSTRATED MAGAZINE. Auckland: New Zealand Illustrated Magazine Co., 1899-1905. Monthly.

This general magazine included one or more short stories in nearly every issue. The editor for most of the magazine's life was Thomas Cottle. A typescript copy of "NEW ZEALAND ILLUSTRATED MAGAZINE, Vols 1-12 (October 1899-September 1905): Index," compiled by G.C. Heron in 1943, is held in the Alexander Turnbull Library.

SPIKE: VICTORIA COLLEGE REVIEW. Wellington: Victoria University Students' Association, 1902-49, 1954-61. Annual.

The subtitle became VICTORIA UNIVERSITY COLLEGE REVIEW. Unnumbered volumes were issued in 1954, 1957, and 1961. Like the other university reviews, SPIKE gradually increased its literary content, becoming in the 1940s almost entirely devoted to comment and the arts.

KIWI: THE MAGAZINE OF THE AUCKLAND UNIVERSITY COLLEGE. Auckland: Auckland University Students' Association, 1905-48, 1949-66. Irregular.

The subtitle varied. Volumes were unnumbered and irregular after 1949. From its beginnings, KIWI was a little more open to literary contributions than the other university reviews, and it became almost exclusively a magazine of comment and the arts in the later 1930s.

SCHOOL JOURNAL. Wellington: Dept. of Education, 1907-- . Irregular.

Volumes 13-43 were issued as NEW ZEALAND SCHOOL JOURNAL. The SCHOOL JOURNAL was published in three parts, graded according to pupils' ability, until 1945, and thereafter in four parts. It was issued monthly during the school year till the mid-1950s; parts one and two then appeared six times and parts three and four, four times a year. Volume numbering ceased in 1963.

In the JOURNAL's early years, the stress fell on informative articles rather than on imaginative literature, but from the 1940s on, fiction by New Zealand authors was more regularly included to encourage children to recognize their independent nationhood. Many of the country's most notable writers, including poets, have written expressly for the SCHOOL JOURNAL. Separate indexes for each part have been issued from time to time.

See Alistair Campbell, "School Publications: The Journal, Parts 3 and 4," EDUCATION, 6 (February 1957), 60-62; Julie Dalzell, "Reading Matters," DESIGNSCAPE, no. 87 (December 1976-January 1977), 9-14; P.R. Earle, "The School Journal," EDUCATION, 20, no. 10 (1971), 24-28; P.M. Hattaway, "The School Journal," NATIONAL EDUCATION, 36 (April 1954), 86-88; D.R. Jenkins, SOCIAL ATTITUDES IN THE NEW ZEALAND SCHOOL JOURNAL ([Wellington]: New Zealand Council for Educational Research, 1939); E.P. Malone, "The New Zealand School Journal and the Imperial Ideology," NEW ZEALAND JOURNAL OF HISTORY, 7 (April 1973), 12-27; "School Publications," DESIGNSCAPE, no. 25 (May 1971), [4 p.]; and K.G. Smythe, "'Cautiously Critical'--Considerations Following an Investigation of the School Journal, Part IV, 1954-1970," EDUCATION, 23, no. 3 (1974), 27-29.

NEW ZEALAND MAGAZINE. Ed. Maurice Hurst. Wellington: New Zealand Magazine Co., 1921-52.

The magazine appeared under a succession of titles in the 1920s, becoming the NEW ZEALAND MAGAZINE in 1930. There were several different publishers. Periodicity varied but there were six issues per year throughout most of its life. Although it was a general magazine, notes and articles on literary matters were frequent, and each issue generally carried a short story.

NEW ZEALAND ARTISTS' ANNUAL. Ed. Pat Lawlor. Wellington: P.A. Lawlor, 1926-32.

A literary and artistic magazine of a generally light character.

ART IN NEW ZEALAND: A QUARTERLY MAGAZINE DEVOTED TO ART IN ITS VARIOUS PHASES IN OUR OWN COUNTRY. Ed. Harry H. Tombs. Wellington: Harry H. Tombs, 1928-46.

The subtitle varied slightly in later volumes. Volume 17 (1945-46) was renamed THE ARTS IN NEW ZEALAND and issued semimonthly. The literary editor until 1942 was C.A. Marris. ART IN NEW ZEALAND was mainly devoted to the pictorial arts, but each number usually carried a short story and several poems, and there was occasionally an essay on a literary topic. It was succeeded by YEAR BOOK OF THE ARTS IN NEW ZEALAND (see p. 217). A typescript copy of "ART IN NEW ZEALAND: Index vols. 1-14," compiled by Elizabeth Arya in 1943, is held in the Alexander Turnbull Library.

PHOENIX. Eds. James Bertram (vol. 1), R.A.K. Mason (vol. 2). Auckland: Auckland University College Literary Club, 1932-33.

A notable independent student magazine devoted to literature and opinion. It was modelled in both content and typographical design on English periodicals, especially the ADELPHI. Under the editorship of Mason, the magazine became distinctly more political than literary in character. Four numbers were published.

TOMORROW: AN INDEPENDENT WEEKLY PAPER. Ed. Kennaway Henderson. Christchurch: K. Henderson, 1934-40. Fortnightly after 4 March 1936.

The subtitle varied, and there was a gap in publication from 10 April to 24 July 1935. TOMORROW covered both national and international affairs of a political, social, and cultural nature. It was not primarily a literary periodical, but it did print many of the early short stories of Frank Sargeson as well as stories and poetry by other authors. It also carried reviews of and occasional essays on New Zealand literature. INDEX TO TOMORROW 1934-40 was compiled by J.J. Herd (Dunedin: University of Otago Press, 1962).

NEW ZEALAND LISTENER. Wellington: Broadcasting Council of New Zealand, 1939-- . Weekly.

The general contents of the LISTENER reflect the fact that it has always been the official organ of the national broadcasting service. However, the first two editors, Oliver Duff and M.H. Holcroft, were both keen to develop the LISTENER's strength in original literary work. Duff was hampered by paper shortages and other difficulties in the war years, but under Holcroft the regular short story became a feature and some important poetry was published. Book reviews and articles on literary topics became more substantial too. This emphasis has not been maintained to the same extent in recent years, but the magazine remains by far the most widely read of all

New Zealand periodicals and its literary journalism is of a generally high standard. Later editors were Alexander MacLeod, Ian Cross, and Tony Reid. The name was changed to LISTENER on 29 October 1973, though the running title has remained N.Z. LISTENER. To avoid confusion with the London weekly of the same name, it is always referred to in this bibliography as the NEW ZEALAND LISTENER.

See Peter Bland et al., "The First Twenty-Five Years," NEW ZEALAND LISTENER, 26 June 1964, pp. 10-22; M.H. Holcroft, RELUCTANT EDITOR: THE "LISTENER" YEARS, 1949-67 (Wellington: Reed, 1969); Dennis McEldowney, "One Thousand New Zealand Listeners," NEW ZEALAND LISTENER, 17 October 1958, pp. 8-9; and the anonymous "Ten Over-Crowded Years," NEW ZEALAND LISTENER, 24 June 1949, pp. 6-7. A selection of stories, N.Z. LISTENER SHORT STORIES, has been edited by Bill Manhire (Wellington: Methuen New Zealand, 1977).

BOOK: A MISCELLANY. Ed. Denis Glover. Christchurch: Caxton, 1941-47. Irregular.

BOOK was both a literary magazine of a generally high standard and an excuse for typographical experiment by the editor-printer. AN INDEX TO BOOK: A MISCELLANY FROM THE CAXTON PRESS, CHRISTCHURCH was compiled by Olive Johnson (Auckland: Dept. of English, University of Auckland, 1960).

NEW ZEALAND NEW WRITING. Ed. Ian Gordon. Wellington: Progressive Publishing Society, [1942]-45. Annual.

This was closely modelled on the PENGUIN NEW WRITING of the same war years. It printed work by some of the best writers of fiction of the time, but, perhaps deliberately, offered little space to poetry. A few essays and other pieces of nonfictional prose were also printed.

ARENA: A QUARTERLY OF NEW ZEALAND WRITING. Ed. Noel F. Hoggard. Wellington: Handcraft Press, 1943-75. Irregular.

Although it began as a quarterly, ARENA soon appeared irregularly. In later years there were usually about two issues per year. It occasionally carried brief essays but, being a small magazine hand-printed by its editor, it existed primarily to publish short stories and poetry. ARENA may not have carried the best work written during its thirty years of life, but few New Zealand authors of the time were not represented in its pages. "An Index to ARENA, Numbers 1-70" was compiled by P. Andrews and issued in cyclostyled typescript form by the compiler in 1970.

YEAR BOOK OF THE ARTS IN NEW ZEALAND. Wellington: Wingfield Press, 1945-51.

Edited successively by Howard Wadman, Harry H. Tombs, and Eric Lee-Johnson. Volumes 6 and 7 appeared as ARTS YEAR BOOK. This annual concentrated on the visual arts, but always carried a selection of the year's verse, and usually an essay on the year's verse too.

LANDFALL: A NEW ZEALAND QUARTERLY. Christchurch: Caxton, 1947-- .

Edited successively by Charles Brasch, Robin Dudding, Leo Bensemann, and Peter Smart. Those who created LANDFALL are agreed that they were determined to reintroduce a magazine of the kind PHOENIX had aspired to be. Both periodicals were modelled quite closely on J. Middleton Murry's ADELPHI, and in the editing of LANDFALL Brasch also had in mind magazines like CRITERION, DUBLIN REVIEW, and HORIZON. LANDFALL has been primarily a literary magazine, offering space to original work in verse and prose and to extensive reviews of New Zealand literary publications. In recent years critical essays on New Zealand writing have become more frequent. For over twenty-five years and until the appearance of ISLANDS it was the country's leading--indeed outstanding--literary periodical. A separate index is issued with each five volumes.

See David G.H. Anido, "The Genesis and Development of LANDFALL, and Its Influence in Relation to the Culture of New Zealand and the Commonwealth" (Thesis, University of Canterbury, 1972); James Bertram, "Landfall Lives," NEW ZEALAND LISTENER, 7 February 1972, p. 46; and Charles Brasch, "Conversation with Charles Brasch," LANDFALL, 25 (December 1971), 344-72, a discussion with Ian Milner, in the course of which Charles Brasch talked about the founding, editing, and publishing of LANDFALL during its first twenty years. Charles Brasch also edited LANDFALL COUNTRY: WORK FROM LANDFALL, 1947-61 (Christchurch: Caxton, 1962).

HERE & NOW: AN INDEPENDENT MONTHLY REVIEW. Auckland: Here & Now, 1949-57.

Edited by a panel. HERE & NOW frequently included a short story or poem and reviewed literary publications, but it was not primarily a literary periodical.

HILLTOP: A LITERARY MAGAZINE. Ed. John M. Thomson. Wellington: Victoria University College Literary Society, April-September 1949. 3 issues.

The subtitle for numbers two and three was A LITERARY PAPER. HILLTOP was not exactly a student magazine: it solicited, and received, work by a variety of New Zealand writers. It was superseded by ARACHNE (Wellington: Crocus Publishing Co., 1950-51), which was a magazine of similar character.

TE AO HOU: THE NEW WORLD. Wellington: Dept. of Maori Affairs, 1952-75. Quarterly.

Edited successively by Eric Schwimmer, Bruce Mason, Margaret Orbell, and Joy Stevenson. The original subtitle (a translation of Te Ao Hou) became THE MAORI MAGAZINE in 1962. TE AO HOU was a magazine of Maori cultural affairs. From 1956 on, original short stories and poems (a few in Maori) became a valuable and increasingly significant section. An index to numbers 1-22 appeared in Number 22. See Margaret Orbell, "The New World," NEW ZEALAND LISTENER, 7 May 1965, pp. 4-5, an article in which the author looks back over fifty issues and discusses the literary contributions to the magazine.

NUMBERS. Wellington: The Editors, 1954-59. Irregular.

Ten issues were published. Louis Johnson is especially associated with NUMBERS though James K. Baxter, Charles Doyle, and others helped with the editing. The magazine's sympathies, it was declared in an early issue, "lie in the direction of younger writers, and/but, its objective is to publish the best work offering in all fields."

FERNFIRE. Ed. Murray Gittos. Auckland: Fernfire Publications, 19[57]-66. Irregular.

It was the aim of the editorial committee to publish literature--especially fiction--for the ordinary working man.

MATE: A LITERARY PERIODICAL. Wellington: The Editor, 1957-77. Irregular.

The subtitle varies. There have been eight different editors, Robin Dudding and Alistair Paterson being the most important. MATE established a position, behind LANDFALL but ahead of its other contemporaries in the 1960s, as a magazine of original writing in verse and prose. It has also occasionally carried essays on New Zealand literature. A separate index to the first twelve numbers was published. (Note: MATE was renamed CLIMATE: A JOURNAL OF AUSTRALASIAN WRITING in 1978. The first issue indicates that the serial numbering will continue unbroken.)

COMMENT: A NEW ZEALAND QUARTERLY REVIEW. Wellington: Comment Publishing Co., 1959-70.

Although a periodical of public affairs generally and of political matters in particular, COMMENT usually carried a few poems in each issue (but not prose fiction) and from time to time printed literary and critical essays and full reviews of important literary publications. INDEX TO NUMBERS 1-24 (VOLUMES 1-6) was issued separately in 1966, and an index to volume 7 appeared in the issue for April 1967. COMMENT was revived in October 1977 (new series volume 1).

NEW ZEALAND UNIVERSITIES LITERARY YEARBOOK. New Zealand Universities Arts Council, 1960-72.

The title and place of publication vary. It was not published in 1964 or 1965.

ACT. Wellington: Downstage Theatre and New Zealand Theatre Federation, 1967-75.

Edited successively by Bruce Mason, Nonnita Mann (Rees), and Laurie Atkinson. ACT began with volumes of varying numbers; later issues appeared under the serial number. It usually appeared quarterly. ACT was a general theatrical magazine but particular attention was increasingly given to articles on and reviews of New Zealand plays. Number 3 and numbers 10-29 carried complete playscripts by New Zealand authors. ACT was replaced in March 1976 by ACT: THEATRE IN NEW ZEALAND (Wellington: Playmarket, 10 issues a year).

FREED. Auckland: Auckland University Students' Association for the Auckland University Literary Society, 1969-72. Irregular.

The editing was largely the work of Alan Brunton, Murray Edmond, and Russell Haley, who, with David Mitchell, were also the most important contributors. Avant-garde both in its verse and in its graphics and lay-out, FREED has been the most notable of a number of small, short-lived and very independent magazines run by young writers and artists in recent years. It is sometimes referred to as THE WORD IS FREED, the title used in the first issue.

EDGE. Ed. D.S. Long. Christchurch: Edge Press, 1971-73. Irregular.

Verse and prose by (on the whole) younger writers. Work by overseas writers was also included. A stray seventh number appeared in Summer 1976.

CAVE: MAGAZINE OF THE ARTS. Eds. Trevor Reeves, Norman Simms. Hamilton: Outrigger Publishers, 1972-75. Irregular.

Later issues are subtitled AN INTERNATIONAL REVIEW OF ARTS AND IDEAS. Deliberately avoiding the policy of LANDFALL, the editors of CAVE published work by American and other overseas writers, but in their attempt to be international, they failed to establish for the magazine any individual identity. CAVE was superseded by NEW QUARTERLY CAVE: AN INTERNATIONAL REVIEW OF ARTS AND IDEAS (Ed. Norman Simms. Hamilton: Outrigger Publishers, 1976--).

ISLANDS: A NEW ZEALAND QUARTERLY OF ARTS AND LETTERS. Ed. Robin Dudding. Auckland: Robin Dudding, 1972-- .

Since its inception, ISLANDS has been the country's premier literary magazine, carrying original verse and prose, critical essays, and reviews. An index to volumes 1-5 was issued in 1977. See "'Landfall' Lives and 'Islands' Is Born," NEW ZEALAND LISTENER, 14 August 1972, p. 15.

NEW ARGOT. Wellington: New Zealand Students' Arts Council, 1973-75. Irregular.

A tabloid newspaper in format, but in content a lively student cultural magazine with an emphasis on the literary arts.

NEW ZEALAND BOOK WORLD. Wellington: John Paul Productions, 1973-- . Monthly since 1975.

This contains light journalistic notes and articles on current literary affairs. There was greater emphasis on New Zealand material in the earlier issues. Twenty numbers had appeared by the end of 1975.

SCRIPT. Ed. Roland Vogt. [Taradale]: Hawkes Bay Community College, 1975-- .

SPLEEN. Wellington: Red Mole Enterprises, 1975-76. Irregular.

A lively and irreverent review of the arts, edited and largely written by Alan Brunton, Martin Edmond, Russell Haley, and Ian Wedde.

Chapter 7
NONFICTION PROSE

New Zealand is a small South Pacific country which has been known to the Western world for little more than two hundred years, and which has been colonized for less than 150 years. Yet within that span of time, and from the very beginnings, an amazingly large number of factual books has been written describing the country and its various inhabitants. The early settlers, at least, might be forgiven for thinking imaginative writing superfluous when there was so much that needed merely factual description. And so early writers recorded their impressions of the land and of its Maori people; scientists described and classified fauna and flora. Later, observers commented on the nature of the evolving society in the country and in the towns, biographies began to be produced, and both regional and national history flourished. Other authors recorded the activities of New Zealand soldiers in several overseas wars. More recently, writing about the arts has made a slow beginning.

"Merely factual" much of this may have been, but there was often a genuinely imaginative quality to these books all the same. Many of their writers were blessed with organizing powers and a lively and apt prose style which make much of the country's prose fiction seem clumsy and even unimaginative by comparison. Historical writing in particular has frequently been excellent. Dennis McEldowney, writing in 1965, even went so far as to say, "I . . . think Dr Curnow and all New Zealand critics define literature too narrowly: that, for instance, Keith Sinclair's THE ORIGINS OF THE MAORI WARS is a greater achievement than any novel so far written in New Zealand."

This chapter, then, allows for a wider definition of "literature" than previous chapters have done. Its contents, however, it should be noted, reflect a highly selective and personal choice. It is not intended, either, to provide a representative list of what has been written in any particular field but simply to indicate a range of examples of good nonfiction books. Generally speaking, only those of a specifically New Zealand interest are recorded here. Scholarly contributions of a more general kind to the arts or sciences, for example, have not been included. And with one exception, only separately published books are listed.

Classification according to subject-matter seemed inappropriate where balanced coverage was not intended, and the chronological arrangement adopted below has its value as a way of indicating the growth in volume and variety of non-fiction New Zealand prose. Note that a few books, especially editions of letters and journals, published only long after the time of writing, are placed according to the date at which they were written.

Cook, James. THE JOURNALS OF CAPTAIN JAMES COOK ON HIS VOYAGES OF DISCOVERY. Vol. 1: THE VOYAGE OF THE ENDEAVOUR, 1768-1771. Vol. 2: THE VOYAGE OF THE RESOLUTION AND ADVENTURE, 1772-1775. Vol. 3: THE VOYAGES OF THE RESOLUTION AND DISCOVERY, 1776-1780. Ed. J.C. Beaglehole. Cambridge: Cambridge University Press for the Hakluyt Society, 1955-67.

James Cook was the first Englishman to visit and explore the coasts of New Zealand. His journals, the records of an expedition commander and navigator but also of a man with a shrewd eye for significant detail about the lands and peoples he visited, are the prime documents of that first period of exploration, even if the journals of others display in different ways a greater sensitivity to the English language. Among those other writers were Joseph Banks on the first voyage (THE "ENDEAVOUR" JOURNAL OF JOSEPH BANKS 1768-1771. 2 vols. Ed. J.C. Beaglehole. [Sydney]: The Trustees of the Public Library of New South Wales in association with Angus & Robertson, 1962), and David Samwell on the third voyage ("Some Account of a Voyage to the South Sea's in 1776-1777-1778." In Vol. 3 of Beaglehole's edition of Cook's journals, pp. 987-1295).

J.C. Beaglehole's editing of the journals, which are here printed in full for the first time, is superb, and his lengthy introductions to each voyage are themselves splendid historical essays.

Nicholas, John Liddiard. NARRATIVE OF A VOYAGE TO NEW ZEALAND, PERFORMED IN THE YEARS 1814 AND 1815, IN COMPANY WITH THE REV. SAMUEL MARSDEN, PRINCIPAL CHAPLAIN OF NEW SOUTH WALES. 2 vols. 1818; rpt. Auckland: Wilson & Horton, [1971].

Written in clear, well-developed prose, with a touch of eighteenth-century formality and balance to it.

Marsden, Samuel. THE LETTERS AND JOURNALS OF SAMUEL MARSDEN, 1765-1838, SENIOR CHAPLAIN IN THE COLONY OF NEW SOUTH WALES AND SUPERINTENDENT OF THE MISSION OF THE CHURCH MISSIONARY SOCIETY IN NEW ZEALAND. Ed. with an introductory biographical chapter by John Rawson Elder. Dunedin: Coulls, Somerville, Wilkie, and A.H. Reed for the Otago University Council, 1932.

Marsden's journals (though this edition of them is not complete) make up the fullest and most ably written account of early New Zealand.

Earle, Augustus. A NARRATIVE OF A NINE MONTHS RESIDENCE IN NEW ZEALAND IN 1827; TOGETHER WITH A JOURNAL OF A RESIDENCE IN TRISTAN D'ACUNHA, AN ISLAND SITUATED BETWEEN SOUTH AMERICA AND THE CAPE OF GOOD HOPE. 1832; rpt. as NARRATIVE OF A RESIDENCE IN NEW ZEALAND; JOURNAL OF A RESIDENCE IN TRISTAN DA CUNHA. Ed. and introd. E.H. McCormick. Oxford: Clarendon Press, 1966.

> Earle combined the advantages of a classical education and a lucid style with a close knowledge and remarkably unprejudiced view of the Maori.

Polack, J.S. NEW ZEALAND: BEING A NARRATIVE OF TRAVELS AND ADVENTURES DURING A RESIDENCE IN THAT COUNTRY BETWEEN THE YEARS 1831 AND 1837. 2 vols. 1838; rpt. Christchurch: Capper Press, 1974.

> Written in slightly formal but good-humored, ebullient prose.

Dieffenbach, Ernest. TRAVELS IN NEW ZEALAND; WITH CONTRIBUTIONS TO THE GEOGRAPHY, GEOLOGY, BOTANY, AND NATURAL HISTORY OF THAT COUNTRY. 2 vols. 1843; rpt. Christchurch: Capper Press, 1974.

> An intelligent if sometimes a little ponderous account of New Zealand and of the Maori during the country's first years of colonization, written with the steady and unprejudiced eye of the scientific observer.

Wakefield, Edward Jerningham. ADVENTURE IN NEW ZEALAND FROM 1839 TO 1844; WITH SOME ACCOUNT OF THE BEGINNING OF THE BRITISH COLONIZATION OF THE ISLANDS. 2 vols. 1845; rpt. Amsterdam: Israel; New York: Da Capo Press, 1971; Auckland: Wilson & Horton, [1971].

> From the historian's point of view, a very biassed account of the colonizing activities of the New Zealand Company; but Jerningham Wakefield wrote, for the most part, a lively and readable narrative, full of spirited local colour.

Godley, Charlotte. LETTERS FROM EARLY NEW ZEALAND BY CHARLOTTE GODLEY: 1850-1853. Ed. John R. Godley. Christchurch: Whitcombe & Tombs, 1951.

> These letters, first printed for private circulation in 1936, give a delightfully sharp and humorous picture of early, well-to-do society in New Zealand.

Shortland, Edward. TRADITIONS AND SUPERSTITIONS OF THE NEW ZEALANDERS, WITH ILLUSTRATIONS OF THEIR MANNERS AND CUSTOMS. London: Longman, Brown, Green & Longmans, 1854.

> An early survey of Maori culture by a highly intelligent and unprejudiced man who was a worthy forerunner of the modern anthropologist.

Grey, Sir George. POLYNESIAN MYTHOLOGY, AND ANCIENT TRADITIONAL HISTORY OF THE NEW ZEALAND RACE AS FURNISHED BY THEIR PRIESTS AND CHIEFS. 1855; rpt. Ed. W.W. Bird. Christchurch: Whitcombe & Tombs, 1956.

> Grey collected and published many legends and songs of the Maori. This book is largely based on his own translations of the legends, which are retold with an appropriately formal directness, and a touch of biblical nobility.

Thomson, Arthur S. THE STORY OF NEW ZEALAND: PAST AND PRESENT, SAVAGE AND CIVILIZED. 2 vols. 1859; rpt. Christchurch: Capper Press, 1974.

> This was the first attempt at a full-scale history of New Zealand. It includes a description of the country and of the Maori inhabitants, as well as an account of early European colonization. Thomson's style is vivid, brisk, and lucid, and the book is still very readable.

Butler, Samuel. A FIRST YEAR IN CANTERBURY SETTLEMENT. 1863; rpt. Eds. A.C. Brassington and P.B. Maling. Auckland: Blackwood & Janet Paul, 1964.

> A lively and, it goes without saying, intelligent record, combining vivid descriptions of the exploring and establishing of a new sheep farm with shrewd observations on the new colonial society.

Maning, Frederick Edward. OLD NEW ZEALAND: A TALE OF THE GOOD OLD TIMES. 1863; rpt. with A HISTORY OF THE WAR IN THE NORTH TOLD BY AN OLD CHIEF OF THE NGAPUHI TRIBE. Auckland: Golden Press in association with Whitcombe & Tombs, 1973.

> Enormously vigorous, comic, and at times even luridly melodramatic autobiographical recollections of the 1830s, not altogether free of fiction. THE WAR IN THE NORTH, though of less blatant attraction, is a finer piece of controlled, imaginative, historical writing.

Gorst, Sir John Eldon. THE MAORI KING; OR THE STORY OF OUR QUARREL WITH THE NATIVES OF NEW ZEALAND. 1864; rpt. as THE MAORI KING. Ed. and introd. Keith Sinclair. Hamilton: Paul's Book Arcade; London: Oxford University Press, 1959.

> A perceptive account of the negotiations and events preceding the wars between Maoris and Europeans in the Waikato in the 1860s, which Gorst as a local magistrate was well placed to observe. His humanitarian sympathy towards the Maori and his intelligent, psychologically shrewd understanding of their leaders make this a fine example of contemporary historical writing.

Barker, Lady Mary Anne (Stewart). STATION LIFE IN NEW ZEALAND. 1870; rpt. (1883 ed.) Auckland: Golden Press in association with Whitcombe & Tombs, 1973.

> This and Lady Barker's STATION AMUSEMENTS IN NEW ZEALAND (1873; rpt. Auckland: Wilson & Horton, [1970]) are delightfully fresh accounts of the daily life, the amusements, and the frequent excitements of a sheep-station owner's wife in North Canterbury.

Taylor, Nancy M., ed. EARLY TRAVELLERS IN NEW ZEALAND. Oxford: Clarendon Press, 1959.

> Nancy Taylor presents the journals and diaries of eleven travellers who recorded, during the years 1840 to 1870, their journeys in various parts of the country. The accounts of Thomas Brunner and A.J. Barrington are especially notable.

Kennaway, Laurence J. CRUSTS: A SETTLER'S FARE DUE SOUTH. 1874; rpt. Christchurch: Capper Press, 1970.

> The experiences of "new chums" and others in colonial Canterbury: an example of vigorous, popular, anecdotal writing.

Gudgeon, Thomas W. REMINISCENCES OF THE WAR IN NEW ZEALAND. London: Sampson Low, Marston, Searle & Rivington; Auckland: E. Wayte, 1879.

> Not so much reminiscences as a detailed and well-written history of the fighting that occured between 1860 and 1871.

Campbell, John Logan. POENAMO. 1881; rpt. slightly abridged, introd. Joan Stevens. Christchurch: Whitcombe & Tombs, 1952.

> Fond recollections of the exploits of youth. Campbell writes with warm enthusiasm and good humour of his experiences during the years just before and just after the settlement of Auckland.

Green, William Spotswood. THE HIGH ALPS OF NEW ZEALAND; OR, A TRIP TO THE GLACIERS OF THE ANTIPODES WITH AN ASCENT OF MOUNT COOK. 1883; rpt. Christchurch: Capper Press, 1976.

> A fine descriptive account both of the mountain terrain and of the mountaineering accomplished.

Hudson, G.V. AN ELEMENTARY MANUAL OF NEW ZEALAND ENTOMOLOGY; BEING AN INTRODUCTION TO THE STUDY OF OUR NATIVE INSECTS. London: West, Newman & Co., 1892.

> Mainly a popular descriptive account of individual species. Although few of these are allowed more than a page each, Hudson succeeds very well not only in avoiding "all unnecessary technicalities" but also in including distinctive personal observations.

Fitzgerald, E.A. CLIMBS IN THE NEW ZEALAND ALPS, BEING AN ACCOUNT OF TRAVEL AND DISCOVERY. London: Fisher Unwin, 1896.

The most substantial account of early mountaineering in New Zealand's highest mountain country, though Fitzgerald's prose style is sometimes ponderous when he strives for literary effect.

Douglas, Charles. MR. EXPLORER DOUGLAS. Ed. and introd. John Pascoe. Wellington: Reed, 1957.

These selections from the letters and official reports of Douglas display a personality in a way unsurpassed in the records of New Zealand explorers. He was a warm, quizzical man of wide, intelligent, and largely self-taught interests, keenly observant of his surroundings, and devoted to his calling of "explorer." The following entry (see Harper below) makes a fascinating contrast.

Harper, Arthur P. PIONEER WORK IN THE ALPS OF NEW ZEALAND: A RECORD OF THE FIRST EXPLORATION OF THE CHIEF GLACIERS AND RANGES OF THE SOUTHERN ALPS. London: Fisher Unwin, 1896.

A formal and "educated" account--and a very readable one--of exploration shared with Charles Douglas (see above), whose own versions of this pioneer work were not published for another sixty years.

Reeves, William Pember. THE LONG WHITE CLOUD--AO TEA ROA. 1898; rpt. (4th ed., 1950) Auckland: Golden Press in association with Whitcombe & Tombs, 1973.

The best of the histories of New Zealand written for the general reader (though of course it covers only the nineteenth century with any thoroughness). Reeves's intellectual grasp of his subject is admirably served by his succinct yet easy and limpid prose. The last edition to be revised by Reeves was published in 1924. This and the fourth edition contain additional material of less interest by other authors.

_____. STATE EXPERIMENTS IN AUSTRALIA & NEW ZEALAND. 2 vols. London: Grant Richards, 1902. Rpt. Ed. and introd. John Child. Melbourne: Macmillan of Australia, 1969.

Reeves's most substantial contribution to historical and political studies. It is less immediately approachable than his more popular histories, but displays the great virtues of his mature, clear, and intelligent prose style.

Salmond, Sir John William. JURISPRUDENCE, OR, THE THEORY OF THE LAW. London: Stevens & Haynes, 1902.

This and the same author's THE LAW OF TORTS (1905) immediately established themselves as classic authorities. They both remain in print today, but with the updating introduced by successive editors, they now offer less of Salmond's own fine jurist's prose.

Thomson, Geo M. A NEW ZEALAND NATURALIST'S CALENDAR; AND NOTES BY THE WAYSIDE. Dunedin: R.J. Stark, 1909.

Personal, random observations designed for a popular audience, in admirably direct and vigorous prose.

Cockayne, Leonard. NEW ZEALAND PLANTS AND THEIR STORY. 1910; rpt. (3rd ed., 1927) Wellington: Government Printer, 1967.

A good general description of the New Zealand flora, with an emphasis on characteristic plant communities.

Buick, T.L. TREATY OF WAITANGI; OR, HOW NEW ZEALAND BECAME A BRITISH COLONY. 1914; rpt. (3rd ed., 1936) Christchurch: Capper Press, 1976.

Buick was a productive historian. This is his best and most original work.

Cradock, Lt. Col. Montagu. DIARY OF THE SECOND NEW ZEALAND MOUNTED RIFLES ON ACTIVE SERVICE IN SOUTH AFRICA FROM 24TH FEBRUARY, 1900, TO 21ST MARCH, 1901, ALSO FROM 1ST APRIL, 1901, TO 8TH MAY, 1901. Dunedin: Evening Star Co., [1915].

These brief, unpretentious diary entries have an immediacy and vividness not matched by the more extended accounts by New Zealanders of the Boer War.

Guthrie-Smith, H. TUTIRA: THE STORY OF A NEW ZEALAND SHEEP STATION. 1921; rpt. (3rd ed., 1953) Wellington: Reed, 1969.

TUTIRA is deservedly regarded as one of the most original and imaginative works to be written in New Zealand--at least in its impact on the reader. In recording, from his own observations of one particular farm over a period of more than forty years, the ecological changes brought about by the European's sudden and utter transformation of a country which less than a hundred years before had been very little altered by man, Guthrie-Smith wrote a book of significance not just for the agricultural scientist but for every inhabitant whose introduced Western culture has had to be accommodated in a land so biologically isolated and unstable.

Cowan, James. THE NEW ZEALAND WARS: A HISTORY OF THE MAORI CAMPAIGNS AND THE PIONEERING PERIOD. 2 vols. Wellington: Government Printer, 1922-23; rpt. New York: AMS Press, 1969.

A detailed history which includes incidents and stories related to Cowan by those who recalled their participation in the wars.

Best, Elsdon. THE MAORI. 2 vols. Wellington: Board of Maori Ethnological Research for the Author and on behalf of the Polynesian Society, 1924.

A general survey by a man who wrote extensively on many aspects of Maori life.

_____. TUHOE: THE CHILDREN OF THE MIST. A SKETCH OF THE ORIGIN, HISTORY, MYTHS AND BELIEFS OF THE TUHOE TRIBE OF THE MAORI OF NEW ZEALAND; WITH SOME ACCOUNT OF OTHER EARLY TRIBES OF THE BAY OF PLENTY DISTRICT. 2 vols. 1925; rpt. Wellington: Reed for the Polynesian Society, 1972-73.

The fullest tribal history, based on oral material collected by the author around the turn of the century. Volume 2 contains genealogies and maps only.

Alpers, O.T.J. CHEERFUL YESTERDAYS. 1928; rpt. Hamilton: Paul's Book Arcade, 1951.

Recollections, urbanely and amusingly recounted, of the life of a Danish immigrant boy who became a judge.

Firth, Raymond. PRIMITIVE ECONOMICS OF THE NEW ZEALAND MAORI. Introd. R.H. Tawney. London: Routledge, 1929; rev. ed., as ECONOMICS OF THE NEW ZEALAND MAORI. Wellington: Government Printer, 1959.

The classic study of late eighteenth- and early nineteenth-century Maori culture.

Condliffe, J.B. NEW ZEALAND IN THE MAKING: A SURVEY OF ECONOMIC AND SOCIAL DEVELOPMENT. London: Allen & Unwin, 1930.

The standard economic history. The second revised edition (London: Allen & Unwin, 1959), incorporating new material and opinions, is less satisfying. THE WELFARE STATE IN NEW ZEALAND (London: Allen & Unwin, 1959) deals, still less adequately from the general reader's point of view, with the period from 1935 to 1957.

Stead, Edgar F. THE LIFE HISTORIES OF NEW ZEALAND BIRDS. London: Search Publishing Co., 1932.

A personal study of eighteen species, admirably conveying the author's sense of the ecological relationship between the birds and their environment.

Guthrie-Smith, H. SORROWS AND JOYS OF A NEW ZEALAND NATURALIST. Dunedin: Reed, 1936.

The best of several books in which are collected the ably written accounts of expeditions undertaken by the author to observe and photograph New Zealand birds.

Beaglehole, J.C. THE UNIVERSITY OF NEW ZEALAND: AN HISTORICAL STUDY. [Wellington]: New Zealand Council for Educational Research, 1937.

A scholarly study by a conscious and witty stylist.

Schroder, J.H.E. REMEMBERING THINGS AND OTHER ESSAYS. Christchurch: Whitcombe & Tombs; London: Dent, 1938.

Good-natured, pleasantly turned essays, mainly on literary topics.

Somerset, H.C.D. LITTLEDENE: A NEW ZEALAND RURAL COMMUNITY. [Wellington]: New Zealand Council for Educational Research, 1938.

A model sociological study for the general reader, warm but not uncritical, entirely free of jargon, and displaying a pleasant wit. It was republished, with a second part called "Littledene Revisited," as LITTLEDENE: PATTERNS OF CHANGE (Wellington: New Zealand Council for Educational Research, 1974).

Baxter, Archibald. WE WILL NOT CEASE. London: Gollancz, 1939; rpt. Christchurch: Caxton, 1968.

A courageous and moving account of the sufferings and privations inflicted upon a conscientious objector during the First World War.

Beaglehole, J.C. THE DISCOVERY OF NEW ZEALAND. Wellington: Dept. of Internal Affairs, 1939; rev. ed. London: Oxford University Press, 1961.

An extended essay, and a good example both of Beaglehole's command of his subject and of his highly wrought prose and his conscious and sardonic wit. His THE EXPLORATION OF THE PACIFIC (3rd rev. ed. London: A. & C. Black; Stanford, Calif.: Stanford University, 1966), while of less direct relevance to New Zealand, is a more substantial historical work.

Pascoe, John. UNCLIMBED NEW ZEALAND: ALPINE TRAVEL IN THE CANTERBURY AND WESTLAND RANGES, SOUTHERN ALPS. London: Allen & Unwin; New York: Macmillan, 1939.

A personal record of several holiday climbing trips into little-known areas, written in serviceable, unpretentious prose.

Simpson, Helen M. (Richmond). THE WOMEN OF NEW ZEALAND. Wellington: Dept. of Internal Affairs, 1940 ; rpt. with a postscript. Auckland: Paul's Book Arcade; London: Allen & Unwin, 1962.

An agreeably written historical study which concentrates on the nineteenth century.

Burdon, R.M. NEW ZEALAND NOTABLES. [Christchurch]: Caxton, 1941.

This, like Burdon's two later collections of NEW ZEALAND NOTABLES, SERIES TWO and THREE (1945 and 1950), contains several novella-length, essay-like biographies.

Duff, Oliver. NEW ZEALAND NOW. Wellington: Dept. of Internal Affairs, 1941; rpt. with a new foreword and postscript by Duff. Hamilton: Paul's Book Arcade; London: Allen & Unwin, 1956.

Though neither a professional sociological study, nor very profound in its insights, this is an urbane, personal essay on the nature of the New Zealand of 1940, enlivened by a pleasantly dry wit.

Sutch, W.B. POVERTY AND PROGRESS IN NEW ZEALAND. Wellington: Modern Books, 1941.

The historical parts of this were given in more extended form in THE QUEST FOR SECURITY IN NEW ZEALAND (Harmondsworth, Middlesex: Penguin, 1942), and this in turn was reprinted, with a long section bringing the work up-to-date, as THE QUEST FOR SECURITY IN NEW ZEALAND: 1840 TO 1966 (Wellington: Oxford University Press, 1966). The original book was reissued in a revised and enlarged form as POVERTY AND PROGRESS IN NEW ZEALAND: A RE-ASSESSMENT (Wellington: Reed, 1969). These books will not be referred to for faultless factual information, but they are unsurpassed as vigorous, polemical, and hard-hitting accounts of New Zealand's social history.

Cotton, Charles A. GEOMORPHOLOGY: AN INTRODUCTION TO THE STUDY OF LAND-FORMS. 3rd rev. ed. Christchurch: Whitcombe & Tombs, 1942.

A widely praised textbook, succinctly and lucidly written. It was first published as THE GEOMORPHOLOGY OF NEW ZEALAND in 1922.

Sinclaire, Frederick. LEND ME YOUR EARS: ESSAYS. Christchurch: Caxton, 1942.

A collection of examples of that no longer very popular literary form: the personal, lively, and eloquently written essay.

Cumberland, Kenneth B. SOIL EROSION IN NEW ZEALAND: A GEOGRAPHIC RECONNAISSANCE. Wellington: Soil Conservation and Rivers Control Council, 1944.

Clear, vigorous, descriptive writing.

Wood, F.L.W. UNDERSTANDING NEW ZEALAND. New York: Coward-McCann, 1944; rev. ed. as THIS NEW ZEALAND. Hamilton: Paul's Book Arcade, 1946.

A balanced and lucid survey of New Zealand life, originally written for an American audience during the Second World War.

Burton, O.E. IN PRISON. Wellington: Reed, 1945.

An observant, well-written, personal account of life in a New Zealand prison during the years of the Second World War.

Henderson, James. GUNNER INGLORIOUS. Wellington: Harry H. Tombs, 1945.

A spirited, very colloquial account of the author's service with a gun-crew in the desert campaign, and of his experiences as a wounded prisoner of war.

Mirams, Gordon. SPEAKING CANDIDLY: FILMS AND PEOPLE IN NEW ZEALAND. Hamilton: Paul's Book Arcade, 1945.

A diverting and knowledgeable study of films and their effect in New Zealand society by the man who, through his own reviews, did most to establish a place for intelligent and serious film criticism.

Plishke, E.A. DESIGN AND LIVING. Wellington: Dept. of Internal Affairs, 1947.

A lucid discussion, unprecedented in New Zealand and influential in its time, of utilitarian and aesthetic considerations in the design of new furniture, new houses, and new towns.

Buck, Sir Peter. THE COMING OF THE MAORI. Wellington: Maori Purposes Fund Board, 1949.

The title is misleading: the importance of this great book lies in its portrayal, based on personal knowledge and experience, of early Maori culture. Buck's account of Maori origins, however, and the Maori's settlement of New Zealand, more fully expounded in his VIKINGS OF THE SUNRISE (New York: Frederick A. Stokes, 1938; rpt. Christchurch: Whitcombe & Tombs, 1954, and, as VIKINGS OF THE PACIFIC, [Chicago]: University of Chicago Press, [1959]), has encountered scholarly disagreement.

Kippenberger, Sir Howard. INFANTRY BRIGADIER. London: Oxford University Press, 1949.

A personal narrative of the Second World War (especially the desert campaign) which, while it well captures the author's admiration of the New Zealand soldier, is in other respects a little too coolly objective to recreate vividly Kippenberger's own experiences.

Llewellyn, S.P. JOURNEY TOWARDS CHRISTMAS: OFFICIAL HISTORY OF THE 1ST AMMUNITION COMPANY, SECOND NEW ZEALAND EXPEDITIONARY FORCE, 1939-45. Wellington: War History Branch, Dept. of Internal Affairs, 1949.

An informal and most readable narrative, written with a literary flair which powerfully evokes the physical sensations and mental strains experienced by the ordinary soldier, especially in the desert campaign.

McLintock, A.H. THE HISTORY OF OTAGO: THE ORIGINS AND GROWTH OF A WAKEFIELD CLASS SETTLEMENT. Dunedin: Otago Centennial Historical Publications, 1949; rpt. Christchurch: Capper Press, 1975.

The finest of the provincial histories. Despite the occasionally stilted eloquence of his prose, McLintock has written a vigorous narrative with a touch of proper pride in his subject.

Duff, Roger. THE MOA-HUNTER PERIOD OF MAORI CULTURE. Wellington: Dept. of Internal Affairs, 1950; rpt. Wellington: Government Printer, 1977.

A splendid scientific study based on the author's archaeological work on the Wairau Bar site. The 1977 edition includes a brief review of recent research written by Michael M. Trotter.

Wilson, Helen. MY FIRST EIGHTY YEARS. Hamilton: Paul's Book Arcade, 1950.

An autobiography which describes a life spent on a variety of farms.

Graham, David H. A TREASURY OF NEW ZEALAND FISHES. Wellington: Reed, 1953.

Graham was a professional biologist who knew how to write with the enthusiasm of the amateur naturalist.

Mackay, Ian K. BROADCASTING IN NEW ZEALAND. Wellington: Reed, 1953.

A lively and not unprejudiced historical survey of the subject, with special emphasis on the question of political control.

Cumberland, Kenneth B. SOUTHWEST PACIFIC: A GEOGRAPHY OF AUSTRALIA, NEW ZEALAND AND THEIR PACIFIC NEIGHBOURHOODS. 1954; 4th rev. ed. Christchurch: Whitcombe & Tombs, 1968; New York: Praeger, [1968].

A readable, general study.

Holloway, John T. "Forests and Climate in the South Island of New Zealand." TRANSACTIONS OF THE ROYAL SOCIETY OF NEW ZEALAND, 82 (September 1954), 329-410.

> Most scientific writing appears in the form of articles in learned journals. Holloway's essay is the only such article to be included in this chapter. It is not only an important botanical study, but is also a splendid example of a hypothesis lucidly and excitingly expounded, supported with a varied range of evidence, and presented in forthright, serviceable prose.

McCormick, E.H. THE EXPATRIATE: A STUDY OF FRANCES HODGKINS. Wellington: New Zealand University Press, 1954.

> A study of the New Zealand artist in exile in Europe, in the form of a biography of the painter Frances Hodgkins.

Burdon, R.M. KING DICK: A BIOGRAPHY OF RICHARD JOHN SEDDON. Christchurch: Whitcombe & Tombs, 1955.

> A vigorous and readable biography, concentrating on the man rather than his political milieu.

Hall, D.O.W. PORTRAIT OF NEW ZEALAND. Wellington: Reed, 1955.

> An affectionate and untendentious study of New Zealand society.

Gardner, W.J. THE AMURI: A COUNTY HISTORY. Culverden, Canterbury: Amuri County Council, 1956.

> A history of a local community up to 1919, written by a professional historian who recognizes and very largely overcomes the problems inherent in local history.

Phillips, N.C. ITALY: VOLUME I, THE SANGRO TO CASSINO. Wellington: War History Branch, Dept. of Internal Affairs, 1957.

> Phillips, a professional historian and distinguished soldier, orders material ranging from atmospheric descriptions of local terrain to discussions of command decisions to produce a finely judged account of the Second New Zealand Division's part in the Italian campaign.

Sinclair, Keith. THE ORIGINS OF THE MAORI WARS. Wellington: New Zealand University Press, 1957; rpt. [Auckland]: Auckland University Press; [Wellington]: Oxford University Press, 1974.

> A fine historical monograph, displaying a masterly understanding of the complex confusions of the time, and well served by a direct, alert prose style.

McLintock, A.H. CROWN COLONY GOVERNMENT IN NEW ZEALAND. Wellington: Government Printer, 1958.

Written with a sense of form, and in an elegant style which some historians think a little grandiloquent for its subject matter.

Miller, John. EARLY VICTORIAN NEW ZEALAND: A STUDY OF RACIAL PROBLEMS AND SOCIAL ATTITUDES 1839-1852. London: Oxford University Press, 1958; rpt. Wellington: Oxford University Press, 1974.

A beautifully written book, and one which is especially interesting on the "racial problems," of which Miller offers a fresh and penetrating study.

Wood, F.L.W. THE NEW ZEALAND PEOPLE AT WAR: POLITICAL AND EXTERNAL AFFAIRS. Wellington: War History Branch, Dept. of Internal Affairs, 1958.

A superbly lucid narrative of the way the New Zealand government arrived at its military decisions during the late 1930s and early 1940s. Wood's book is notable for its balanced grip on the complexities of both national and international issues.

McCormick, E.H. THE INLAND EYE. [Auckland]: Auckland Gallery Associates, 1959.

A short autobiographical essay concentrating on the growth of the author's cultural awareness. Its slightly heightened style occasionally betrays its origins as a public lecture.

Sinclair, Keith. A HISTORY OF NEW ZEALAND. 1959. Rev. ed. Harmondsworth, Middlesex: Penguin, 1969.

This book, which might have been included with other brief histories (see the following entry), deserves its own individual mention. Not only is it considerably longer than the others, it is also based, especially in its first half, on more original material and original views. And for all that it was published by Penguin for a world market, it is a New Zealand-centred book, an attempt to explain present-day New Zealand through its own history with as little regard to European influences as possible. This is Sinclair's finest piece of sustained writing--succinct, alert, witty, and deft.

Oliver, W.H. THE STORY OF NEW ZEALAND. London: Faber, 1960.

New Zealand has been fortunate in its short, popular histories. This, like W.P. Reeves's NEW ZEALAND (London: Horace Marshall & Son, [1898]), J.C. Beaglehole's NEW ZEALAND: A SHORT HISTORY (London: Allen & Unwin, 1936), and Harold Miller's NEW ZEALAND (London: Hutchinson's University Library, 1950), was a contribution to a series with a predominantly overseas audience. They have all depended, and successfully, on their authors' ability to present, within a brief span, a coherent, imaginative account of New Zealand without becoming either one-sided or blandly general. Nevertheless, besides reflecting its author's interests, each book has also reflected the times in which it was written. Reeves celebrates the successful colonization of the country and the radical legislation of the nineties; Beaglehole analyzes the economic factors which had produced the Depression as it was experienced in New Zealand; Miller is strongest on early race relations and on the rise of the socialist state; and Oliver concentrates on political and cultural history. All four authors have their own fine individual prose style.

Turnbull, Michael. THE CHANGING LAND: A SHORT HISTORY OF NEW ZEALAND FOR CHILDREN. London: Longmans, 1960; rev. and enl. as THE CHANGING LAND: A SHORT HISTORY OF NEW ZEALAND. Auckland: Longman Paul, 1975.

An accurate and lively rendering of scholarly knowledge for young teenagers.

Woollaston, M.T. THE FAR-AWAY HILLS: A MEDITATION ON NEW ZEALAND LANDSCAPE. [Auckland]: Auckland Gallery Associates, 1960.

An autobiographical account of the development of one of the country's most important painters.

Duff, Oliver. A SHEPHERD'S CALENDAR. Hamilton: Paul's Book Arcade, 1961.

Duff's essays are notable for their sensitive and honest reflections on man's place in the countryside, and for their strong, muscular, very attractive prose.

McDonald, J.D., ed. THE PITCHER AND THE WELL. Hamilton: Paul's Book Arcade, 1961.

An edited selection of letters said to have been written by an airman dying of burns in a German prisoner-of-war hospital. The author has not been identified, and it is possible that the letters are partly or even wholly fictional. The book is in any case a penetrating and sensitive account of the experiences of a New Zealand Air Force navigator in the Second World War, and, whatever its proper classification, is a fine piece of writing.

Rutherford, J. SIR GEORGE GREY, K.C.B., 1812-1898: A STUDY IN COLONIAL GOVERNMENT. London: Cassell, 1961.

A lengthy volume which attempts to cover the historical material of its subtitle through its biographical subject. Even if Rutherford does not solve the fascinating problems of Grey's complex personality, he clearly sets out the available evidence.

Sinclair, Keith, and W.F. Mandle. OPEN ACCOUNT: A HISTORY OF THE BANK OF NEW SOUTH WALES IN NEW ZEALAND, 1861-1961. Wellington: Whitcombe & Tombs, 1961.

This is "not a house journal but an economic history of New Zealand seen from a bank manager's parlour" (D. Sloane). The book successfully avoids the dangers of centennial adulation.

May, Philip Ross. THE WEST COAST GOLD RUSHES. Christchurch: Caxton, 1962; rev. ed., 1967.

A splendid monograph, both scholarly and readable, even if, given its considerable length, rather narrowly limited to a celebration of its subject. May's GOLD TOWN: ROSS, WESTLAND ([Christchurch]: Pegasus, [1970]), a history of the township of Ross, is a model illustrated history.

Aitken, Alexander. GALLIPOLI TO THE SOMME: RECOLLECTIONS OF A NEW ZEALAND INFANTRYMAN. Introd. Sir Bernard Fergusson. London: Oxford University Press, 1963.

First written immediately after the war, and revised some years later, this narrative combines the immediacy of youthful experience with the balanced judgment of an older man. It is the finest personal account of war to be written by a New Zealander.

Cumberland, Kenneth B., and James W. Fox. NEW ZEALAND: A REGIONAL VIEW; 2nd rev. ed. Christchurch: Whitcombe & Tombs, 1975.

A secondary-school textbook of interest beyond its intended audience.

Lee, John A. SIMPLE ON A SOAP-BOX. Auckland: Collins Publishers, 1963; rpt. Christchurch: Whitcombe & Tombs, 1975.

Gossipy, tendentious, and eminently readable recollections of the Labour Party and of the early years of the first Labour government.

O'Farrell, P.J. HARRY HOLLAND: MILITANT SOCIALIST. Canberra: Australian National University, 1964.

A good political biography, clear and succinct and free of partisan distortion.

Richardson, E.S. IN THE EARLY WORLD. Wellington: New Zealand Council for Educational Research, 1964; rpt. New York: Pantheon Books, [1969].

A fascinating record of enlightened experimental teaching at a small, rural primary school.

Allan, Ruth M. NELSON: A HISTORY OF EARLY SETTLEMENT. Ed. and introd. J.C. Beaglehole. Wellington: Reed, 1965.

A splendid account of the early years of a planned "Wakefield" settlement. Allan died before the book was finished, and Beaglehole, with the help of others, put the final version together.

Sinclair, Keith. WILLIAM PEMBER REEVES: NEW ZEALAND FABIAN. Oxford: Clarendon Press, 1965.

Scholarly and undemonstrative, but also a warm and sympathetic biography. Keith Sinclair's WALTER NASH ([Auckland]: Auckland University Press; [Wellington]: Oxford University Press, 1976) is a more substantial and important but less well-written book.

Sharell, Richard. THE TUATARA, LIZARDS AND FROGS OF NEW ZEALAND. London: Collins, 1966.

A good popular treatise written by an amateur enthusiast.

Metge, Joan. THE MAORIS OF NEW ZEALAND. London: Routledge & Kegan Paul, 1967; rev. ed. as THE MAORIS OF NEW ZEALAND: RAUTAHI. 1976.

A simple lucid study, especially good on modern Maori society.

Orbell, Margaret, ed. and trans. MAORI FOLKTALES IN MAORI AND ENGLISH. Auckland: Blackwood & Janet Paul; London: C. Hurst, 1968.

Stories, some of very ancient origins, all first recorded (in Maori) in written form between 1843 and 1876.

Wards, Ian. THE SHADOW OF THE LAND: A STUDY OF BRITISH POLICY AND RACIAL CONFLICT IN NEW ZEALAND 1832-1852. Wellington: Historical Publications Branch, Dept. of Internal Affairs, 1968.

Although Wards' topic is "racial conflict" in a military sense rather than the wider subject of "racial relationships," this detailed study nevertheless displays a fine ability to see military events against the wider historical background.

McCaskill, L.W. MOLESWORTH. Wellington: Reed, 1969.

The history of a large high-country sheep and cattle run.

Docking, Gil. TWO HUNDRED YEARS OF NEW ZEALAND PAINTING. Wellington: Reed, 1971.

An impressive survey.

Oliver, W.H., and Jane M. Thomson. CHALLENGE AND RESPONSE: A

STUDY OF THE DEVELOPMENT OF THE GISBORNE EAST COAST REGION. [Gisborne]: East Coast Development Research Association, [1971].

An excellent example of that difficult genre, the regional history. Oliver, writing with his accustomed grace, and with the help of his research assistant, always senses the way the region reflects the experiences of the nation as a whole.

Rolleston, Rosamond. WILLIAM AND MARY ROLLESTON: AN INFORMAL BIOGRAPHY. Wellington: Reed, 1971.

A slight but entertainingly written study, especially of Mary Rolleston.

Stuart, Peter. EDWARD GIBBON WAKEFIELD IN NEW ZEALAND: HIS POLITICAL CAREER, 1853-4. Wellington: Price Milburn for Victoria University of Wellington, 1971.

A brisk account of Wakefield's part in the early colonial struggle for political power.

Grimshaw, Patricia. WOMEN'S SUFFRAGE IN NEW ZEALAND. [Auckland]: Auckland University Press; [Wellington]: Oxford University Press, 1972.

A clearly written history of the successful women's franchise movement of the last decades of the nineteenth century, but one which may be considered a little too dispassionate given the emotional nature of the struggle.

Stone, R.C.J. MAKERS OF FORTUNE: A COLONIAL BUSINESS COMMUNITY AND ITS FALL. [Auckland]: Auckland University Press; [Wellington]: Oxford University Press, 1973.

An account of the city of Auckland's economic boom and slump in the 1880s and 1890s, and a significant contribution to economic history.

Beaglehole, J.C. THE LIFE OF CAPTAIN JAMES COOK. London: Adam & Charles Black, 1974.

Magisterial in its command of the material and in its style, this biography was the final fruit of the author's lifelong devotion to the history of the Pacific.

McCormick, E.H. ALEXANDER TURNBULL: HIS LIFE, HIS CIRCLE, HIS COLLECTIONS. Wellington: Alexander Turnbull Library, 1974.

A scholarly book both in its style and in its material, though lacking a little in warmth and imaginative insight.

Clark, Paul. "HAUHAU": THE PAI MARIRE SEARCH FOR MAORI IDENTITY. [Auckland]: Auckland University Press; [Wellington]: Oxford University Press, 1975.

A thoroughly researched study of the Maori response to the wars of the 1860s.

Stirling, Amiria. AMIRIA: THE LIFE STORY OF A MAORI WOMAN. Ed. Anne Salmond. Wellington: Reed, 1976.

An autobiography based on a number of taped interviews.

Archey, Sir Gilbert. WHAOWHIA: MAORI ART AND ITS ARTISTS. Auckland and London: Collins, 1977.

An authoritative, fully illustrated introduction, devoted chiefly to wood-carving.

King, Michael. TE PUEA: A BIOGRAPHY. Auckland: Hodder & Stoughton, 1977.

"Oral history" has always been the natural form of historical record amongst the Maori, and in this fine life of Te Puea Herangi, an important Maori leader, King has made extensive use of taped interviews with people who knew her.

AUTHOR INDEX

This index includes all authors, editors, translators, and other contributors to works cited in the text. It is alphabetized letter by letter and numbers refer to page numbers. In the case of individual authors, underlined numbers refer to main entries.

A

B

Author Index

C

C

D

E

F

G

H

N

O

P

R

S

T

Author Index

Y

Z

TITLE INDEX

This index includes titles of all books, theses, and bibliographical exercises. Titles of journal essays are excluded. Titles of theses and other unpublished material are given in full; otherwise, subtitles are not usually provided except where needed to assist in identification. This index is alphabetized letter by letter and numbers refer to page numbers.

A

B

C

D

E

F

G

H

I

O

P

Q

R